REAL ESTATE
FINANCE

REAL ESTATE FINANCE

John P. Wiedemer

University of Houston

Reston Publishing Company, Inc.
A Prentice-Hall Company
Reston, Virginia

Library of Congress Cataloging in Publication Data

Wiedemer, John P
   Real estate finance.

   1. Real estate business—United States—Finance.
2. Mortgages—United States. I. Title.
HD1375.W53   332.7'2   74-11210
ISBN 0-87909-704-3

© 1974 by
Reston Publishing Company, Inc.
A Prentice-Hall Company
Reston, Virginia 22090

10 9 8 7 6

Printed in the United States of America

The forms used in this text are for information only and are not intended for use as legal documents. In such matters, an attorney should
be consulted.

CONTENTS

TABLES

FIGURES

FOREWORD

Land is a scarce and limited resource. Its availability and use are so basic to human life that they form the foundation upon which societies are organized and function. Inherent in the structure of every society is a system designed to deal with the multiltude of relationships concerning land.

In this society, private ownership of real property is an established and guarded right. Here too, systems have been developed that recognize this right and facilitate the individual's exercise of this right.

The economic importance of real estate transactions is obvious. So obvious, in fact, that most people are only vaguely aware of the tremendous impact of real estate transactions on the financial market. The potential size and number of these transactions give the appearance of something too complicated to understand. This appearance is both deceiving and dangerous.

An individual purchasing a home is obligating a large portion of his personal income. The real estate salesperson is concerned with the economic well-being of his or her client. Complications notwithstanding, buyers, sellers, brokers, and others are faced with an urgent need to know.

Admittedly, the field of real estate finance is in a state of continuous change; change in practices, methods, clientele, and sources. This circumstance should not be viewed with alarm, for change is inherent in progress. Professionals in real estate, like professionals in every field, must stay abreast of these changes if they are to remain professionals.

Newcomers to the field must gain a solid foundation in the basic principles and terminology of real estate finance. The real estate profession's clientele need at least a working knowledge of these same principles and terms.

In order to fulfill these needs, access to accurate, current information is necessary. The information required is available from many sources. Unfortunately, information of this type is normally presented in an obscure and unimaginative form that makes learning a labor and is of limited educational value to all but the specialist.

In this sense, Wiedemer's book is unique. Not only is the information current and technically accurate, it is presented as an informal discussion. His discussion of methods and elements of real estate finance are objective and complete.

His book contains the information necessary to fulfill the needs of the beginner and is thorough enough to be a valuable resource for the established professional. The book has been written in such a way that the novice can understand the language of the professional.

Mr. Wiedemer has been a lecturer in real estate at the University of Houston since 1970. He has brought to his classroom the knowledge and enthusiasm of a leader in his field. He approaches his teaching duties with a sincere desire for his students to learn. This approach is immediately evident in his book.

A true professional, Wiedemer wants to give back something to the profession that has been good to him. This book and his continuing work in education are overt expressions of this willingness and desire.

James C. Taylor, J. D.
Dean, Continuing Education
University of Houston

INTRODUCTION

The financing of real estate, which includes our homes, shopping centers, office buildings, farms, and factories, is one of the largest responsibilities of our financial system. The multifaceted operation of this system today has resulted from long experience with a great variety of requirements, from the harsh realities of the depression years of the 1930s, and from the efforts of many men and women working through private industry and governmental agencies to achieve more and better housing along with better living conditions for all of us. One might say that it is this system that attempts to match dreams with reality and make them come true.

The goal of this book is to acquaint us with the most commonly used methods of financing real property and to acquire some familiarity with the terminology used in our financial community. We recognize that differences in methods, in institutions, and even in terminology, do exist across the country, but for our purposes, and within our time limitations, this material will be focused on common practices with minimal reference to local geographic areas.

This text does not cover the "how to make a fortune in real estate your first year in business" that is popularized in some current books. It is the author's belief that well-selected land and buildings represent some of the soundest investments available, and that their value increases by two basic factors: (1) by the influx of people into any specific area, and (2) by the normal inflationary cycle we now live with. There are other influences, of course, such as the discovery of minerals, massive irrigation work, and the site selection for a major construction project; but we will concern ourselves primarily with the fundamentals and the normal pressures rather than the speculative ones.

Since World War II, the influence and power of the federal government have been an ever-increasing force in the real estate business, with many bureaus, agencies, and departments exercising authority. In this book, however, we will attempt to cover only the major procedures and programs now in use, along with the conventional money market and the areas of overlap.

JOHN P. WIEDEMER

ACKNOWLEDGMENTS

The author gratefully acknowledges the expert advice, assistance, and encouragement of the following persons who made possible the preparation and writing of this book.

REGINALD C. CAPSHAW Houston Sales Manager, Wood Brothers Homes

BREAUX B. CASTLEMAN Management Consultant, Booz: Allen and Hamilton, Dallas, Texas

R. L. COBB Loan Guaranty Officer, Veterans Administration, Houston

JOSEPH P. CONTE President, Conte Investments, Inc. Houston

JOHN W. CRADDOCK CLU, Great Southern Life Insurance Co.

JACK DANIELS Chairman, Executive Committee, Fidelity National Bank, Albuquerque, New Mexico

BERT KADELL Executive Vice President, U S Life Title Company of Houston

FLOYD KOWALSKI Chief Underwriter, Federal Housing Administration, Houston

PATRICIA McAULIFFE Real Estate Sales, Houston

ROBERT M. MEGGINSON Executive Vice President, Milton and Megginson Mortgage Company, Jackson, Mississippi

ARTHUR MORALES Executive Vice President, San Jacinto Savings Association, Houston

WILLIAM A. PAINTER Director, Houston Office, HUD, Federal Housing Administration

HARRY RODEY Federal National Mortgage Association, Dallas

MANUEL A. SANCHEZ President, Gulf-Tex Brokerage, Inc. Brownsville, Texas

RUDY C. SCHUBERT Real Estate and Investments, Houston

JAMES C. TAYLOR, J.D. Dean, Continuing Education, University of Houston

JOE P. WALLACE Wallace and Associates, Realtors, Houston

VERLYNE WALLACE Wallace and Associates, Realtors, Houston

BEN H. WARD Real Estate Investments, Houston

GEORGE YOUNG Assistant Dean, Continuing Education, University of Houston

AND A SPECIAL ACKNOWLEDGEMENT to my wife, Margaret I. Wiedemer, for organization and editing assistance plus her kind patience.

REAL ESTATE FINANCE

HISTORY
AND
BACKGROUND

The history of real estate financing presents a fascinating record of man's learning to live with, and enjoy the benefits of, the land he lives on. While private ownership of land can be traced back to civilizations existing over 2500 years ago, only in the last several hundred years has it become possible for the average person to own property.

EARLY FINANCING METHODS

In ancient Rome, men of means were most often the hereditary large landlords whose land in the provinces had gained them admission to the Curia. This membership required their residence in the city, allowing them to extend their political, religious, and economic influence throughout Rome. Other members included administrators and shareholders of the tax gathering societies whose treasuries were assured of capital funds. Of course, these societies were open only to the privileged few, unlike our modern investment institutions.

In medieval times under the feudal system, land was owned primarily by the king, the nobility, or the church. Thus land ownership

1

was restricted to the very few, and those who did possess rights to land could pledge their property rights as security for a loan. In these earlier times there were no savings banks or other institutions capable of accumulating investment capital, and so only these few individuals of great wealth were capable of making loans. Besides the severe limitations on investment capital imposed by there being very few property owners, an equally severe limitation was caused by the lack of money—a problem that still exists with many of us today! Historically the growth of widespread land ownership parallels the increase in pools of money available for long-term loans.

With the advent of the Industrial Revolution in the eighteenth century, more individuals became capable of producing wealth with their ideas and their machinery. People began to find that they had another option opened to them: the life of a serf grubbing an existence from land owned by the nobility was no longer the only way to make a living. With the more widespread wealth came the demand for ways to make better use of accumulated money, and the seeds of our publicly owned savings institutions started to grow.

COLONIAL AMERICA

Prior to the Industrial Revolution, colonial America felt the need for capital to build its new homes and businesses. Many groups began to join together for mutual protection and mutual help. Savings were pooled in informal clubs or fraternal groups in order to provide lendable funds for members wishing to build a house, make an addition to their building, or to construct a barn. Organizations were created to provide fire protection for their members. And some groups arranged for periodic payments into the club treasury, which provided for a lump sum payment to the member's family at his death. The only problem here was that without regulation and accurate reserves based on mortality rates, the groups grew older, failed to attract younger members, and often went broke.

In spite of these setbacks, the desire for economic security and the need for the protection of capital helped spawn the banks, savings associations, and life insurance companies of the nineteenth century which have become great assets to our nation today. These older institutions, along with their many younger brothers, plus some exciting new pools of money such as pension funds and trust funds, are now providing us with the funds needed to own and develop our land. Table 1–1 gives a chronological outline of when the major institutions were formed in this country.

TABLE 1–1

Chronology of Key Agencies and Institutions Associated with Real Estate Finance in the United States

1759	Charter date of the oldest life insurance company in the United States. The Presbyterian Ministers Fund issued its first policy in 1761. The name was changed to Presbyterian Annuity and Life Insurance Company in 1889, thereafter insuring Protestant ministers, their wives, and theological students.
1781	Bank of North America, the oldest commercial bank in this country, opened in Philadelphia. It was chartered by the Pennsylvania legislature and incorporated by the Continental Congress for the purpose of providing money to wage the Revolutionary War against England through pooling of private and public resources.
1791	First Bank of the United States was the original effort to establish a national bank. This institution was promoted by Alexander Hamilton and chartered by the Congressional Federalists. The initial capitalization was $10 million, of which 20% was owned by the national government. The bank terminated in 1811 due to considerable opposition in Congress.
1812	The first public life insurance company was formed under the name of Pennsylvania Company for Insurance on Lives and Granting Annuities.
1816	The second Bank of the United States was established to exert some controls over private banks and to regulate the U. S. monetary system. This second attempt to establish a national banking system was successfully opposed by President Andrew Jackson and closed down in 1836. The federal government did not again resume responsibility for regulating bank notes until 1863, which was important since the state chartered banks could issue their own notes, which circulated as currency.

TABLE 1-1 (Continued)

1816	The first mutual savings bank was established and still operates under its original name—Philadelphia Savings Fund Society. The bank was organized to operate for the interests of its shareholders (its depositors) and it encouraged savings by factory workers and persons of modest means.
1831	The first savings and loan association was chartered in Philadelphia expressly to accumulate capital for building houses.
1835	New England Mutual was chartered as the first of the modern forms of life insurance companies.
1913	The Federal Reserve Bank was established by the federal government as a national bank to administer currency and to regulate federal chartered commercial banks and member state chartered banks.
1916	The government created the Federal Land Bank as a system to raise money through the sale of bonds for the purpose of making loans to farmers.
1932	Under the administration of Herbert Hoover, the Reconstruction Finance Corporation was established to provide direct loans to private business.
1932	The Federal Home Loan Bank was created as a regulatory agency to charter national savings and loan associations and to supervise their operations.
1933	On March 6, 1933, President Franklin D. Roosevelt closed all banks in the country to halt disastrous runs. Thereafter, those deemed in satisfactory condition could reopen. Within one year, the number of operating banks in this country was reduced from 30,000 to 16,000.
1933	Securities and Exchange Commission (SEC) was established to regulate the issuance and sale of all types of securities to the general public.
1934	Federal Housing Administration (FHA) created an organization to utilize the credit of the federal government to insure home loans and thus encourage lending from private sources.
1934	Farmer's Home Administration (FmHA) set up a federal program to provide direct home loans to low income farmers.

TABLE 1-1 (Continued)

1934 Federal Deposit Insurance Corporation (FDIC) provided a means to insure deposits in commercial banks against bank failure.

1934 Federal Savings and Loan Insurance Corporation (FSLIC) provided a corporate body similar to the FDIC that insures deposits in savings associations.

1937 Local Housing Authority (LHA) allowed for the creation of local bodies for the purpose of developing low-cost housing.

1938 Federal National Mortgage Association (FNMA) was the government agency established to provide funds for the purchase of FHA insured loans.

1944 Veterans Administration (VA) created during World War II to organize all assistance programs for veterans.

1965 Department of Housing and Urban Development (HUD) resulted from the reorganization of various government operations intended to coordinate and expand housing programs.

1968 Government National Mortgage Association (GNMA) created by the partitioning of the Federal National Mortgage Association as an agency under HUD to handle housing assistance programs and loan management functions.

1970 Federal Home Loan Mortgage Corporation (FHLMC) established by the Federal Home Loan Bank Board to sell bonds and use the proceeds to purchase mortgages from member savings associations.

1970 Environmental Protection Agency (EPA) created to develop rules and procedures for the improvement of our natural heritage with requirements for proper land development.

DEVELOPMENT OF MORTGAGE BANKING

In a growing country like the United States, the pools of lendable money were not always readily available where needed, or were not always known to a potential borrower. To help bridge the gap, a new industry gradually developed that is now known as mortgage banking. The precise date of its origin would be difficult to state because the mortgage banking business has developed from a small service or brokerage facility in the late 1800s into a major banking industry today. Initially, a lawyer, or perhaps a real estate broker with contacts in the investment world, would arrange a loan for his client and charge a service fee; and as some individuals became quite adept at this business, the placement of loans became their principal occupation. Even today, a large number of mortgage bankers come from first- or second-generation family-owned businesses.

LENDING REFORMS FROM THE GREAT DEPRESSION

Going back to the early 1900s just after the turn of the century, a potential borrower had three main sources from which he could seek a loan—a bank, an insurance company, or a wealthy individual. Or he could minimize his search by turning his problem over to a loan broker, who usually had several potential sources of funds available for a small fee. But the rules were quite different. A house loan might be 50% of the lender's estimate, to be repaid in full in five years—no amortization, no escrow account—a system that could cause an instant collapse—and did. Also, without some regulation, an individual or company could sell mortgage bonds up to the appraised value of a projected development, say a Florida resort hotel. And the "appraisal" could be made by no less an authority than the man trying to sell the bonds! In the 1920s these were the "gold bonds," which pretty much disappeared from circulation during the Depression.

The collapse of the real estate loan market in the early 1930s brought a flood of foreclosures with farms, houses, and businesses swept away. It is the now-passing generation who determined then for us that there must be a better way.

Many historic changes were wrought in our economy under the administration of Franklin Delano Roosevelt to prevent future economic disasters. The call by some economists in those days to "control the economy" or to "eliminate depressions" was the source of many jokes and was not taken too seriously by most people, including much of the business community. But controls were established nonetheless.

The Securities and Exchange Commission was brought into existence to regulate the sale of all types of securities to the general public. The bankruptcy laws were revised to deter one or two creditors from destroying a cash-short business at the expense of all the other creditors.

But the area of change bearing on our special interests encompasses the sweeping reforms made in real estate finance beginning with the closing of all banks in 1933. To start patching up the economy, the Home Owners Loan Corporation was formed that same year to issue government-guaranteed bonds and to use the proceeds to refinance home owners' indebtedness. Over one million houses were refinanced through this agency, and with the new liquidity in our financial institutions, stability was gradually restored.

A year later, in 1934, the Federal Housing Administration was created to provide home loan insurance. It did not then, and does not today, make loans. It provides a loan insurance policy, insuring the lender against loss through default, if the FHA qualifications are met. However, many bankers and other lenders, inherently opposed to any government intrusion, especially in an area where character judgment was considered all important, simply refused to recognize a government-insured commitment.

Hence, a few years later, in 1938, the Federal National Mortgage Association, FNMA or "Fannie Mae," was established to buy FHA insured mortgage loans and then to resell them as markets could be found. This agency provided the real beginnings of the so-called secondary market for mortgage loans, which may be broadly defined as any purchaser of a mortgage loan who does not participate in its origination. Money to finance FNMA purchases was derived from the sale of bonds.

By 1940, the pressures of a war economy brought an expansion of FHA activities to encourage housing in defense-designated areas and to permit financing of large apartment or multifamily projects. In 1944, Congress passed legislation permitting the Veterans Administration to guarantee mortgage loans made by private lenders to veterans.

POST-WORLD WAR II EXPANSION

The post-World War II growth of government-assisted financing has paralleled and supported the growth of the mortgage banking industry. Were it not for the lubrication provided by multiservice mortgage bankers, the government would be much less efficient in spreading its insured programs to those needing loan assistance. Both the FHA and the VA lean heavily on mortgage bankers approved by these agencies as having met their standards, and who are therefore qualified (1) to disseminate correct requirements and data to the public, (2) to secure the necessary information on a loan applicant's qualifications, and (3) to proceed to arrange prompt funding for the loan upon issuance of a government commitment.

The growth of government programs parallels and in no way diminishes the continuing expansion of savings associations and insurance companies in providing mortgage loans either direct to clients, or through correspondents, for houses, apartments, and commercial buildings.

In addition, the recent years have seen a new pool of money entering the real estate field in pension and trust funds. Since most of these funds have little contact with the general public, such moneys move primarily through the mortgage banking industry.

FUTURE REAL ESTATE DEVELOPMENT

Looking toward the future, we foresee demands for ever larger land developments where financing requirements will exceed the capacity and capability of the average developer. Community-type developments offering a wide range of recreational, educational, visual, and other amenities could make traditional financing methods inadequate. The New Communities Act of 1968 and the Tax Reform Act of 1969 are indications that the federal government will become increasingly involved in financing large developments of the future. On the private side, many major companies as diverse as Westinghouse, Ford Motor Company, and Exxon have entered the real estate development field where large amounts of cash are essential. But as some companies have learned, considerably more than money is needed to succeed with land developments.

Probably the greatest impact on real estate growth will be made by the growing national real estate firms and developers who are large enough to bypass the traditional financing channels and can generate their own funds through the sale of stocks and bonds, through real estate trust funds, and through their ability to sell commercial paper or borrow short-term funds at commercial banks without resort to mortgages. These concerns are becoming large enough to cope with the multiplying problems of environmental impact and other land-use restrictions that are springing up throughout the country. This is important since environmental clearances alone have added tremendously to the time and cost factors required to successfully launch any major development.

MONEY
AND
INTEREST RATES

No commodity is more widely used and less well understood than money. In a limited sense, we know very well what money can do: its value lies primarily in our confidence that other people will accept the money in exchange for their goods and services. A brief reference to history shows that money has long been with us in all civilizations as a means to improve the barter system of trading goods and services among people. Commodities of high intrinsic value have always been used in trade, including precious metals, gem stones, furs, and even salt and other spices. In fact, many areas of the world still use such standards today. Our modern business, however, floats on an intangible— the trust and confidence that individuals and nations place in currency and credit lines extended for bonds or other promissory certificates issued under a recognized government's authority. Certainly, the confidence placed in a government and its international trading power is indicated by the relative values placed on a nation's money in the realm of international trade.

So in a broad and sweeping context, the movement of money from the government, the interrelationship with the Federal Reserve Bank

System, the controls exercised over the banking system itself, the role played by large investment institutions, and additionally, the relationship of U. S. currency to that of other nations pose complex questions not easily answered.

Some of the rules are clearly defined, but money does not respond to regulation according to a precisely defined and predictable pattern. For instance, one basic aspect of our *monetary* policies, that is, the manner in which our government controls the money supply, depends on a blend of pressures and influences to encourage or discourage the flow of private money resources. In dealing with our *fiscal* policies, i.e., the manner in which the government controls its budget with tax and spending programs, we are dealing with more tangible pressures such as the actual expenditure of cash by the government. More and more, we are accepting deficit, and therefore inflationary, spending as a normal procedure.

As an economist views the current situation, the government's fiscal policy must balance an acceptable level of inflation with an acceptable level of unemployment. In implementing monetary or fiscal policies, the government necessarily works through the same basic forces of supply and demand that control prices and movements of other commodities in the free, competitive market system within which our country is supposed to operate.

Under this free market system, savings or nonspent money will tend to move where it earns the greatest yield. If interest rates are much higher in Europe, investing companies, banks, and giant multinational corporations tend to move their cash reserves overseas. And this movement would effectively reduce the supply of money available for mortgage and other lending purposes in the United States.

MONEY SUPPLY

There is, of course, a limit on the total money supply in our country. Only recently has foreign money started to flow into investments in the United States in large amounts— and the expectation is that it will continue as a growth factor, especially as the result of the billions that will be poured into the Middle East for oil. Prior to the influx of foreign money into the United States, the total increase or decrease in currency and deposits had been under the tight control of the Federal Reserve Board, whose directors are appointed by the President of the United States, with tenure, so as to minimize direct political pressures. When the United States Treasury sells bonds to the Federal Reserve, payment is made in the form of newly printed currency or deposits posted to the government's account with the Federal Reserve Bank. However, the Federal Reserve Board itself exercises an independent, discretionary judgment and decides when and how much new money will be released. The Board tries to increase the money supply commensurate with the normal needs and growth requirements of our economy and population, rather than releasing it simply as a means of financing the government's spending programs.

For obvious reasons, the Federal Reserve Board does not announce its decisions on the money supply in advance since the effect on the various markets could be precipitous. But the results of these decisions can be observed in the weekly reports published on money supply in the United States.

THE MEANING OF M_1 AND M_2

In order to obtain greater clarity of analysis, economists use two categories of money supply, which are designated as M_1 and M_2.

M_1 is the currency in circulation outside the banks plus the demand deposits in the banks. This is the active money, and it has shown a steady increase in quantity. In a sample period from 1965 to 1974, the currency and demand deposits (M_1) increased from a total of $167 billion to $276 billion— a 65% increase in ten years. These figures are only a part of the money available, as the rest of the total money supply is represented in the time deposits held by savings associations, mutual banks, and commercial banks. And in the time deposits during the same 1965 to 1974 period, the total more than doubled—from $145 billion to $308 billion.

Now add them all together—the currency, the demand deposits and the time deposits—and you have what is called M₂ or total money supply. During the sample ten-year period (1965 to 1974), these totals increased from $311 billion to $558 billion. During this climb in money supply, it is interesting to note that the year 1969 showed the first actual drop in total money supply since 1948. The drop in M₂ from $404 billion to $398 billion in that year was one of the major causes triggering the credit crunch of 1969–1970.

ROLE OF THE FEDERAL GOVERNMENT

A number of agencies and branches of the federal government exert an influence on the movement of money and on the overall economy. As a branch of the government and the guardian of our money supply, the Federal Reserve prints the money and establishes credit within its banks for the federal government in exchange for bonds. The Federal Reserve also influences money supply through its control of member banks. It does this by determining reserve and liquidity requirements, plus the purchase and sale of government bonds held by the member banks. This topic will be covered further in the section on "Interest Rates."

The United States Treasury issues the government bonds, and sets the policies controlling the funding and refunding of our national debt. The methods used to fund the annual deficits play an important role in both the money market and the capital market. In 1972, with a large federal deficit to finance, the Treasury elected to sell bonds in the short-term money market—an unusual procedure, although economically reasonable. The short-term market is more liquid and far more absorptive of the new issues than the long-term capital markets. The interest rates therefore are generally higher in the short-term market and require faster refunding. But the administration knew that a sustained soaking-up of long-term funds through the sale of government bonds would reduce the money available for mortgage loans and would force curtailment of a booming construction industry

—and, it should be recalled, 1972 was an election year.

The Secretary of the Treasury is also charged with administering certain controls over other federal agencies in their handling of government commitments. Some of these agencies with major influence in the capital markets are the Federal Housing Administration, the Veterans Administration, the Government National Mortgage Association, the Federal Home Loan Bank System, the Farmers Home Administration, the Federal Land Banks, and the various governmental pension and trust funds.

ROLE OF PRIVATE LENDING INSTITUTIONS

Private lending institutions are subject to a number of governmental regulations and supervising authorities designed to insure the safekeeping of the public's invested savings. Within these regulations, the lending institutions are faced with their own internal money supply problems.

All lending institutions exercise limits on the amount of a single loan, and are, of course, limited by their own assets as to total money available for loans. The three prime sources of lendable cash are: (1) new deposits into savings accounts (2) new premium payments to life insurance companies, and (3) the repayments of previous loans, which would include the interest earned on these loans. In the 1968–1969 period, new deposits almost dried up, insurance companies were hit by demands for loans by policyholders, and many lenders found themselves overcommitted on future loans. Cash for mortgage loans was hard to find.

Insurance companies are not so dependent on mortgage lending and can shift their investments as the market changes. But the thrift institutions, savings associations, and mutual savings banks are deeply committed to mortgage loans. In order to give savings associations greater liquidity, the Federal Home Loan Bank Board established the Federal Home Loan Mortgage Corporation (Freddie Mac) in 1970, whose purpose is to buy mortgage loans from member associations and thus enable them to restore their cash position.

Freddie Mac is another example of the government's efforts to improve and stabilize the flow of mortgage money through privately owned institutions. The availability of an additional source of money to liquidate or reduce a mortgage loan portfolio in a savings association gives support to the market when money becomes tight. However, all private lenders exercise their own judgment as to how they will use the various sources available to them to sell loans and thus have more cash available for further lending. Some associations actively sell most of their loans, but continue to service the collections, while many of the more conservative associations confine their lending exclusively to their own assets.

INTEREST RATES

As indicated in the first section of this chapter, investment money flows to the highest yields, specifically to that type of loan that offers the highest return commensurate with the safety and security of the money. The question, then, is: Who sets the interest rates and what forces change them?

Contrary to much popular opinion, neither the government nor a mysterious "banking monopoly" actually determines interest rates, although both can influence them. Underlying all interest rates are the forces of open market supply and demand over the long-term basis. The continuing day-to-day analysis and interpretation of these complex forces of supply and demand rest in the hands of the major lending institutions and of the government itself.

It is important to recognize that the interest rate quoted is only a part of the story, since the real fluctuation in money costs is in the total yield that money earns. The yield includes all income received from a loan, which includes the initial loan fee, if any; a discount deducted from the loan, which increases the return to the lender; plus any other participation or fees that may be assessed for making a loan.

A good example of the incongruity of attempting to set an interest rate in a free market exists in the Federal Housing Administration's fixed interest rates for mortgage loans. The rate established by the Secretary of Housing and Urban Development under the authority of Congress often has to be adjusted in the private money market through changes in the amount of discount required to make a loan. The FHA loans would otherwise be noncompetitive in attracting the private money market, where all FHA-insured commitments must be funded.

In 1973, the FHA held steadfastly to a 7% interest rate while the discount reached 9% of the loan (or nine points), as mortgage yields climbed. Finally, recognizing the considerable imbalance that existed, an adjustment was made to a 7¾% interest rate, and the discount subsequently fell about five points, thus keeping the actual yield to the investor virtually unchanged. In the face of continued upward pressures on interest rates, the Secretary of HUD shortly advanced the rate to 8½%.

The loan manager of a lending institution would not long retain his job if he continued to make loans at a 7% interest rate on FHA-insured loans when he could obtain an 8% rate on comparable conventional loans. Hence, there is a need for a means of adjusting yields in a competitive market that insures a more even flow of lendable funds. And this is the purpose of the discount.

Since there is, as yet, no national market in mortgages with quoted rates on yields such as we find in commodity markets or the stock exchanges, the industry relies on many guides, which certainly would include some individual intuition. One of the more important guides in determining interest rates is the movement of yields on other long-term investments. These include the daily published rates on government and corporate bonds. If a new government bond issue sells rapidly at its offered price, the strength is duly noted by other lenders, and there is a tendency to move interest rates upward. If an issue finds few buyers, the market moves downward.

The rapidly fluctuating short-term money market exerts an influence on long-term interest rates by the direction of its trend. Short-term rates trending upward eventually force long-term rates higher, or else the flow of money temporarily shifts to the short-term arena.

It is evident then that the major forces acting upon these rates are those of supply and demand. Looking at the supply aspect, that large source of our mortgage money, the savings association, provides us with an example. Over the years, our nation has enjoyed a considerable increase in the individual savings held by millions of families. The interest rate paid by associations to their depositors is fixed by government regulation at a relatively low return. By contrast, rates on other forms of savings such as Treasury bills can fluctuate widely. Hence, from time to time, these associations suffer massive withdrawals of funds by individuals looking for higher yields in other forms of investment or perhaps simply trying to wage the battle against constantly inflating prices.

In times of heavy withdrawals, the supply of money available for loans diminishes, in some cases to the point of a complete lack of lendable funds. But as the supply diminishes, savings associations are under pressure to increase interest rates for loans in an effort to discourage further borrowing.

Turning now to the demand factor, the need for mortgage money is strongly influenced by the need for housing. And this need follows the population growth pattern, with young married adults becoming the central, dominating group. The demand for commercial mortgage money, for such investments as shopping centers, office buildings, and warehouses, also grows with the population but is more subject to the economics of prevailing interest rates. As interest rates rise, the prudent developer will tend to postpone a new shopping center, whereas a home buyer may simply look to a smaller house than otherwise, as his need for living space is not only a question of economics but also a basic need to provide housing for his family.

So it can be seen that the movement of interest rates is the result of a variety of factors. These may include the cold facts of business economics for the developers, the social requirements of a family, or the side effects of other business activities such as energy needs, plus other intangible factors. One of these might be psychological pressures, such as panic buying, or fears of uncertain income in an inflationary cycle, or fears of a recession or depression. All of these things, and more, affect the cost of money.

Specific Influences on Interest Rates

The interplay of influences and pressures in our economic world as they affect the rise and fall of interest rates can be outlined in the following four categories:

Supply of Money. For lending purposes, we must find and understand those factors that influence the inflow of funds into the large sources. One of these, the inclination to save a portion of one's earnings, both by individuals and corporations, for the "rainy day," is still quite strong. As this money flows into the great pools of private funds (commercial banks, thrift institutions, and life insurance companies), their capacity for lending more money obviously increases. As our economy has grown, the increase in savings has been correspondingly steady, although more so in some years than others. Situations arise, for instance, in which the movement of funds between various institutions causes periodic shortages of money in certain areas. The competitive efforts among the savings associations, among the banks, and between banks and savings associations to garner more deposits, mostly at each other's expense, may cause some changes in the availability of money for mortgage lending. For example, competition has surfaced in such ways as changes in interest rates offered for various types of deposits; gifts or premiums for opening new accounts or substantially enlarging old ones; and even the introduction of a checking account procedure into savings associations, currently carried on in the New England area associations by means of an instrument called a Negotiable Order of Withdrawal (or NOW). Whether or not savings will be allowed to accumulate in the banks, thrift institutions, and life insurance companies portfolios also depends on the condition of business in general. In times of increasing inflationary pressures it is often necessary to draw against savings reserves to meet rising costs. Or inflation could spur an interest in spending money on major appliances or a car before prices increase further. The element of mass psychology is inherently involved in this area and complicates the problems of analysis and prediction.

Demand for Money. The basic supply of money in the country does not fluctuate nearly as much as the demand. There are four major areas of demand covering both long-term and short-term needs that compete with each other for the available supply. These are:

1. *Business borrowing*—all forms of loans, inventory needs, tax requirements, long-term funds, and others.
2. *Consumer and personal loans*—installment loans, auto financing, personal requirements.
3. *Government financing*—federal, state, and municipal bond issues, short-term needs, government agency issues.
4. *Mortgage loans*—all types: construction, development, income properties, housing, etc.

In a booming economy, all segments have needs that add to the upward pressures on interest rates in their efforts to attract the necessary financing. Regulations have been eased that previously restricted the interest rates that could be paid on bond issues by cities and states, and their issues have now become more competitive. Efforts to reduce demand by forcing acceptance of higher interest rates have not always been effective, however, because businesses can afford the higher rates if its competitors are forced to pay the same costs. The federal government is not restricted as to what interest it can pay in the bill and bond markets, and Congress has never publicly expressed concern for money costs when voting for a deficit spending program.

The lower end of the capability spectrum includes people on fixed incomes who are not always able to pay the extra interest costs required to purchase a car or new house. In a sagging economy, the lowering of interest rates does not in itself create much new demand for money. The inclination to borrow for an expansion of facilities or for an increase in inventory is neither strong nor urgent when business declines.

Monetary Policies of the Federal Reserve Bank. The Board of Governors of the Federal Reserve has the power to influence and, to a substantial degree, to exercise control over interest rates. The economic tools it uses to achieve and maintain these controls are:

1. *The rate of increase in money supply.* The amount of money in circulation is a direct responsibility of the Federal Reserve. In order to maintain a stable condition, the money supply should be allowed to increase at a rate comparable to our normal economic growth. To dampen inflationary pressures, the Fed can reduce the rate of increase, which simply makes less funds available to be loaned out by our banking system. Conversely, to spur a lagging economy, the rate of increase can be accelerated to place more lendable funds in circulation.

2. *Open market operations.* By buying government bonds in the market, the Fed puts money into the accounts of sellers and thus increases bank deposits, which in turn provides more lendable funds. When the Fed sells bonds, money is withdrawn from the bank accounts of the buyers, and this has a dampening effect on money available for loans.

3. *Changes in member bank reserve requirements.* All Federal Reserve member banks, which includes all the major banks in the country, are subject to rules that specify the percentage of their assets that must be held in reserve, i.e., assets unavailable for any loans, together with the percentage of liquidity, that is, cash and deposits that must be held in the Federal Reserve Bank. The reserve requirement varies between 12% and 17% of a bank's assets depending on its size. By increasing the reserve requirement, the Federal Reserve is simply ordering withdrawal of a certain amount of cash from availability for loans. And by reducing this reserve requirement, more money is placed in the hands of the banking system to be loaned out.

4. *Discount rate.* The Federal Reserve member banks are permitted to borrow money from the Federal Reserve Bank system, but the loans must be fully collateralized. The use of this privilege is intended more as a standby security measure

than as a normal commercial procedure. The rate that the Fed charges its member banks is called the *discount rate*. By adjusting this discount rate, the Fed tries to exercise some influence over the potential borrowings of its member banks, and thus control the amount of money they could make available for loans to their own customers. A change in the discount rate is an important signal to the banks, encouraging a change in their own lending rates. However, in actual practice, it has not proved to be a very effective tool. The attempt in 1973 to hold down the inflationary boom with successive increases in the discount rate proved of small value. The rate in that one year increased from 4½% at the beginning of the year to an all-time record of 8% by the following fall. The member banks managed to follow each raise with an equivalent increase in their own lending rates to all-time highs. And business demand for loans seldom wavered in the face of rising interest costs, largely because prices were increasing at a rapid enough rate to cover the costs. The effect of a lowering in the discount rate does have a positive effect, but if the business climate is not good, then businesses will not borrow money even at low rates. The need for borrowing must be present.

Fiscal Policies of the U.S. Government. The manner in which the government handles its tax and spending programs is a major factor in controlling the business cycle and, in turn, the demand for money. Within ill-defined bounds, an increase in taxes, primarily the income taxes on persons and corporations, will take money out of the hands of people who would otherwise spend it for more goods; whereas a decrease in taxes should serve as a spur to the economy. As for the spending side of the policy, a big deficit spending program is intended to increase a lagging economy and bring forth some inflationary pressures; whereas restricted spending programs should dampen business activity and slow down the economy. The economic interaction isn't quite so simple as suggested, however, since deficit spending creates the corresponding problem of raising the cash to finance the loss, which is done by selling more government bonds, thus soaking up lendable funds that might have been used for other purposes in the private sector of the economy.

CAPITAL MARKET—MONEY MARKET

Reference has been made to the terms *capital market* and *money market* in this text. Investment money that moves into short-term loans is generally designated for a term of less than three years. Examples of short-term loans are Treasury bills, commercial paper (corporation promissory notes), certificates of deposit, federal funds, and installment loans. This is the *money* market.

The long-term *capital* market is investment money loaned for periods of ten years or longer. This is the market that deals in mortgage loans. Other examples of long-term loans that compete with mortgage loans for the available funds are government bonds and corporate bonds. Government bonds include both the federally issued bonds of many types and maturities, and the income tax-exempt municipal bonds. Corporate bonds are classed as industrial, utility, and railroad bonds.

MORTGAGE LOANS BY TYPE OF PROPERTY AND FINANCING

To give the reader a better idea of the total amount of money invested in mortgage loans and how it is invested, the tables on the following pages show the growth over the past ten years. The figures are published periodically by the Federal Reserve Bank under the heading of "Real Estate Credit."

It is interesting to note that over the ten-year span (1964 through 1973), the amount invested in one- to four-family houses has declined from 65 percent to 60 percent of the total of all mortgage money invested. The mortgage demands for multi-family housing and commercial properties has shown a larger percentage increase. On the division between the amount of money invested in conventional loans versus the federally underwritten loans, the conventional type has had a small increase from 72 percent to 75 percent of the total outstanding loans.

TABLE 2–1

Mortgage Debt Outstanding 1964–1973
(In billions of dollars)

End of period	*All properties*				*Farm*		
			Other holders [2]				
	All holders	*Financial institutions* [1]	*U.S. agencies*	*Individuals and others*	*All holders*	*Financial institutions* [1]	*Other holders* [3]
1964	300.1	241.0	11.4	47.7	18.9	7.0	11.9
1965	325.8	264.6	12.4	48.7	21.2	7.8	13.4
1966	347.4	280.8	15.8	50.9	23.3	8.4	14.9
1967	370.2	298.8	18.4	53.0	25.5	9.1	16.3
1968	397.5	319.9	21.7	55.8	27.5	9.7	17.8
1969	425.3	339.1	26.8	59.4	29.5	9.9	19.6
1970	451.7	355.9	33.0	62.8	31.2	10.1	21.1
1971	499.9	394.4	39.4	66.2	32.9	9.9	23.0
1972	565.4	450.6	45.8	69.0	35.4	10.5	24.9
1971–III	485.6	383.5	37.4	64.6	32.4	9.8	22.6
IV	499.9	394.4	39.4	66.2	32.9	9.9	23.0
1972–I	511.7	404.2	41.2	66.4	33.5	9.9	23.6
II	529.1	418.9	42.7	67.5	34.4	10.2	24.2
III	547.3	434.6	44.3	68.3	35.0	10.3	24.7
IV	565.4	450.6	45.8	69.0	35.4	10.5	24.9
1973–I	580.1	463.3	47.3	69.5	36.5	10.7	25.8
II	600.4	480.5	49.0	71.0	37.7	11.0	26.7
III[p]	619.9	494.9	53.0	71.9	38.7	11.4	27.3

[1] Commercial banks (including nondeposit trust companies but not trust depts.), mutual savings banks, life insurance companies, and savings and loan assns.

[2] U.S. agencies include former Federal National Mortgage Assoc. and, beginning fourth quarter 1968, new Government National Mortgage Assoc. as well as Federal Housing Admin., Veterans Admin., Public Housing Admin., Farmers Home Admin. They also include U.S. sponsored agencies—new FNMA, Federal land banks, GNMA (Pools), and the Federal Home Loan Mortgage Corp. Other U.S. agencies (amounts small or separate data not readily available) included with "individuals and others."

[3] Derived figures; includes debt held by Federal land banks and farm debt held by Farmers Home Admin.

| | Nonfarm | | | | | | | |
| | 1- to 4-family houses [4] | | | Multifamily and commercial properties [5] | | | Mortgage type [6] | |
All holders	Total	Financial institutions [1]	Other holders	Total	Financial institutions [1]	Other holders	FHA-VA-underwritten	Conventional
281.2	197.6	170.3	27.3	83.6	63.7	19.9	77.2	204.0
304.6	212.9	184.3	28.7	91.6	72.5	19.1	81.2	223.4
324.1	223.6	192.1	31.5	100.5	80.2	20.3	84.1	240.0
344.8	236.1	201.8	34.2	108.7	87.9	20.9	88.2	256.6
370.0	251.2	213.1	38.1	118.7	97.1	21.6	93.4	276.6
395.9	266.8	223.7	43.2	129.0	105.5	23.5	100.2	295.7
420.5	280.2	231.3	48.9	140.3	114.5	25.8	109.2	311.3
467.0	307.8	254.2	53.7	159.2	130.3	28.9	120.7	346.3
530.0	346.1	288.7	57.4	183.9	151.3	32.6	131.1	398.9
453.2	299.7	248.0	51.7	153.5	125.8	27.7	117.5	335.7
467.0	307.8	254.2	53.7	159.2	130.3	28.9	120.7	346.3
478.2	314.1	259.6	54.5	164.1	134.6	29.4	123.7	354.5
494.8	324.6	268.8	55.8	170.2	140.0	30.3	126.6	368.2
512.3	335.8	279.2	56.6	176.5	145.1	31.3	129.0	383.3
530.0	346.1	288.7	57.4	183.9	151.3	32.6	131.1	398.9
543.6	353.9	296.3	57.6	189.7	156.4	33.4	132.5	411.1
562.7	365.7	306.9	58.8	197.0	162.5	34.5	133.6	429.1
581.2	376.6	315.0	61.6	204.5	168.5	36.0	. . . .	. . . .

[4] For multifamily and total residential properties, see tables below.

[5] Derived figures; includes small amounts of farm loans held by savings and loan assns.

[6] Data by type of mortgage on nonfarm 1- to 4-family properties alone are shown in table below.

Note: Based on data from Federal Deposit Insurance Corp., Federal Home Loan Bank Board, Institute of Life Insurance, Depts. of Agriculture and Commerce, FNMA, FHA, PHA, VA, GNMA, FHLMC, and Comptroller of the Currency.

Figures for first three quarters of each year are F.R. estimates.

TABLE 2-2

Mortgage Debt Outstanding
on Residential Properties
(In billions of dollars)

End of period	All residential			Multifamily [1]		
	Total	Financial institutions	Other holders	Total	Financial institutions	Other holders
1964	231.1	195.4	35.7	33.6	25.1	8.5
1965	250.1	213.2	36.9	37.2	29.0	8.2
1966	264.0	223.7	40.3	40.3	31.5	8.8
1967	280.0	236.6	43.4	43.9	34.7	9.2
1968	298.6	250.8	47.8	47.3	37.7	9.7
1969	319.0	265.0	54.0	52.2	41.3	10.8
1970	338.2	277.1	61.1	58.0	45.8	12.2
1971	374.7	306.1	68.5	66.8	52.0	14.9
1972	422.5	347.9	74.6	76.4	59.1	17.3
1971—III ..	364.0	298.4	65.6	64.3	50.4	13.9
IV ..	374.7	306.1	68.5	66.8	52.0	14.9
1972—I	382.9	312.9	70.0	68.8	53.3	15.4
II ...	395.8	324.1	71.7	71.3	55.3	16.0
III ..	409.3	336.1	73.2	73.5	56.9	16.6
IV ..	422.5	347.9	74.6	76.4	59.1	17.3
1973—I	432.8	357.4	75.5	79.0	61.1	17.9
II ...	447.9	370.4	77.5	82.2	63.5	18.7
III[p] ..	461.6	380.0	81.6	85.0	65.0	20.0

[1] Structures of five or more units.

Note: Based on data from same source as for "Mortgage Debt Outstanding" table above.

In these tables the role of our financial institutions, which are the savings associations, commercial banks, life insurance companies, and mutual savings banks, are lumped into

TABLE 2–3

Mortgage Debt Outstanding on
Nonfarm 1- to 4-Family Properties
(In billions of dollars)

| End of period | Total | Government-underwritten | | | Con-ven-tional |
		Total	FHA-in-sured	VA-guaran-teed [1]	
1964	197.6	69.2	38.3	30.9	128.3
1965	212.9	73.1	42.0	31.1	139.8
1966	223.6	76.1	44.8	31.3	147.6
1967	236.1	79.9	47.4	32.5	156.1
1968	251.2	84.4	50.6	33.8	166.8
1969	266.8	90.2	54.5	35.7	176.6
1970	280.2	97.3	59.9	37.3	182.9
1971	307.8	105.2	65.7	39.5	202.6
1972	346.1	113.0	68.2	44.7	233.1
1971–III	299.7	102.9	64.4	38.5	196.8
IV	307.8	105.2	65.7	39.5	202.6
1972–I	314.1	107.5	66.8	40.7	206.6
II	324.6	109.6	67.6	42.0	215.0
III	335.8	111.5	68.4	43.1	224.3
IV	346.1	113.0	68.2	44.7	233.1
1973–I	353.9	113.7	67.9	45.8	204.2
II	365.7	114.7	67.5	47.2	251.0
III[p]	376.6	. . . .	. . . .	. . . .	. . . .

[1] Includes outstanding amount of VA vendee accounts held by private investors under repurchase agreement.

Note: For total debt outstanding, figures are FHLBB and F.R. estimates. For conventional, figures are derived.

Based on data from FHLBB, Federal Housing Admin., and Veterans Admin.

one column. The breakdown of how each of these institutions is involved in mortgage lending is detailed in further explanatory tables in Chapter 4.

NOTES
AND
MORTGAGES

Loans made with real estate as the collateral security can be traced back as far as the ancient Pharaohs of Egypt and the Romans of a pre-Christian era. Even then, some form of pledge or assignment of the property was used to ensure repayment of an obligation to the lender. The development over many centuries of this type of property assignment illustrates the interplay of individual rights, more specifically, the rights of a borrower as against the rights of a lender.

HISTORY AND DEVELOPMENT

The Mortgage as a Grant of Title to Property

In its earliest forms, a property pledge to secure a debt was an actual assignment of that property to the lender. During the term of the loan, the lender might even have the physical use of that land and was entitled to any rents or other revenues derived from the land pledged. Thus, the earliest form of land as security for a loan was the actual granting of title to the lender for the term of the loan.

Due to the primitive conditions of communications and transportation then in existence, the practice of granting title to property for a loan tended to foster a number of abuses by lenders. For example, a slight delay in payments, which might even be encouraged by the lender, easily created a default and forfeited the borrower's rights for any recovery of his land. Sometimes borrowers who felt they had been unjustly deprived of their property appealed to the king, or perhaps to an appointed minister, to seek a hearing for their grievances and to petition for just redress. And if it was subsequently determined that a wrong had been committed, the borrower might be given a chance to redeem his land with a late payment of the obligation. Thus the *right of redemption* came into being.

However, lenders were not happy with this redemption privilege and initiated a countermove by inserting a clause in future loan agreements that specifically waived the right of redemption. The borrower had to accept this clause or be denied the loan. As our civilization developed away from the unchallenged rule of an absolute monarch into written codes of law, the granting or refusal of redemption became a matter of law or of statute often referred to as *statutory redemption*. Variations in such laws among the states are substantial, going all the way from a total lack of redemption rights upon default up to two full years after default to pay off the loan and recover the property.

The Mortgage as a Lien

Another way in which land can be pledged as security for a loan is by means of granting a lien. A *lien* constitutes an encumbrance on property. It is a declaration of a claim to a parcel of land for some purpose that is recorded in the public record. In states where the lien form is prevalent, a pledge of land as security for a loan grants no title except under default of the obligation. So when a default does occur, the lender must convert his lien rights into an actual title to the property through court action, as the particular state may require.

While there is some variation in the precise usage of the lien as a form of pledge, and the limited assignment of title as another form of pledge, all property laws concerning mortgages can be classified into one or the other forms. The advantages and disadvantages of each can be weighed as legal arguments, but for purposes of finance, it is important mainly to be aware of the existing differences and to know under what laws a particular property can be mortgaged.

Lenders have learned to live with various requirements, and can obtain adequate security for their loans by adapting their pledges to the many different laws. For example, they have adjusted even to the unique law spelled out in the original constitution of the State of Texas protecting a family homestead from all creditors with just three exceptions—one of these being a loan for purchase of the property, the second is mechanics and materialmen's liens, and the third is property tax.

STATE LAWS CONTROL PROPERTY RIGHTS

Property rights in the United States are spelled out primarily under state laws, not by the federal government. And each state has written into its code of law specific rights that must be adhered to with regard to land ownership in that state. The local variations and shadings in these laws reflect the background and origins of the particular region. In the East, for example, the great body of English parliamentary law and common law guided the New England and mid-Atlantic states in setting up their constitutions and subsequent statutes. In the South, on the other hand, the French legal codes were reflected in the Louisiana Territory and were especially evident in the growing city of New Orleans. In still another section of the country, the Southwest, Spanish heritage determined the laws, and these laws recognized Catholic religious ties in marriage, as well as patriarchal protection of wife, children, and family relationships. As a result, community property statutes were enacted, and for many years special protections, as well as special limitations regarding women's property rights, were in force in this region of the country.

An attempt to cover such a broad field of law as real

property rights on a national basis would be out of place in this text since it is a subject more properly handled by qualified attorneys, skilled in interpreting these rights according to the laws of each state. It can be pointed out, however, that most states have laws specifically limiting any conveyance of property rights to written agreements, and that all states require certain procedures to record conveyances of land in the public records. The result has been an increasingly accurate record of land titles, with a corresponding increase of protection for property owner's rights and those of any other interested parties.

THE MORTGAGE AND PROMISSORY NOTE

There are certain basic instruments used in real estate loans that have essentially the same purposes throughout the country. The most important of this group—and in fact the one that has given its name to the entire field of real estate finance—is the *mortgage*. A mortgage is simply a pledge of property to secure a loan. It is not a promise to pay anything. As a matter of fact, without a debt to secure, the mortgage itself becomes null and void by its own terms; or, as the French derivative of the word mortgage indicates, a "dead pledge." Due to the differences in state laws, the precise definition would vary somewhat, but for our purposes a mortgage can best be defined as a limited conveyance of property as security for the debt recited therein, which can only be activated by failure to comply with its terms.

It is the promissory note, the actual promise to pay, which must accompany, or in some cases becomes a part of, the mortgage instrument that is the real proof of the debt and calls out the payment terms including the rate of interest. It is the note that defaults for nonpayment, not the mortgage instrument. The expression *mortgage default* is a technical misnomer. When the promissory note falls into default, the mortgage instrument is activated and becomes the means of protecting the lender's collateral.

In 1970, the Federal National Mortgage Association decided to expand its lending activities from exclusively FHA-

and VA-underwritten loans into the larger area of conventional loans, that is to say, those loans without government underwriting. In order to provide a more uniform standard of collateral, the FNMA devised a mortgage instrument with a wider application than previously used. No one form could be used throughout the country because of variations in state laws. By way of illustration then, the following pages show some reproductions of forms in general usage—a note and deed of trust as used in California, and a note and mortgage as used in Michigan. The text of the mortgage instruments delineates between uniform covenants and nonuniform covenants, which simplifies a comparison. It should be noted that due to the strong position of the FNMA, this particular form may be considered closest to a national standard mortgage instrument.

The reader should also note the reproduction of the FNMA promissory note that must accompany, and is essential to, the contract completion of the mortgage pledge.

CLAUSES FOUND IN MORTGAGE INSTRUMENTS

Identification of *parties* in the initial clause spells out the precise names of all parties involved, the borrower or mortgagor, and the lender or mortgagee. In many states a wife must join her husband to create a binding pledge on real property. As in all such legal instruments, the parties must be legally qualified (of legal age, of sound mind, etc.) to undertake the contract. It is important for the lender to make sure that *all* parties holding an interest in the title to any pledged property are a party to the mortgage pledge.

Identification of the *property* used as security must be accurately described so as to distinguish it from any other property in the world (see Chapter 7). A street address is never acceptable, nor are boundary lines based on physical features, such as the "big live oak by the river bend." Accurate legal descriptions are normally used either by "metes and bounds" (a surveyor's description of boundary lines from a fixed starting point, thence proceeding in specific compass directions and distances around the prop-

NOTE

US $ ...., California

City

...., 19 ....

FOR VALUE RECEIVED, the undersigned promise to pay...
...., or order, the principal sum of
....Dollars, with interest
on the unpaid principal balance from the date of this Note, until paid, at the rate of..............................
percent per annum. The principal and interest shall be payable at..
...., or such other place as the holder hereof may designate in
writing, in consecutive monthly installments of..
Dollars (US $ ....), on the.. day of each month beginning
...., 19 ...., until the entire indebtedness evidenced hereby is fully
paid, except that any remaining indebtedness, if not sooner paid, shall be due and payable on the
....day of...

    If any monthly installment under this Note is not paid when due and remains unpaid after a date specified by a notice sent by certified mail to the undersigned at the address stated below or at such address as the undersigned may designate to the holder hereof by certified mail, which date shall be not less than thirty days from the date such notice is mailed, the entire principal amount outstanding hereunder and accrued interest thereon shall at once become due and payable at the option of the holder hereof. Failure to exercise such option shall not constitute a waiver of the right to exercise such option if the undersigned is in default hereunder. In the event of any default in the payment of this Note and if suit is brought hereon, the holder hereof shall be entitled to collect in such proceeding all reasonable costs and expenses of suit, including, but not limited to, reasonable attorney's fees.

    The undersigned shall pay to the holder hereof a late charge of 4 percent of any monthly installment not received by the holder hereof on or before the 15th day after the installment is due.

    The undersigned shall have the right to prepay the principal amount outstanding in whole or in part, provided that the holder hereof may require that any partial prepayments shall be made on the date monthly installments are due and shall be in the amount of that part of one or more installments which would be applicable to principal. Any partial prepayment shall be applied against the principal amount outstanding and shall not extend or postpone the due date of any subsequent monthly installments or change the amount of such installments, unless the holder hereof shall otherwise agree in writing.

    Presentment, notice of dishonor, and protest are hereby waived by all makers, sureties, guarantors and endorsers hereof. This Note shall be the joint and several obligation of all makers, sureties, guarantors and endorsers, and shall be binding upon them and their heirs, personal representatives, successors and assigns.

    The indebtedness evidenced by this Note is secured by a Deed of Trust, dated of even date herewith, and reference is made thereto for rights as to acceleration of the indebtedness evidenced by this Note.

....

....

....
        Property Address

(Execute Original Only)

a

Figure 3–1

WHEN RECORDED MAIL TO

SPACE ABOVE THIS LINE FOR RECORDER'S USE

DEED OF TRUST

THIS DEED OF TRUST is made this............day of....................., 19........, among the
Trustor,...
....(herein "Borrower"),
....(herein "Trustee"),
and the Beneficiary,.., a corporation
organized and existing under the laws of..,whose address is
....(herein "Lender").

BORROWER, in consideration of the indebtedness herein recited and the trust herein created, irrevocably grants and conveys to Trustee, in trust, with power of sale, the following described property located in the County of..., State of California:

TOGETHER with all the improvements now or hereafter erected on the property, and all easements, rights, appurtenances, rents (subject however to the rights and authorities given herein to Lender to collect and apply such rents), royalties, mineral, oil and gas rights and profits, water, water rights, and water stock, and all fixtures now or hereafter attached to the property, all of which, including replacements and additions thereto, shall be deemed to be and remain a part of the property covered by this Deed of Trust; and all of the foregoing, together with said property (or the leasehold estate in the event this Deed of Trust is on a leasehold) are herein referred to as the "Property";

TO SECURE to Lender (a) the repayment of the indebtedness evidenced by Borrower's note of even date herewith (herein "Note"), in the principal sum of...
....Dollars, with interest thereon, providing for monthly installments of principal and interest, with the balance of the indebtedness, if not sooner paid, due and payable on.......................................
.... ; the payment of all other sums, with interest thereon, advanced in accordance herewith to protect the security of this Deed of Trust; and the performance of the covenants and agreements of Borrower herein contained; and (b) the repayment of any future advances, with interest thereon, made to Borrower by Lender pursuant to paragraph 20 hereof (herein "Future Advances").

Borrower covenants that Borrower is lawfully seised of the estate hereby conveyed and has the right to grant and convey the Property, that the Property is unencumbered, and that Borrower will warrant and defend generally the title to the Property against all claims and demands, subject to any easements and restrictions listed in a schedule of exceptions to coverage in any title insurance policy insuring Lender's interest in the Property.

Figure 3–2a

UNIFORM COVENANTS. Borrower and Lender covenant and agree as follows:

1. Payment of Principal and Interest. Borrower shall promptly pay when due the principal of and interest on the indebtedness evidenced by the Note, late charges as provided in the Note, and the principal of and interest on any Future Advances secured by this Deed of Trust.

2. Funds for Taxes and Insurance. Subject to Lender's option under paragraphs 4 and 5 hereof, Borrower shall pay to Lender on the day monthly installments of principal and interest are payable under the Note, until the Note is paid in full, a sum (herein "Funds") equal to one-twelfth of the yearly taxes and assessments which may attain priority over this Deed of Trust, and ground rents on the Property, if any, plus one-twelfth of the yearly premium installments for hazard insurance, plus one-twelfth of the yearly premium installments for mortgage insurance, if any, all as reasonably estimated initially and from time to time by Lender on the basis of assessments and bills and reasonable estimates thereof. Lender shall hold the Funds in an account which is insured by a Federal or state agency and shall apply the Funds from said account to pay said taxes, assessments, insurance premiums and ground rents. Lender shall make no charge for so holding and applying the Funds, analyzing said account or verifying and compiling said assessments and bills. Borrower and Lender may agree in writing at the time of execution of this Deed of Trust that interest on the Funds shall be paid to Borrower, and unless such agreement is made, Lender shall not be required to pay Borrower any interest on the Funds. Lender shall give to Borrower, without charge, an annual accounting of the Funds showing credits and debits to the Funds, interest, if any, paid to Borrower on the Funds and the purpose for which each debit to the Funds was made. The Funds are pledged as additional security for the sums secured by this Deed of Trust.

If the amount of the Funds held by Lender, together with the future monthly installments of Funds payable prior to the due dates of taxes, assessments, insurance premiums and ground rents, shall exceed the amount required to pay said taxes, assessments, insurance premiums and ground rents as they fall due, such excess shall be, at Borrower's option, either promptly repaid to Borrower or credited to Borrower on monthly installments of Funds. If the amount of the Funds held by Lender shall not be sufficient to pay taxes, assessments, insurance premiums and ground rents as they fall due, Borrower shall pay to Lender any amount necessary to make up the deficiency within 30 days after notice from Lender to Borrower requesting payment thereof.

Upon payment in full of all sums secured by this Deed of Trust, Lender shall promptly refund to Borrower any Funds held by Lender. If under paragraph 17 hereof the Property is sold or the Property is otherwise acquired by Lender, Lender shall apply, no later than immediately prior to the sale of the Property or its acquisition by Lender, any Funds held by Lender at the time of application as a credit against the sums secured by this Deed of Trust.

3. Application of Payments. Unless applicable law provides otherwise, all payments received by Lender under the Note and paragraphs 1 and 2 hereof shall be applied by Lender first in payment of amounts payable to Lender by Borrower under paragraph 2 hereof, then to interest payable on the Note and on Future Advances, if any, and then to the principal of the Note and to the principal of Future Advances, if any.

4. Charges; Liens. Borrower shall pay all taxes, assessments and other charges, fines and impositions attributable to the Property which may attain a priority over this Deed of Trust, and ground rents, if any, at Lender's option in the manner provided under paragraph 2 hereof or by Borrower making payment, when due, directly to the payee thereof. Borrower shall promptly furnish to Lender all notices of amounts due under this paragraph, and in the event Borrower shall make payment directly, Borrower shall promptly furnish to Lender receipts evidencing such payments. Borrower shall promptly discharge any lien which has priority over this Deed of Trust; provided, that Borrower shall not be required to discharge any such lien so long as Borrower shall agree in writing to the payment of the obligation secured by such lien in a manner acceptable to Lender, or shall in good faith contest such lien by, or defend enforcement of such lien in, legal proceedings which operate to prevent the enforcement of the lien or forfeiture of the Property or any part thereof.

5. Hazard Insurance. Borrower shall keep the improvements now existing or hereafter erected on the Property insured against loss by fire, hazards included within the term "extended coverage", and such other hazards as Lender may require and in such amounts and for such periods as Lender may require; provided, that Lender shall not require that the amount of such coverage exceed that amount of coverage required to pay the sums secured by this Deed of Trust.

The insurance carrier providing the insurance shall be chosen by Borrower subject to approval by Lender; provided, that such approval shall not be unreasonably withheld. All premiums on insurance policies shall be paid at Lender's option in the manner provided under paragraph 2 hereof or by Borrower making payment, when due, directly to the insurance carrier.

All insurance policies and renewals thereof shall be in form acceptable to Lender and shall include a standard mortgage clause in favor of and in form acceptable to Lender. Lender shall have the right to hold the policies and renewals thereof, and Borrower shall promptly furnish to Lender all renewal notices and all receipts of paid premiums. In the event of loss, Borrower shall give prompt notice to the insurance carrier and Lender, and Lender may make proof of loss if not made promptly by Borrower.

Unless Lender and Borrower otherwise agree in writing, insurance proceeds shall be applied to restoration or repair of the Property damaged, provided such restoration or repair is economically feasible. Borrower shall have the right to effect minor repairs to the Property with the insurer's approval and receive payment therefor. If Borrower and Lender are unable to agree whether such restoration or repair would be economically feasible, the determination of economic feasibility shall be made by independent appraisal at Lender's expense. If such restoration or repair is not economically feasible, the insurance proceeds shall be applied to the sums secured by this Deed of Trust, with the excess, if any, paid to Borrower. If the Property is abandoned by Borrower or if Borrower fails to respond to Lender within 30 days after notice by Lender to Borrower that the insurance carrier offers to settle a claim for insurance benefits, Lender is authorized to collect and apply the insurance proceeds at Lender's option either to restoration or repair of the Property or to the sums secured by this Deed of Trust.

Unless Lender and Borrower otherwise agree in writing, any such application of proceeds to principal shall not extend or postpone the due date of the monthly installments referred to in paragraphs 1 and 2 hereof or change the amount of such installments. If under paragraph 17 hereof the Property is acquired by Lender, all right, title and interest of Borrower in and to any insurance policies and in and to the proceeds thereof resulting from damage to the Property prior to the sale or acquisition shall pass to Lender to the extent of the sums secured by this Deed of Trust immediately prior to such sale or acquisition.

6. Preservation and Maintenance of Property; Leaseholds; Condominiums. Borrower shall keep the Property in good repair and shall not permit or commit waste, impairment, or deterioration of the Property and shall comply with the provisions of any lease, if this Deed of Trust is on a leasehold. If this Deed of Trust is on a condominium unit, Borrower shall perform all of Borrower's obligations under the declaration of condominium or master deed, the by-laws and regulations of the condominium project and constituent documents.

7. Protection of Lender's Security. If Borrower fails to perform the covenants and agreements contained in this Deed of Trust, or if any action or proceeding is commenced which materially affects Lender's interest in the Property, including, but not limited to, eminent domain, insolvency, code enforcement, or arrangements or proceedings involving a bankrupt or decedent, then Lender at Lender's option, upon notice to Borrower, may make such appearances, disburse such sums and take such action as is necessary to protect Lender's interest, including, but not limited to, disbursement of reasonable attorney's fees and entry upon the Property to make repairs. Any amounts disbursed by Lender pursuant to this paragraph 7, with interest thereon, shall become additional indebtedness of Borrower secured by this Deed of Trust. Unless Borrower and Lender agree to other terms of payment, such amounts shall be payable upon notice from Lender to Borrower requesting payment thereof, and shall bear interest from the date of disbursement at the rate stated in the Note unless payment of interest at such rate would be contrary to applicable law, in which event such amounts shall bear interest at the highest rate permissible by applicable law. Nothing contained in this paragraph 7 shall require Lender to incur any expense or do any act hereunder.

8. Inspection. Lender may make or cause to be made reasonable entries upon and inspections of the Property, provided that Lender shall give Borrower notice prior to any such inspection specifying reasonable cause therefor related to Lender's interest in the Property.

9. Condemnation. The proceeds of any award or claim for damages, direct or consequential, in connection with any condemnation or other taking of the Property, or part thereof, or for any conveyance in lieu of condemnation, are hereby assigned, and shall be paid, to Lender.

Figure 3–2b

In the event of a total taking of the Property, the proceeds shall be applied to the sums secured by this Deed of Trust, with the excess, if any, paid to Borrower. In the event of a partial taking of the Property, unless Borrower and Lender otherwise agree in writing, there shall be applied to the sums secured by this Deed of Trust such proportion of the proceeds as is equal to that proportion which the amount of the sums secured by this Deed of Trust immediately prior to the date of taking bears to the value of the Property immediately prior to the date of taking, with the balance of the proceeds paid to Borrower. If Borrower and Lender are unable to agree as to the value of the Property immediately prior to the date of taking, such value shall be established by independent appraisal at Lender's expense.

If the Property is abandoned by Borrower or if after notice by Lender to Borrower that the condemnor offers to make an award or settle a claim for damages, Borrower fails to respond to Lender within 30 days of the date of such notice, Lender is authorized to collect and apply the proceeds at Lender's option either to restoration or repair of the Property or to the sums secured by this Deed of Trust.

Unless Lender and Borrower otherwise agree in writing, any such application of proceeds to principal shall not extend or postpone the due date of the monthly installments referred to in paragraphs 1 and 2 hereof or change the amount of such installments.

10. Borrower Not Released. Extension of the time for payment or modification of amortization of the sums secured by this Deed of Trust granted by Lender to any successor in interest of Borrower shall not operate to release, in any manner, the liability of the original Borrower and Borrower's successors in interest. Lender shall not be required to commence proceedings against such successor or refuse to extend time for payment or otherwise modify amortization of the sums secured by this Deed of Trust by reason of any demand made by the original Borrower and Borrower's successors in interest.

11. Forbearance by Lender Not a Waiver. Any forbearance by Lender in exercising any right or remedy hereunder, or otherwise afforded by applicable law, shall not be a waiver of or preclude the exercise of any right or remedy hereunder. The procurement of insurance or the payment of taxes or other liens or charges by Lender shall not be a waiver of Lender's right to accelerate the maturity of the indebtedness secured by this Deed of Trust.

12. Remedies Cumulative. All remedies provided in this Deed of Trust are distinct and cumulative to any other right or remedy under this Deed of Trust or afforded by law or equity, and may be exercised concurrently, independently or successively.

13. Successors and Assigns Bound; Joint and Several Liability; Captions. The covenants and agreements herein contained shall bind, and the rights hereunder shall inure to, the respective successors and assigns of Lender and Borrower. All covenants and agreements of Borrower shall be joint and several. The captions and headings of the paragraphs of this Deed of Trust are for convenience only and are not to be used to interpret or define the provisions hereof.

14. Notice. Any notice from Lender to Borrower provided for in this Deed of Trust shall be mailed by certified mail to Borrower at the Property Address stated below or at such address as Borrower may designate by notice by certified mail to Lender's address, except for any notice given to Borrower in the manner prescribed by applicable law as provided in paragraph 17 of this Deed of Trust.

15. Uniform Deed of Trust; Governing Law; Severability. This form of deed of trust combines uniform covenants for national use and non-uniform covenants with limited variations by jurisdiction to constitute a uniform security instrument covering real property. This Deed of Trust shall be governed by the law of the jurisdiction in which the Property is located. In the event that any provision or clause of this Deed of Trust or the Note conflicts with applicable law, such conflict shall not affect other provisions of this Deed of Trust or the Note which can be given effect without the conflicting provision, and to this end the provisions of this Deed of Trust and the Note are declared to be severable.

16. Borrower's Copy. Borrower shall be furnished a conformed copy of this Deed of Trust at the time of execution or after recordation hereof.

NON-UNIFORM COVENANTS. Borrower and Lender further covenant and agree as follows:

17. Acceleration; Remedies. Upon Borrower's breach of any covenant or agreement of Borrower in this Deed of Trust, including the covenants to pay when due any sums secured by this Deed of Trust, Lender prior to acceleration shall mail notice to Borrower as provided in paragraph 14 hereof specifying: (1) the breach; (2) the action required to cure such breach; (3) a date, not less than thirty days from the date the notice is mailed to Borrower, by which such breach must be cured; and (4) that failure to cure such breach on or before the date specified in the notice may result in acceleration of the sums secured by this Deed of Trust and sale of the Property. If the breach is not cured on or before the date specified in the notice, Lender at Lender's option may declare all of the sums secured by this Deed of Trust to be immediately due and payable without further demand and may invoke the power of sale and any other remedies permitted by applicable law. Lender shall be entitled to collect all reasonable costs and expenses incurred in pursuing the remedies provided in this paragraph 17, including, but not limited to, reasonable attorney's fees.

If Lender invokes the power of sale, Lender shall execute or cause Trustee to execute a written notice of the occurrence of an event of default and of Lender's election to cause the Property to be sold and shall cause such notice to be recorded in each county in which the Property or some part thereof is located. Lender or Trustee shall mail copies of such notice in the manner prescribed by applicable law to Borrower and to the other persons prescribed by applicable law. Trustee shall give public notice of sale to the persons and in the manner prescribed by applicable law. After the lapse of such time as may be required by applicable law, Trustee, without demand on Borrower, shall sell the Property at public auction to the highest bidder at the time and place and under the terms designated in the notice of sale in one or more parcels and in such order as Trustee may determine. Trustee may postpone sale of all or any parcel of the Property by public announcement at the time and place of any previously scheduled sale. Lender or Lender's designee may purchase the Property at any sale.

Trustee shall deliver to the purchaser Trustee's deed conveying the Property so sold without any covenant or warranty, expressed or implied. The recitals in the Trustee's deed shall be prima facie evidence of the truth of the statements made therein. Trustee shall apply the proceeds of the sale in the following order: (a) to all reasonable costs and expenses of the sale, including, but not limited to, reasonable Trustee's and attorney's fees and costs of title evidence; (b) to all sums secured by this Deed of Trust; and (c) the excess, if any, to the person or persons legally entitled thereto.

18. Borrower's Right to Reinstate. Notwithstanding Lender's acceleration of the sums secured by this Deed of Trust, Borrower shall have the right to have any proceedings begun by Lender to enforce this Deed of Trust discontinued at any time prior to five days before sale of the Property pursuant to the power of sale contained in this Deed of Trust or at any time prior to entry of a judgment enforcing this Deed of Trust if: (a) Borrower pays Lender all sums which would be then due under this Deed of Trust, the Note and notes securing Future Advances, if any, had no acceleration occurred; (b) Borrower cures all breaches of any other covenants or agreements of Borrower contained in this Deed of Trust; (c) Borrower pays all reasonable expenses incurred by Lender and Trustee in enforcing the covenants and agreements of Borrower contained in this Deed of Trust, and in enforcing Lender's and Trustee's remedies as provided in paragraph 17 hereof, including, but not limited to, reasonable attorney's fees; and (d) Borrower takes such action as Lender may reasonably require to assure that the lien of this Deed of Trust, Lender's interest in the Property and Borrower's obligation to pay the sums secured by this Deed of Trust shall continue unimpaired. Upon such payment and cure by Borrower, this Deed of Trust and the obligations secured hereby shall remain in full force and effect as if no acceleration had occurred.

19. Assignment of Rents; Appointment of Receiver; Lender in Possession. As additional security hereunder, Borrower hereby assigns to Lender the rents of the Property, provided that Borrower shall, prior to acceleration under paragraph 17 hereof or abandonment of the Property, have the right to collect and retain such rents as they become due and payable.

Upon acceleration under paragraph 17 hereof or abandonment of the Property, Lender, in person, by agent or by judicially appointed receiver shall be entitled to enter upon, take possession of and manage the Property and to collect the rents of the Property including those past due. All rents collected by Lender or the receiver shall be applied first to payment of the costs of management of the Property and collection of rents, including, but not limited to, receiver's fees, premiums on receiver's bonds and reasonable attorney's fees, and then to the sums secured by this Deed of Trust. Lender and the receiver shall be liable to account only for those rents actually received.

Figure 3–2c

20. Future Advances. Upon request of Borrower, Lender, at Lender's option prior to full reconveyance of the Property by Trustee to Borrower, may make Future Advances to Borrower. Such Future Advances, with interest thereon, shall be secured by this Deed of Trust when evidenced by promissory notes stating that said notes are secured hereby.

21. Reconveyance. Upon payment of all sums secured by this Deed of Trust, Lender shall request Trustee to reconvey the Property and shall surrender this Deed of Trust and all notes evidencing indebtedness secured by this Deed of Trust to Trustee. Trustee shall reconvey the Property without warranty and without charge to the person or persons legally entitled thereto. Such person or persons shall pay all costs of recordation, if any.

22. Substitute Trustee. Lender at Lender's option may from time to time remove Trustee and appoint a successor trustee to any Trustee appointed hereunder. Without conveyance of the Property, the successor trustee shall succeed to all the title, power and duties conferred upon the Trustee herein and by applicable law.

23. Request for Notices. Borrower requests that copies of the notice of default and notice of sale be sent to Borrower's address which is the Property Address stated below.

24. Statement of Obligation. Lender may collect a fee not to exceed $15 for furnishing the statement of obligation as provided by Section 2943 of the Civil Code of California.

In Witness Whereof, Borrower has executed this Deed of Trust.

.... —Borrower

.... —Borrower

....

Property Address

STATE OF CALIFORNIA, County of .... ss:
On.......................... , 19......, before me, the undersigned, a Notary Public in and for said State,
personally appeared.. , known
to me to be the person(s) whose name(s) ....subscribed to
the within instrument, and acknowledged that ....executed the same.

Witness my hand and official seal.

....
Notary Public in and for said State

REQUEST FOR RECONVEYANCE

TO TRUSTEE:
The undersigned is the holder of the note or notes secured by this Deed of Trust. Said note or notes, together with all other indebtedness secured by this Deed of Trust, have been paid in full. You are hereby directed to cancel said note or notes and this Deed of Trust, which are delivered hereby, and to reconvey, without warranty, all the estate now held by you under this Deed of Trust to the person or persons legally entitled thereto.

Date : ....

Figure 3–2d

NOTE

US $ ...., Michigan
City

...., 19..........

FOR VALUE RECEIVED, the undersigned promise to pay...
...., or order, the principal sum of
.... Dollars, with interest
on the unpaid principal balance from the date of this Note, until paid, at the rate of...................
percent per annum. The principal and interest shall be payable at..
...., or such other place as the holder hereof may designate in
writing, in consecutive monthly installments of ....
Dollars (US $ ....), on the..day of each month beginning
...., 19......, until the entire indebtedness evidenced hereby is fully
paid, except that any remaining indebtedness, if not sooner paid, shall be due and payable on the
...................................day of...

    If any monthly installment under this Note is not paid when due and remains unpaid after a
date specified by a notice sent by certified mail to the undersigned at the address stated below or at
such address as the undersigned may designate to the holder hereof by certified mail, which date
shall be not less than thirty days from the date such notice is mailed, the entire principal amount
outstanding hereunder and accrued interest thereon shall at once become due and payable at the
option of the holder hereof. Failure to exercise such option shall not constitute a waiver of the right
to exercise such option if the undersigned is in default hereunder. In the event of any default in the
payment of this Note and if suit is brought hereon, the holder hereof shall be entitled to collect in
such proceeding all reasonable costs and expenses of suit, including, but not limited to, reasonable
attorney's fees.

    The undersigned shall pay to the holder hereof a late charge of 4 percent of any monthly install-
ment not received by the holder hereof on or before the 15th day after the installment is due.

    The undersigned shall have the right to prepay the principal amount outstanding in whole or
in part. Any partial prepayment shall be applied against the principal amount outstanding and shall
not extend or postpone the due date of any subsequent monthly installments or change the amount of
such installments, unless the holder hereof shall otherwise agree in writing.

    Presentment, notice of dishonor, and protest are hereby waived by all makers, sureties, guaran-
tors and endorsers hereof. This Note shall be the joint and several obligation of all makers, sureties,
guarantors and endorsers, and shall be binding upon them and their heirs, personal representatives,
successors and assigns.

    The indebtedness evidenced by this Note is secured by a Mortgage, dated of even date herewith,
and reference is made thereto for rights as to acceleration of the indebtedness evidenced by this
Note.

....

....

....
    Property Address

(Execute Original Only)

f

Figure 3–3

MORTGAGE

THIS MORTGAGE is made this................................day of.., 19........,
between the Mortgagor, ...
...., whose address
is ...., (herein "Borrower"),
and the Mortgagee, ..., a corporation
organized and existing under the laws of..., whose address
is .... (herein "Lender").

WHEREAS, Borrower is indebted to Lender in the principal sum of..
....Dollars, which indebtedness is evidenced by Borrower's note of even date herewith (herein "Note"), providing for monthly installments of principal and interest, with the balance of the indebtedness, if not sooner paid, due and
payable on..;

To SECURE to Lender (a) the repayment of the indebtedness evidenced by the Note, with interest
thereon, the payment of all other sums, with interest thereon, advanced in accordance herewith to
protect the security of this Mortgage, and the performance of the covenants and agreements of
Borrower herein contained, and (b) the repayment of any future advances, with interest thereon,
made to Borrower by Lender pursuant to paragraph 20 hereof (herein "Future Advances"),
Borrower does hereby mortgage, grant and convey to Lender, with power of sale, the following
described property located in the County of ...., State of Michigan:

TOGETHER with all the improvements now or hereafter erected on the property, and all easements, rights, appurtenances, rents, royalties, mineral, oil and gas rights and profits, water, water
rights, and water stock, and all fixtures now or hereafter attached to the property, all of which,
including replacements and additions thereto, shall be deemed to be and remain a part of the property covered by this Mortgage; and all of the foregoing, together with said property (or the leasehold estate in the event this Mortgage is on a leasehold) are herein referred to as the "Property".

Borrower covenants that Borrower is lawfully seised of the estate hereby conveyed and has the
right to mortgage, grant and convey the Property, that the Property is unencumbered, and that
Borrower will warrant and defend generally the title to the Property against all claims and demands,
subject to any easements and restrictions listed in a schedule of exceptions to coverage in any title
insurance policy insuring Lender's interest in the Property.

Figure 3—4a

UNIFORM COVENANTS. Borrower and Lender covenant and agree as follows:

1. Payment of Principal and Interest. Borrower shall promptly pay when due the principal of and interest on the indebtedness evidenced by the Note, late charges as provided in the Note, and the principal of and interest on any Future Advances secured by this Mortgage.

2. Funds for Taxes and Insurance. Subject to Lender's option under paragraphs 4 and 5 hereof, Borrower shall pay to Lender on the day monthly installments of principal and interest are payable under the Note, until the Note is paid in full, a sum (herein "Funds") equal to one-twelfth of the yearly taxes and assessments which may attain priority over this Mortgage, and ground rents on the Property, if any, plus one-twelfth of the yearly premium installments for hazard insurance, plus one-twelfth of the yearly premium installments for mortgage insurance, if any, all as reasonably estimated initially and from time to time by Lender on the basis of assessments and bills and reasonable estimates thereof. Lender shall hold the Funds in an account which is insured by a Federal or state agency and shall apply the Funds from said account to pay said taxes, assessments, insurance premiums and ground rents. Lender shall make no charge for so holding and applying the Funds, analyzing said account or verifying and compiling said assessments and bills. Borrower and Lender may agree in writing at the time of execution of this Mortgage that interest on the Funds shall be paid to Borrower, and unless such agreement is made, Lender shall not be required to pay Borrower any interest on the Funds. Lender shall give to Borrower, without charge, an annual accounting of the Funds showing credits and debits to the Funds, interest, if any, paid to Borrower on the Funds and the purpose for which each debit to the Funds was made. The Funds are pledged as additional security for the sums secured by this Mortgage.

If the amount of the Funds held by Lender, together with the future monthly installments of Funds payable prior to the due dates of taxes, assessments, insurance premiums and ground rents, shall exceed the amount required to pay said taxes, assessments, insurance premiums and ground rents as they fall due, such excess shall be, at Borrower's option, either promptly repaid to Borrower or credited to Borrower on monthly installments of Funds. If the amount of the Funds held by Lender shall not be sufficient to pay taxes, assessments, insurance premiums and ground rents as they fall due, Borrower shall pay to Lender any amount necessary to make up the deficiency within 30 days after notice from Lender to Borrower requesting payment thereof.

Upon payment in full of all sums secured by this Mortgage, Lender shall promptly refund to Borrower any Funds held by Lender.

If under paragraph 17 hereof the Property is sold or the Property is otherwise acquired by Lender, Lender shall apply, no later than immediately prior to the sale of the Property or its acquisition by Lender, any Funds held by Lender at the time of application as a credit against the sums secured by this Mortgage.

3. Application of Payments. Unless applicable law provides otherwise, all payments received by Lender under the Note and paragraphs 1 and 2 hereof shall be applied by Lender first in payment of amounts payable to Lender by Borrower under paragraph 2 hereof, then to interest payable on the Note and on Future Advances, if any, and then to the principal of the Note and to the principal of Future Advances, if any.

4. Charges; Liens. Borrower shall pay all taxes, assessments and other charges, fines and impositions attributable to the Property which may attain a priority over this Mortgage, and ground rents, if any, at Lender's option in the manner provided under paragraph 2 hereof or by Borrower making payment, when due, directly to the payee thereof. Borrower shall promptly furnish to Lender all notices of amounts due under this paragraph, and in the event Borrower shall make payment directly, Borrower shall promptly furnish to Lender receipts evidencing such payments. Borrower shall promptly discharge any lien which has priority over this Mortgage; provided, that Borrower shall not be required to discharge any such lien so long as Borrower shall agree in writing to the payment of the obligation secured by such lien in a manner acceptable to Lender, or shall in good faith contest such lien by, or defend enforcement of such lien in, legal proceedings which operate to prevent the enforcement of the lien or forfeiture of the Property or any part thereof.

5. Hazard Insurance. Borrower shall keep the improvements now existing or hereafter erected on the Property insured against loss by fire, hazards included within the term "extended coverage", and such other hazards as Lender may require and in such amounts and for such periods as Lender may require; provided, that Lender shall not require that the amount of such coverage exceed that amount of coverage required to pay the sums secured by this Mortgage.

The insurance carrier providing the insurance shall be chosen by Borrower subject to approval by Lender; provided, that such approval shall not be unreasonably withheld. All premiums on insurance policies shall be paid at Lender's option in the manner provided under paragraph 2 hereof or by Borrower making payment, when due, directly to the insurance carrier.

All insurance policies and renewals thereof shall be in form acceptable to Lender and shall include a standard mortgage clause in favor of and in form acceptable to Lender. Lender shall have the right to hold the policies and renewals thereof, and Borrower shall promptly furnish to Lender all renewal notices and all receipts of paid premiums. In the event of loss, Borrower shall give prompt notice to the insurance carrier and Lender, and Lender may make proof of loss if not made promptly by Borrower.

Unless Lender and Borrower otherwise agree in writing, insurance proceeds shall be applied to restoration or repair of the Property damaged, provided such restoration or repair is economically feasible. Borrower shall have the right to effect minor repairs to the Property with the insurer's approval and receive payment therefor. If Borrower and Lender are unable to agree whether such restoration or repair is economically feasible, the determination of economic feasibility shall be made by independent appraisal at Lender's expense. If such restoration or repair is not economically feasible, the insurance proceeds shall be applied to the sums secured by this Mortgage, with the excess, if any, paid to Borrower. If the Property is abandoned by Borrower or if Borrower fails to respond to Lender within 30 days after notice by Lender to Borrower that the insurance carrier offers to settle a claim for insurance benefits, Lender is authorized to collect and apply the insurance proceeds at Lender's option either to restoration or repair of the Property or to the sums secured by this Mortgage.

Unless Lender and Borrower otherwise agree in writing, any such application of proceeds to principal shall not extend or postpone the due date of the monthly installments referred to in paragraphs 1 and 2 hereof or change the amount of such installments.

If under paragraph 17 hereof the Property is acquired by Lender, all right, title and interest of Borrower in and to any insurance policies and in and to the proceeds thereof resulting from damage to the Property prior to the sale or acquisition shall pass to Lender to the extent of the sums secured by this Mortgage immediately prior to such sale or acquisition.

6. Preservation and Maintenance of Property; Leaseholds; Condominiums. Borrower shall keep the Property in good repair and shall not permit or commit waste, impairment, or deterioration of the Property and shall comply with the provisions of any lease, if this Mortgage is on a leasehold. If this Mortgage is on a condominium

Figure 3–4b

unit, Borrower shall perform all of Borrower's obligations under the declaration of condominium or master deed, the by-laws and regulations of the condominium project and constituent documents.

7. Protection of Lender's Security. If Borrower fails to perform the covenants and agreements contained in this Mortgage, or if any action or proceeding is commenced which materially affects Lender's interest in the Property, including, but not limited to, eminent domain, insolvency, code enforcement, or arrangements or proceedings involving a bankrupt or decedent, then Lender at Lender's option, upon notice to Borrower, may make such appearances, disburse such sums and take such action as is necessary to protect Lender's interest, including, but not limited to, disbursement of reasonable attorney's fees and entry upon the Property to make repairs. Any amounts disbursed by Lender pursuant to this paragraph 7, with interest thereon, shall become additional indebtedness of Borrower secured by this Mortgage. Unless Borrower and Lender agree to other terms of payment, such amounts shall be payable upon notice from Lender to Borrower requesting payment thereof, and shall bear interest from the date of disbursement at the rate stated in the Note unless payment of interest at such rate would be contrary to applicable law, in which event such amounts shall bear interest at the highest rate permissible by applicable law. Nothing contained in this paragraph 7 shall require Lender to incur any expense or do any act hereunder.

8. Inspection. Lender may make or cause to be made reasonable entries upon and inspections of the Property, provided that Lender shall give Borrower notice prior to any such inspection specifying reasonable cause therefor related to Lender's interest in the Property.

9. Condemnation. The proceeds of any award or claim for damages, direct or consequential, in connection with any condemnation or other taking of the Property, or part thereof, or for any conveyance in lieu of condemnation, are hereby assigned, and shall be paid, to Lender.

In the event of a total taking of the Property, the proceeds shall be applied to the sums secured by this Mortgage, with the excess, if any, paid to Borrower. In the event of a partial taking of the Property, unless Borrower and Lender otherwise agree in writing, there shall be applied to the sums secured by this Mortgage such proportion of the proceeds as is equal to that proportion which the amount of the sums secured by this Mortgage immediately prior to the date of taking bears to the value of the Property immediately prior to the date of taking, with the balance of the proceeds paid to Borrower. If Borrower and Lender are unable to agree as to the value of the Property immediately prior to the date of taking, such value shall be established by independent appraisal at Lender's expense.

If the Property is abandoned by Borrower or if after notice by Lender to Borrower that the condemnor offers to make an award or settle a claim for damages, Borrower fails to respond to Lender within 30 days of the date of such notice, Lender is authorized to collect and apply the proceeds at Lender's option either to restoration or repair of the Property or to the sums secured by this Mortgage.

Unless Lender and Borrower otherwise agree in writing, any such application of proceeds to principal shall not extend or postpone the due date of the monthly installments referred to in paragraphs 1 and 2 hereof or change the amount of such installments.

10. Borrower Not Released. Extension of the time for payment or modification of amortization of the sums secured by this Mortgage granted by Lender to any successor in interest of Borrower shall not operate to release, in any manner, the liability of the original Borrower and Borrower's successors in interest. Lender shall not be required to commence proceedings against such successor or refuse to extend time for payment or otherwise modify amortization of the sums secured by this Mortgage by reason of any demand made by the original Borrower and Borrower's successors in interest.

11. Forbearance by Lender Not a Waiver. Any forbearance by Lender in exercising any right or remedy hereunder, or otherwise afforded by applicable law, shall not be a waiver of or preclude the exercise of any right or remedy hereunder. The procurement of insurance or the payment of taxes or other liens or charges by Lender shall not be a waiver of Lender's right to accelerate the maturity of the indebtedness secured by this Mortgage.

12. Remedies Cumulative. All remedies provided in this Mortgage are distinct and cumulative to any other right or remedy under this Mortgage or afforded by law or equity, and may be exercised concurrently, independently or successively.

13. Successors and Assigns Bound; Joint and Several Liability; Captions. The covenants and agreements herein contained shall bind, and the rights hereunder shall inure to, the respective successors and assigns of Lender and Borrower. All covenants and agreements of Borrower shall be joint and several. The captions and headings of the paragraphs of this Mortgage are for convenience only and are not to be used to interpret or define the provisions hereof.

14. Notice. Any notice from Lender to Borrower provided for in this Mortgage shall be mailed by certified mail to Borrower at the Property Address stated below or at such address as Borrower may designate to Lender by certified mail to Lender's address, except for any notice given to Borrower in the manner prescribed by applicable law as provided in paragraph 17 of this Mortgage.

15. Uniform Mortgage; Governing Law; Severability. This form of mortgage combines uniform covenants for national use and non-uniform covenants with limited variations by jurisdiction to constitute a uniform security instrument covering real property. This Mortgage shall be governed by the law of the jurisdiction in which the Property is located. In the event that any provision or clause of this Mortgage or the Note conflicts with applicable law, such conflict shall not affect other provisions of this Mortgage or the Note which can be given effect without the conflicting provision, and to this end the provisions of this Mortgage and the Note are declared to be severable.

16. Borrower's Copy. Borrower shall be furnished a conformed copy of this Mortgage at the time of execution or after recordation hereof.

NON-UNIFORM COVENANTS. Borrower and Lender further covenant and agree as follows:

17. Acceleration; Remedies. Upon Borrower's breach of any covenant or agreement of Borrower in this Mortgage, including the covenants to pay when due any sums secured by this Mortgage, Lender prior to acceleration shall mail notice to Borrower as provided in paragraph 14 hereof specifying: (1) the breach; (2) the action required to cure such breach; (3) a date, not less than thirty days from the date the notice is mailed to Borrower, by which such breach must be cured; and (4) that failure to cure such breach on or before the date specified in the notice may result in acceleration of the sums secured by this Mortgage and sale of the Property. If the breach is not cured on or before the date specified in the notice, Lender at Lender's option may declare all of the sums secured by this Mortgage to be immediately due and payable without further demand and may invoke the power of sale herein granted pursuant to applicable law, and any other remedies permitted by applicable law. Lender

Figure 3–4c

shall be entitled to collect, all reasonable costs and expenses incurred in pursuing the remedies provided in this paragraph 17, including, but not limited to, reasonable attorney's fees.

If Lender invokes the power of sale, Lender shall mail a copy of a notice of sale to Borrower in the manner provided in paragraph 14 hereof. Lender shall publish and post the notice of sale and the Property shall be sold in the manner prescribed by applicable law. Lender or Lender's designee may purchase the Property at any sale. The proceeds of the sale shall be applied in the following order: (a) to all reasonable costs and expenses of the sale, including, but not limited to, reasonable attorney's fees; (b) to all sums secured by this Mortgage; and (c) the excess, if any, to the person or persons legally entitled thereto.

18. Borrower's Right to Reinstate. Notwithstanding Lender's acceleration of the sums secured by this Mortgage, Borrower shall have the right to have any proceedings begun by Lender to enforce this Mortgage discontinued at any time prior to five days before sale of the Property pursuant to the power of sale contained in this Mortgage or at any time prior to entry of a judgment enforcing this Mortgage if: (a) Borrower pays Lender all sums which would be then due under this Mortgage, the Note and notes securing Future Advances, if any, had no acceleration occurred; (b) Borrower cures all breaches of any other covenants or agreements of Borrower contained in this Mortgage; (c) Borrower pays all reasonable expenses incurred by Lender in enforcing the covenants and agreements of Borrower contained in this Mortgage and in enforcing Lender's remedies as provided in paragraph 17 hereof, including, but not limited to, reasonable attorney's fees; and (d) Borrower takes such action as Lender may reasonably require to assure that the lien of this Mortgage, Lender's interest in the Property and Borrower's obligation to pay the sums secured by this Mortgage shall continue unimpaired. Upon such payment and cure by Borrower, this Mortgage and the obligations secured hereby shall remain in full force and effect as if no acceleration had occurred.

19. Assignment of Rents; Appointment of Receiver; Lender in Possession. (Omitted.)

20. Future Advances. Upon request of Borrower, Lender, at Lender's option prior to release of this Mortgage, may make Future Advances to Borrower. Such Future Advances, with interest thereon, shall be secured by this Mortgage when evidenced by promissory notes stating that said notes are secured hereby.

21. Release. Upon payment of all sums secured by this Mortgage, Lender shall prepare and file a discharge of this Mortgage without charge to Borrower, and shall pay the fee for recording the discharge.

In Witness Whereof, the Borrower has executed this Mortgage.

Witnesses:

....   ——————————————— —Borrower

....   ——————————————— —Borrower

....

Property Address

State of Michigan, County of .... ss :

On this ....day of .... , 19........ , before me, the subscriber, a Notary Public in and for said county, personally appeared ....

to me known to be the same person(s) described in and who executed the within instrument, and acknowledged execution of the same as .... free act and deed.

My Commission expires: ....
.... Notary Public
.....................................County, Michigan

This instrument was prepared by .... of... ,

....

Figure 3–4d

erty back to the starting point), or more commonly in urban areas, by lot and block taken from a subdivision plat registered and approved by a local governmental authority. An erroneous description of the property, even a typographical error, can render the mortgage instrument void but does not necessarily invalidate the promissory note.

Principal Amount Due

The mortgage instrument must spell out the pledge of the property as security for an initial debt. But the mortgage claim cannot exceed the value of the unpaid balance of the debt. As payments are made on the principal amount of the debt, the value of the mortgage pledge is correspondingly reduced. In this context, the word *estoppel* is sometimes used. Since the mortgage instrument may have a term of 20 or 30 years, and is recorded in the public records only in its original form, we may ask, "How, then, does one determine the exact balance still due on the promissory note at any point in the life of the loan?" The balance due becomes important when a mortgage is sold between lenders, and the estoppel form can be used. This is a statement of the balance due as of a specific date, acknowledged by the lender, and the borrower, and in effect, "stops" the subsequent purchaser of the loan from claiming any greater amount due from the borrower. While most mortgage loans are repaid on a monthly installment basis and the reduction of principal due after each payment is accurately projected by an amortization table, there can always be breaks in the payment pattern. A greater reduction of principal may be made in any one year, or payments could be delinquent. So the estoppel form is used to determine an exact balance due.

Prepayment

One of the clauses contained in most mortgages prior to 1972 provides the manner in which the loan may be paid off ahead of the full term. This particular privilege has caused many arguments and misunderstandings. From the lender's viewpoint, he is making a loan of say $25,000 for a period of 30 years. Under the terms of the promissory note, the borrower agrees to make certain monthly payments, which include both principal and interest. The 360 payments agreed to can amount to as much as $40,000 in interest for the lender over the 30-year period. The lender can claim a contractual right to this interest, which has obvious value. Why should he then be required to forfeit this right to the interest? Earlier mortgages usually provided a compromise to this position by calling for a specific payment against the unearned portion of the interest at the time of early principal payment in order to obtain a release of the mortgage claim. This *prepayment premium,* or conversely, prepayment penalty from the homeowner's viewpoint, varies widely within the industry and may run from 1% to 3% of the balance due at the time of prepayment up to all interest due for the first ten years of the loan. A more common provision allows up to 20% of the original loan to be paid off in any one year without any premium for the unearned interest, plus 1% of the balance that may exceed that payment if paid off in full.

With the rise in popularity of "consumerism," many attacks have been made on the prepayment provision insofar as residential loans are concerned. A number of lenders, under the leadership of FNMA and supported by subsequent rules eliminating prepayment requirements in FHA underwriting procedures, have dropped all such requirements. The reasoning behind this action is that when the principal sum has been returned to the lender, he is free to put this money back to work in a new loan and thus suffers no compensable loss.

Acceleration

One of the essential clauses in a mortgage instrument provides for the payment in full of the balance due, that is, the "acceleration" of each monthly payment to the present date in case of a default in the mortgage terms. While there can be other possible reasons for a default in the mortgage terms, such as improper usage of the property, or selling of the premises without specific permission of the mortgagee, the most probable cause of default is nonpayment of the debt secured. Without an acceleration clause, it is conceivable that a lender would be forced to foreclose his claim each and every month as the installment payments came due.

Right to Sell

As a general rule, mortgaged property can be freely sold by the owner or mortgagor, either with an assumption of the existing debt by the new buyer, or by paying off the balance due on the existing mortgage. In a sale the common assumption is that the original borrower remains liable on the obligation along with the new buyer. Some lenders may grant a release of liability to the original borrower, but they are under no obligation to do so.

When interest remained at lower and more level rates, lenders were more cooperative in allowing sales and assumptions of their loans. But as interest rates moved upward in the late sixties, more lenders eyed the loss of value in their older loans, which had been made at much lower rates. And many began to insert clauses in their mortgage instruments that required specific approval by the lender before the borrower could make any sale of the property. The price of that approval often proved to be an adjustment of the interest rate upward on the balance of the loan to a percentage closer to the then existing market rate. This interest adjustment is sometimes demanded without releasing the original borrower from the obligation.

The reservation of the right to approve a sale by the lender should not be confused with the term *interest escalation,* although this can be the result. More specifically, the escalation of interest is called for in a promissory note when payments become delinquent or when default occurs. The purpose of increasing the interest in such cases is to help offset the increased costs to the lender in collecting a delinquent account or in undertaking foreclosure proceedings.

Insurance

Mortgages require property insurance coverage for the lender's protection. This is also termed *hazard insurance.*

Principally, it includes fire and extended coverage and is required by the lender where any buildings are involved in an amount at least equal to that of the loan. To make certain that insurance payments are made, the lender generally requires a full year's paid-up insurance policy before releasing the loan proceeds, plus two or three months of the annual premium paid into an escrow account. Then with each monthly payment, one-twelfth of the annual premium must be paid. The original policy is held by the lender, and it is part of his responsibility to maintain the coverage with timely payments made from the borrower's escrow account.

Insurance companies in most states have another requirement controlling the amount of insurance coverage, which is that the borrower (mortgagor) carry an amount of insurance equal to at least 80% of the total property value or become liable himself as a co-insurer of the property. Under this restriction, an insurance company protects itself from paying small losses out of proportion to the policy premium. For example, if a homeowner of a $30,000 house decides that he can "get by" with a $20,000 insurance policy, he is covering only two-thirds of the property value, or less than the 80% co-insurance requirement. For a total loss on this property, the insuror would pay the full $20,000 face value; but for a partial loss (say $10,000, the insuror would pay two-thirds of the $10,000 loss, or $6,666. If the homeowner had carried a policy for $24,000, or 80% of the $30,000 value, then the $10,000 partial loss would be paid in full. In periods of rising property values and laxness in watching insurance coverages, lenders can expose themselves to underinsured losses.

Another insurance problem to be considered in a mortgage involves determining just how the proceeds should be paid in case of an actual loss. Earlier mortgages required payment of the insurance money to the lender, who in turn then decided how to apply the funds, i.e., whether to permit the funds to be used for restoration of the property, which is the usual procedure on smaller losses, or to apply the insurance proceeds to the payoff of the loan. As time has passed, recent mortgages have given the borrower a stronger position in the distribution of insurance proceeds, as is apparent in the FNMA standard conventional mortgage terms.

Taxes

Lenders long ago learned that the real first lien on any property is in the hands of the property taxing authority, that is, the agency that levies the ad valorem property taxes. It can be categorically stated that the full documented and properly recorded "first" mortgage instrument securing the lender's position takes only a poor second place to a tax levy. And in some states, this tax levy includes an assessment by a properly authorized neighborhood maintenance association!

It is evident then, that the timely payment of property taxes becomes another essential requirement in mortgage loans. Lenders usually require that a sum equal to two to four months of the annual taxes be paid into an escrow account by the borrower before the loan is funded. One-twelfth of the annual taxes is also added to each monthly payment of principal and interest. In this manner, the lender accumulates sufficient cash each year to pay the borrower's property taxes directly to the tax authorities and thus protect himself against any tax priority lien on the pledged property.

In regard to federal taxes, these take priority over state laws regarding property and do carry lien rights and highest priority. However, federal taxes, including federal income taxes, become property liens only when they are filed as a delinquent assessment against an individual or corporation, not when the tax liability is incurred. A federal tax lien is a general lien and may apply to any and all property owned by the taxpayer. The ad valorem, or property tax, is a specific lien (applying only to the designated property liable for the tax), and becomes a lien against the property from the minute the taxing authorities levy the assessment.

Foreclosure

The right of the lender to foreclose on a property is limited by the terms of the mortgage instrument and by the applicable state laws. In general, foreclosure is the last recourse of the lender, often a costly procedure and usually an open admission that an error in judgment was made in making the loan. Lenders will normally put forth considerable effort to cooperate with a borrower who has unforeseen financial problems and needs some relief. But the lender must depend on the borrower to seek the relief, and this is more easily arranged before a serious delinquency occurs. Lenders have an obligation to their own investors, depositors, insurance policy holders, trust funds, etc., to exercise control over their borrower's accounts and not allow a property mortgage note to slide into default so that such laxity would compromise the lender's security. When failure to comply with the terms of the note and mortgage occurs on the part of the borrower, generally due to nonpayment of the obligation, then the lender must seek foreclosure of the property.

The real purpose of a foreclosure is to sell the property under the authority of a court order, usually referred to as a *sheriff's sale*, and to distribute the proceeds to the various creditors holding claims on the property. Contrary to popular belief, the lender has no more right to take title to the property than anyone else who has a claim on it, in a foreclosure proceeding.

Accordingly, the court orders a property to be sold in a foreclosure proceeding, and whoever offers the highest cash price at the subsequent public sale acquires a deed to the property by court order, in some places referred to as a *sheriff's deed*. In practice, the lender is allowed to submit his claim, that is, the balance due on his promissory note, as part or all of the cash offer for the property. In many states, the lender need not even offer the full amount of his claim if he deems it too high.

Because the lender has a claim against the property and can use that as payment in a foreclosure sale, the lender or his agent usually ends up taking title to the foreclosed property. If the claim against the borrower is not fully satisfied from the proceeds of the sale, then the lender can seek a deficiency judgment for the balance due.

The above considerations strongly suggest that the foreclosure is apt to be a difficult, distasteful, and discouraging procedure. The lender is faced with the costs of litigation, with the possibility of an unpleasant eviction, and with the risk of property damage through owner abuse, or vandalism, along with the costs of renovating and maintaining the property, plus payment of delinquent taxes and insurance—so that foreclosure is seldom a satisfactory solution.

TYPES OF MORTGAGES

The most common forms of mortgage instruments have some important variations, namely, in how and when they are used. The underlying purpose of providing a pledge of property as security for a loan remains the same however. Some of the principal variations are discussed below.

Deed of Trust

The *deed of trust* introduces a third party, a trustee, into the pledging instrument. Under these terms, the borrower actually makes an assignment, and the wording is very similar to a warranty deed of the property to the trustee, but restricts the effectiveness of the assignment to when a default occurs under the mortgage terms. The trustee is normally selected by the lender with the right of substitution in case of death or dismissal.

The deed of trust form is used in many areas and is almost universally used in Texas as a means of simplifying "homestead" law procedures. It substantially reduces the problems of foreclosure, limiting the process to an action by the trustee, with proper notice and in accordance with prevailing laws, rather than by litigation conducted in a court hearing.

Open-end Mortgages

The open-end mortgage permits a lender to advance additional money under the same security and priority as the original mortgage. This type of mortgage is often employed in farm loans where the lender maintains continuing relations with his customer-borrower. As the borrower pays his mortgage principal down, he may wish to add a new barn, or perhaps a new loading corral to his property. The additional loan can easily be accommodated under the terms of an open-end mortgage.

In some areas a borrower may elect to leave a minimal mortgage balance of, say, one dollar outstanding on his mortgage loan. This record of balance due, no matter how small, sustains the life of the mortgage instrument and, most significantly, its priority over any other subsequent lien except, of course, property taxes. This provision gives rural banks a means of making loans to their farm- or ranch-owning customers without the expense and delay of researching a title and recording a new mortgage instrument with each loan.

Construction Mortgages

A loan to build a house or other building is a construction loan, sometimes called *interim* financing. The security requirement is the same—a first lien on real property—but in this type of loan, proceeds are disbursed as the building is constructed. Under the construction mortgage, the borrower or builder draws a portion of the total loan at various stages, or at set time intervals, such as monthly, for work completed. It takes a construction-wise lender to make sure his disbursement of funds does not exceed the value of a building at each stage of construction.

A construction loan is considered a high-risk loan. It carries high-interest rates and is never intended to extend beyond three years. Commercial projects, such as a warehouse or apartment, usually require assurance of permanent financing or a "take-out commitment," i.e., an agreement by a reputable lender that the lending organization will make a permanent loan upon completion of the project.

Homebuilders frequently build for speculative sales, in which case the construction lender must look to the actual sale of the property to pay off the construction loan. The promissory note for a construction loan allows for funding as the work progresses and is expected to be paid off at completion of the building or shortly thereafter.

Mortgages with Release Clauses

When money is borrowed for the purpose of development on a piece of land, it is necessary to have specific release procedures that will permit the developer to sell lots and pay an agreed amount of the development loan, to obtain a release of the lots sold. Under the terms of regular mortgages, there is no provision allowing a partial sale of the property. A deal of this type would be subject to negotiation with the lender.

Therefore, when the purpose is to sell off the property a portion at a time, a special clause is needed in the mortgage stating the terms and amount of repayment required for the release of each portion. These clauses are also known as *partial releases* since the remainder of the land continues to be held as security for the loan.

Junior Mortgages

The term *junior mortgages* applies to those mortgages that carry a lower priority than the prime or first mortgage. These are *second* and even *third* mortgages.

The mortgage instrument carries no designation in its text describing its lien position. The order of priority, which determines the exact order of claims against a piece of property, is established by the time of the recording of that instrument. This becomes of extreme importance in a foreclosure proceeding. For example, if a property considered to be worth $50,000 carries a first mortgage for $30,000, and a second mortgage for $8000, and that property is forced into a foreclosure sale that results in a recovery of $35,000 in cash after payment of legal fees—how, then, should the money be distributed? The priority of the liens exercise control, and assuming that no other liens, taxes, or otherwise, have shown priority, then the first mortgage holder is in a position to recover his full $30,000 from the $35,000 proceeds, and the remaining $5000 is awarded to the second mortgage holder, leaving him $3000 short of recovering his $8000 loan. Due to the promissory note, the second mortgage holder has a right to seek a deficiency judgment against the borrower to recover that $3000. However, it becomes evident that the security of the land has been wiped out in the foreclosure sale and resulting settlement.

Later in this text, the subjects of recording and of title protection, as related to the question of establishing the priority of mortgage liens, will be discussed in more detail.

Purchase Money Mortgages

In some states, a distinctive, special protection is given to a loan for the initial purchase of a property, usually a residence. This type of mortgage is referred to as a *purchase money mortgage*.

Chattel Mortgages

Although we have been discussing mortgages primarily in terms of real property as security, the term *mortgage* can also be used to describe a pledge of personal property such as furniture or a car. This personal property can be referred to as *chattel*. Chattel, then, may be defined as a movable object—any property, exclusive of land or objects permanently attached to the land. With a chattel mortgage, the pledge of personal property as security for a loan can be similar to that for real property. It is the movable quality of the collateral and the difficulty of properly identifying an object such as a table or a washing machine that make the pledge a less secure procedure than it is in regard to real property.

Nevertheless, the form is widely used in small loan companies and for installment financing. Some states, it should be noted in this connection, use a conditional sales contract procedure for installment purchases that does not legally pass title to the chattel until it is fully paid for, thus eliminating the need for a mortgage pledge.

Package Mortgages

The *package mortgage* occurs in a hybrid form and attempts to include in the mortgage indenture both real property and personal property. It is used in residential loans when considerable built-in equipment is included with the house. Such a mortgage would list various household appliances, such as an oven, a range, a dishwasher, or disposal equipment, that might be considered attached to and a part of the real property, but that can be removed rather easily. By adding these various items to the mortgage as security, the lender may better protect his complete property loan. Although the procedure is often ignored or not enforced, it is definitely a violation of the mortgage terms to sell or dispose of a mortgaged range or dishwasher without the express consent of the mortgagee.

Contract for Deed

In listing types of mortgages, a *contract for deed* would be considered out of place, except for the fact that many people believe this instrument to be similar to a mortgage procedure. It is not.

In essence a contract for deed is another method of selling real estate. It is exactly what its name implies, a contract for a deed, and no more. It is used to sell real property on an installment payment basis without delivering title to the property until payment has been made in full. Properly drawn, a contract for deed is enforceable against either signatory party, as is any contract under the state's codes providing for contracts. However, it is not a deed to real property and grants to the buyer only the rights of possession and enjoyment; and these rights exist only as long as the grantor holds control of the land.

If fully understood by both parties, the contract for deed can be helpful in transferring property usage when a buyer has temporary credit problems or the seller does not yet hold a fully marketable title. However, this form of contract has gained a poor reputation through abuses, failure to fully disclose the facts, and outright frauds. The real pitfall lies in the possible inability of the seller to deliver a valid title after full payment has been made. During the installment paying period, anything that might happen to the seller, such as a damage claim resulting in a heavy adverse judgment, a divorce causing property settlements, dissolution of a corporate seller through bankruptcy, or any lien filed against the property under contract, can defeat the intent of the contract and can cause the seller to be unable to deliver a good title. If the seller cannot produce a good title to the property at completion of payment, the buyer may have a claim for damages against the seller, but he has no direct claim to the property involved.

Contract for deed sales are most commonly used in the sale of resort-type lots and also in smaller rent houses where a tenant becomes a buyer if he completes the payments. In the latter case, the property owner may wish to give a tenant the right to buy the house, but because of some prior credit problems or some temporary family troubles of the tenant, the owner does not want his land encumbered by the tenant buyer if a default occurs.

In regard to the resort-type lot sales, there have been flagrant abuses in the past. In 1969, the Department of Housing and Urban Development established the Office of Interstate Land Sales as a policing agency for developers of property containing more than 50 lots in any one development. The thrust of the legislation is not to establish sales patterns as minimum requirements, but to make sure the developer fully discloses the development plans and the legal status of the land title itself. And the buyer must acknowledge the receipt of all the information required, which also has the effect of protecting the developer against unwarranted claims from the buyer.

MORTGAGE PROCEDURES

Again, the practices and procedures by which mortgage rights are established and protected vary among the states, but certain elements are common to all. In the following discussion, the common procedures and reasons for them will be considered.

Recording

Of all the statutes written regarding ownership of land, the requirement to record a transaction has had the greatest long-range effect on improving our records of land ownership and the claims against that land. In fairly recent times and due to the lack of controlling legislation, courts have held that a valid title to land was actually passed by such procedures as a handwritten entry in the family Bible. How can a mortgage lender determine who really owns a piece of land? The answer lies in the recorded instruments of land transactions filed in the county records wherein the land is located. As the laws have made the recording of land transactions a necessary procedure and as our methods of handling this documentation have improved, the actual determination of proper title is becoming more and more accurate.

What is *recording?* In legal terms it is a form of notice— notice to the world—that a transaction of some kind has affected the title to a specific piece of land. Another form of legal notice is actual possession of the land, and historically, possession is the highest form of notice. The procedure for recording a transaction is to take the document to the record office of the county where the land is located and pay the fee for filing. The county officer responsible for the recording, copies the instrument in its entirety for the record book and certifies on the original as to the time, date, volume, and page or pages that contain the record.

Most state laws that require instruments affecting land titles to be recorded do not challenge the contractual rights of any parties to buy, sell, or encumber a piece of land. What they actually do is to declare any such transaction invalid against a third party *only in regard to the title to land.* For example, *A* can agree to sell ten acres of land to *B* and actually deliver a deed for the ten acres to *B*. The contract may be valid and the consideration (payment for the land) accepted, but actual title to the land is not secure until the deed has been recorded. If the seller *A*, in this example, should suffer a heavy casualty loss and be subjected to a court judgment against him before the deed to buyer *B* has been recorded, the ten acres of land would be subject to the claim of *A*'s new creditors since the title would still be in *A*'s name on the public record.

It is important to emphasize that the failure to record an instrument affecting land title does not invalidate the instrument insofar as the parties involved in the transaction are concerned. It places the burden on whichever party is asserting a claim to the land to give notice of his claim in the public records, or lose the effectiveness of that claim against any other claimant. The rules apply to all instruments applicable to land titles, conveyances, claims, or debts against the land itself or against the landowner, and, of course, all mortgage instruments. Contracts for deed and leases are instruments affecting land title and can be recorded, but for various reasons of privacy or other interests often are not recorded.

State laws are usually lenient as to what instruments can be recorded, but most require that the signature to the instrument be acknowledged before a duly authorized officer of the state such as a Notary Public, or be properly witnessed. Because any instrument affecting a title to land is a legal matter that can involve many state laws, it is customary, though not always required, that such an instrument be prepared by a licensed attorney. The preparation of any instrument conveying a land title is considered the practice of law in most states and, therefore, is restricted to that state's licensed attorneys. Few, if any, lenders would permit a loan to be made based on a mortgage instrument prepared by anyone other than a qualified attorney regardless of the requirements for recording.

Mortgage Priorities

The expression *first mortgage* or *second mortgage* is so commonly used that it is not unusual for a person to expect to find such an identification spelled out in the mortgage instrument. Such is not the case. The priority by which a mortgage, or any other claim to land, is established is by the time of recording. And this is determined not only by the day of recording, but by the time of that particular day.

In handling a mortgage instrument, the lender is most concerned about the proper priority of his security claim; i.e., what prior claims, if any, could jeopardize the lender's claim to the land. Most lenders do not rely on the record alone, but require an insuring agent to guarantee the priority of the claim backed by an insurance policy, called a *title policy*.

The statutory priorities given workmen and material suppliers in most states may be a source of additional problems for construction loan mortgages. For example, in a mortgage to secure construction money, any work permitted on the land prior to the recording means that a workman may have a claim on the land itself in case of nonpayment. Such a claim held by a workman or contractor need not be recorded to establish its priority, but there must be some positive proof that the work was accomplished before the mortgage was recorded. One method of establishing priority for the lender is to photograph the raw land, have the date of the picture certified, and retain the print as proof that the land was untouched prior to recording the mortgage.

Any claim to land that is of lower priority, i.e., recorded or incurred at a later date, is said to be junior to the prior claim. Thus, as noted earlier, second and third mortgages are sometimes referred to as junior mortgages.

Subordination

Another method of establishing priorities for mortgage instruments is by contract. For various reasons it may be beneficial to the parties involved in a land transaction to establish a claim of lower value or lesser importance to another, a procedure called *subordination*.

An example might be a hypothetical case where a piece of land is sold to a developer who plans to erect an office building for lease to one of his customers. The seller of the land, for taxes or other reasons, prefers to take his payment in ten annual installments. But the developer needs to mortgage the land immediately with first priority for payment going to the mortgage lender for construction money to build the office building. In such a case, and assuming credit worthiness of the developer, the land seller would agree specifically to subordinate his land ownership claim to the lender's mortgage, securing his ten annual payments with a second mortgage.

Limitation Statutes

In the codes of law established by the various states, *time limitations* have been established on the validity of most claims or debts. These limitations may vary somewhat, but usually place time limits within which a creditor can file a claim for an open account, such as one to two years, and probably a longer limit within which a written promissory note can be recovered, perhaps five to ten years. Time limits for secured debts may be extended for even longer periods.

There are also limiting statutes imposed for general contractors and subcontractors filing claims for unpaid work and materials on construction projects. Failure to file a claim, usually in the form of a lien recorded in the county records, within the prescribed time limits, would make that claim invalid insofar as the land itself is concerned. It does not void the debt, however.

There are also time limitations in most states affecting title to real property. These have been established in an effort to clarify claims to ownership of land. The time limitations vary with what is called the "color of title" that can be asserted to the land claimed. Two factors are essential to establishing a valid claim to land over a period of time and within the statutes of limitation: (1) actual possession and use of the land plus, and (2) possession and use considered adverse or use without the express consent of the opposing claimant.

An example of a short time limitation might be cited here as, for instance, the purchase of a house from the heirs of a family who previously owned the property. All the known heirs have agreed to the sale of the property and have joined in signing the deed; the purchaser has duly paid the full price agreed to. Then several years later someone claiming to be an heir comes forward to assert his interest in the house that was sold. Because a deed was delivered in good faith and the consideration was paid, the new claimant might be limited to three years within which his claim would be considered by the courts.

The longest time limits are usually granted in any transaction involving minor children or mentally incapacitated persons. Most states draw a line at 25 years and simply rule that possession of land for that period precludes anyone else asserting a claim against it.

The result of these limiting statutes is an effective scrubbing of the records after the prescribed number of years. Title insurance policies lapse after the maximum years within which claims can be filed. And many property owners are careful to establish their own property lines with special markers and to assert their own usage and ownership of land by restricting access to private roadways, etc., for perhaps one day a year, so as to prevent or offset the workings of time limitation statutes.

LAND TITLES

Ownership of land is a right. It is not a deed, it is not a title insurance policy, it is not living on the land. All of these characteristics are important evidences of ownership, but the right itself is broader and covers four definable areas:

1. *Possession*—the right to occupy the land, such as a residence.
2. *Use*—the right to work the land, which covers what may be grown, what minerals may be recovered, etc.
3. *Enjoyment*—the use and occupancy of the land free of harassment or interference.
4. *Disposition*—the right to sell, lease, or otherwise dispose of the land.

In today's complex living patterns, the free and unfettered ownership of land that once existed in earlier rural areas is difficult to find. Possession is about the only element of ownership that remains clearly distinguishable, and even that has become more difficult to determine.

The usage of land is complicated by leases on mineral rights (oil, gas, coal, etc.) and by restrictions set up by some state governments forbidding the use of water except by separate grants of water rights, as well as by federal restrictions as to what can or cannot be grown on the land. The enjoyment of the land is also subject to many restrictions in urban areas, particularly in the form of zoning laws, health and safety restrictions, and possible conflicts in neighborhood associations.

The rights to dispose of land are complicated by the practice of bequeathing life estates, say, to a widow upon the death of a husband; or by the assignment of property by will to a charitable foundation or educational institution; or by a gift of land to a community for a specific use such as a park, with the land reverting back to the estate of the former owner should his wishes be violated.

With all the complications in land ownership, as outlined above, it becomes necessary to find a way to establish where and in whose hands ownership and control of the land actually lie. In order for a mortgage instrument to be valid and to provide security for a loan, it is necessary that sufficient rights to the land be pledged and that the pledge be made by the person or persons holding the rights to do so. Loans are made against various portions of real property ownership, such as oil production loans on oil leases, development loans on mining claims, and crop loans on surface and water rights. It rarely happens today that much more than a portion of the ownership rights is pledged, but that portion must include the essential rights that would enable a lender to use the property as a last resort in recovering the balance of his loan.

The area under study in this text is land development and the buildings occupying the land, which would mean the ownership rights to at least the surface, the access rights thereto, and protection against infringement by any other user of rights to that land. The researching of these rights of ownership to land is the special province of land title companies, which are basically insurance companies. Title companies sell insurance policies that guarantee to the purchaser a good title to a certain piece of property. The guarantee is in the form of a promise to protect the land title against any adverse claim or to pay the holder of the policy the face amount (purchase price of the property) in cash, should the title fail for any reason. At the time the initial owner's policy is issued, a second policy covering the same property may be purchased that makes a similar pledge of title protection to the lender or mortgagee. In this manner the mortgage lender avails himself of the recorded information regarding property title, which is researched by the title company to protect its own insurance pledge and is backed by the title insurance company's resources to pay off in cash if the title fails.

A second method of obtaining title information and of determining the validity of a mortgage pledge is to employ an attorney to research the title. In this procedure, the attorney will order an abstract from an abstract or title company. The abstract is a certified collection of all instruments that have been recorded and, therefore, have affected the chain of title since the inception of that title. The inception of the title could be a land grant by a foreign monarch who once claimed the land, or more commonly by a state granting title to a purchaser, or it could be by quit claim deed from the federal government. From its original grant, the land may have been broken into many segments and passed through many hands, and the abstracts can be quite voluminous. The result of the research is an attorney's opinion on the title stating any adverse claims to the land that are exceptions to the title. The opinion will then identify those title problems that must be corrected, or "cured" before a mortgage can be made securely.

In certain areas of the country another method is employed to handle property titles, a method flowing from the Torrens Act procedure. This is a process whereby a state has adopted a program for recording title, mostly for urban property lots, by registering property title in the public record established for that purpose. The procedure is very similar to that used in registering the ownership of a car. Any sale of the property must be registered, and a new certificate of title is then issued by the state. The plan has some inherent advantages in minimizing legal expenses and title costs in the sale of property, but because of the complex nature of land owner-ship, this plan has not become too widespread in usage.

Accepting the fact that land titles in today's urban society are seldom completely clear, the mortgage lender has learned to live with certain kinds of exceptions. For instance, title insurance companies have standard clauses of exceptions that they customarily make in any insurance policy they issue. One of these exceptions has to do with the rights of anyone then in possession of the property. The title company does not physically inspect the property, leaving that to the buyer. Since the seller is usually in possession of the property when it is sold, his rights are clearly determined when he signs a warranty deed granting title to the buyer. If a tenant is in possession, it is necessary to establish his rights before a sale is consummated.

Another standard exception made by the title company is in the zoning requirements or sometimes in regard to deed restrictions. The title company is not insuring any specific usage of the property; it is only making certain that the ownership rights of possession and disposition are clearly assignable.

The title insuring policy will usually list any easements crossing the property, which are generally utility easements and street rights-of-way. The easements are exceptions to the insurance policy and are simply claims to the land, which are accepted as normal and necessary.

Often the title company will list certain requirements in the initial title opinion that involve a question of encroach-ments on the property lines, or perhaps a dispute among heirs, or a problem arising from a divorce settlement that is undecided. The requirements must be resolved to the satis-faction of the title company, or the insurance policy can be refused, or it can be issued with the unsatisfied requirement listed as an exception to the coverage.

What these questions involving title problems lead to is not always a completely clear title, but what is called a "merchantable" or "marketable" title. There can be exceptions or unsatisfied requirements, which, at the discretion of the mortgage lender, may be so unimportant or insignificant to the total property value that they can be ignored. The ultimate question is whether or not a knowledgeable buyer would be willing to accept the minor title defects in a subsequent sale should foreclosure become necessary.

SOURCES OF
MORTGAGE MONEY

The great pools of money that are available in the United States for investment can be classified into five major sources and a number of lesser sources as follows:

Major Sources

1. Savings and Loan Associations
2. Mutual Savings Banks
3. Commercial Banks
4. Life Insurance Companies
5. Government Agencies

Lesser Sources

1. Pension and Trust Funds
2. Individuals
3. Real Estate Investments Trusts
4. Miscellaneous Others

Of the principal sources for all types of investments, long-term and short-term, the commercial banks rank as the largest. The second in volume of loans are the thrift institutions or savings banks and associations, followed by industrial corporations as the third largest source.

Fourth in size are the investment accounts of the various governments, with the life insurance companies ranking fifth.

What about foreign investments in this country? While it is true that more foreign money is coming in to purchase securities and real estate itself, as a present source of lendable funds foreign investment has added very little to this country's totals so far. Furthermore, the continuing instability of the world money markets holds poor prospects for any increase of funds from this source for lending purposes.

In examining the major sources of lendable funds, we are limiting our coverage to those making substantial investments in long-term mortgage loans. One of the largest sources of investment funds—the industrial corporations—does not make long-term loans to the general public. Its investments are generally limited to growth within its own organization and private sphere of business. The need for outside mortgage money by industrial corporations is discussed in Chapter 11, but as a source of funds for the purposes of this text these corporations are not considered.

The sources covered in this chapter are the mortgage lenders—all subject to various regulations that control and direct their loans. But within the rules, each lender is free to exercise his judgment in the selection of loans that will achieve a maximum yield for his money compatible with the risk exposure. Only a portion of the many government bureaus and agencies making loans have their programs coupled to social and political purposes such as subsidized housing, aid to the victims of a natural disaster, assistance for displaced families, and aid for military personnel. The major thrust of the government programs is to facilitate the flow of money through the private lending institutions and to help protect the savings of the individuals and companies whose cash, in the form of deposits, insurance premiums, and security purchases, is the real underlying source of all our lendable funds.

Institutions making long-term real estate mortgage loans have a variety of reasons for making each loan. They might wish to increase an investment yield, or to satisfy and maintain a business relationship with a particularly good customer; or perhaps they wish to attract some new business from a competitor; or they might want to shift a portion of the investments within their own portfolio of loans; or there could be a need to comply with a statutory requirement or a new regulation. Whatever the specific reason may be for a loan, there are four basic qualifications common to all mortgage lenders, which are as follows:

1. A substantial pool of available cash with a reasonable and predictable inflow.
2. A satisfactory method for controlling the outflow of funds.
3. Adequate personnel knowledgeable in the field of mortgage lending.
4. Legal qualifications permitting long-term loans.

In considering the qualifications listed above, the predictable inflow is excellent with insurance companies and pension funds. Savings associations have grown by being allowed to offer a slightly higher interest rate for savings accounts, but such accounts are subject to withdrawal— legally upon 30-day notice, but in practice almost on demand. The protection of the inflow for thrift institutions lies in their ability to borrow additional money against their loan portfolio or to sell some of the loans in the secondary market when they are faced with substantial withdrawals. Commercial banks must limit their long-term loans to a percentage of their time deposits rather than their demand deposits. In regard to the outflow of funds, then, the life insurance companies and the pension funds are in almost complete control, whereas the thrift institutions and banks must rely on borrowed funds or the sale of loans to offset any massive withdrawals.

On the succeeding pages, we will analyze those institutions that can be considered sources of mortgage money, relating them to the guidelines indicated above, and discussing the role each one plays in the financing of real estate.

SAVINGS AND LOAN ASSOCIATIONS

The number one source of mortgage funds is the savings and loan associations across the country. The origin of this type of institution was the loosely formed associations of people with common interests: farmers, storekeepers, religious groups, fraternal organizations, and others who pooled their capital to provide funds for building houses, improving land, or adding to their farms. The modern counterpart of these groups might be found in company credit unions; although there are differences in the purposes and types of loans of these institutions from those of the earlier associations.

Until the 1930s there was little regulation of these associations, but the Depression showed up many problems. Resources were restricted to local deposits, and the long-term loans allowed little liquidity or flexibility. In 1932 the federal government established the Federal Home Loan Bank system—still very much in operation today—which provides member associations a continuing source of funds for emergency needs or for financing additional mortgage loans. In 1933 the Federal Home Loan Bank Board was authorized to issue federal charters to newly formed savings associations, charters that required certain standards of compliance and a supervised method of operations. A year later, in 1934, the Federal Savings and Loan Insurance Corporation (FSLIC) was established to provide deposit insurance, and all federally chartered associations were required to belong and to comply with its rules. The insurance coverage now protects any one depositor up to the amount of $20,000.

Along with the efforts of the federal government to improve our savings associations, most states undertook reforms of all kinds to establish regulatory authorities and more stringent lending laws for their own state-chartered institutions. Some states have established their own deposit insurance procedures and have set rules with limits and procedures different from those of the federal patterns. But most states find it a good policy to follow the guidance of the Federal Home Loan Bank Board in order to establish a more uniform set of rules. The growing dependence on the secondary market for the sale of mortgage loans has increased the pressure toward more uniform standards; and unless certain procedures are required by state policies, the lending institution tries to follow the more nationalized procedures.

State-Chartered Savings and Loan Associations. Until 1933 all savings associations were state-chartered and operated under whatever rules and administrative procedures the various state legislatures established. State-chartered associations thus can be found under a variety of rules. They may be either mutually owned by the depositors, or they may be stock corporations owned by stockholders. Further, state charters may be required to carry deposit insurance, or they may not. Some states operate their own insurance funds to protect the depositors; others may require compliance with the Federal Savings and Loan Insurance Corporation. State chartered associations are permitted to become members of the FSLIC and to be insured by it. To be eligible, the association must also become a member of the Federal Home Loan Bank System and is subject to its supervision. Thus, the state-chartered association would be subject to the rules established by the FSLIC, subject to the supervision of the FHLBB, plus meet the requirements of the state regulatory authorities. In spite of the overlapping of authorities, many state charters elect to join the federal system because of the protection it provides for the depositor.

State regulatory bodies can and do set their own limitations on the types of loans that can be made, the amounts that limit any one type of loan, and the general mix of investments permitted to the associations under their jurisdiction. In practice the upper limits of loans are being set by the federal authorities—the FHLBB and the newer Federal Home Loan Mortgage Corporation, which purchases mortgage loans—in order to maintain a portfolio of loans that can be more easily converted to cash should the need arise.

Federal-Chartered Savings and Loan Associations. The authority granted to the Federal Home Loan Bank Board in 1933 to issue savings and loan association charters created a new pattern that is uniform across the country. All federal-chartered associations must be mutually owned by the depositors. They must be members of the Federal Home Loan Bank system and have their deposits insured by the FSLIC.

The general requirements of the Federal Home Loan Bank Board imposed on its members are (1) an economically sound policy for mortgage loans and (2) the condition that the interest rates charged be reasonable. The Board also required that a portion of each association's assets be held in liquid form; i.e., cash or demand deposits. Prior to August, 1971, this requirement was 7½% of savings deposits and short-term borrowed funds. After that date the requirement was lowered to 7% in an effort to free more funds to relieve the pressures of the 1969–1970 credit crunch.

For some years the Federal Home Loan Bank Board has been reviewing its policy that does not permit its charters to be stockholder-owned. From the depositors' viewpoint, a change to a stockholder form is important. Over the years these thrift institutions have built up substantial undistributed surpluses, which technically belong to the depositors. Since the individual depositors continue to change through the years, the proper allocation of the accumulated surplus to the current depositors is a major problem to any transition of ownership. From the lending viewpoint, the same rules and regulations would apply to the institution regardless of the form of ownership. A stockholder form of ownership might be considered more aggressive and could tend to channel loans into areas of higher yields.

Investment Policies of Savings Associations

Two important rules guide the thrust of a savings and loan investment policy. One of these is the requirement that 80% of a savings association's assets be held in residential mortgage loans, as that is the purpose for which it is chartered. The other is a policy of the Internal Revenue Service that allows a savings association to transfer earnings to a non-taxable surplus account, providing that loans classified as commercial do not exceed 18% of the association's assets.

The tax rule was designed to assist the purpose of the savings associations. The pooling of the depositors' funds is intended to provide them with a source of money to purchase or improve their homes. By permitting any earnings to accumulate tax-free, the association's ability to assist its members would be increased, and this would promote the growth of the economy. If any of the earnings are distributed as a dividend to the association's owners, that distribution is taxed at the corporate level and also as income to the member owner. Consequently, many associations prefer to accumulate surpluses.

But surpluses have not always been enough to stabilize the inflow of funds when new deposits slow or reverse themselves into an outflow. From experiences learned in the 1969–1970 credit crunch, the Federal Home Loan Bank Board made several changes in the regulations governing member associations to improve their ability to handle fluctuating market conditions. As mentioned earlier, the regular pass book deposits are subject to withdrawal only after 30 days prior notice according to the rules. In practice, no association can really enforce this rule for fear of causing some alarm with a refusal to return a depositor's money upon demand. However, it is this legal limitation on immediate withdrawal that gives an association a technical position to make the long-term loans that cannot be permitted with a commercial bank's demand checking accounts.

To give savings associations greater stability than the 30-day withdrawal notice was supposed to provide, the FHLB in 1971 created a savings certificate to pay 6% interest, which was a full 1% over the existing pass book rate, provided that the certificate was held for two years. The new savings form was very popular, and some areas of the country reported over half of their deposits were coming from the long-term certificates. Another practice that had a tendency to improve the savings associations' long-term stability of deposits was the increase of branch offices into the smaller communities and rural areas. The effect has been to attract depositors who keep their money in the association and ignore interest-rate cycles.

The FHLBB also relaxed some of the restrictions on the types of loans that savings associations could make, allowing them to finance mobile homes and household appliances and to grant more liberal property-improvement loans. These are short-term loans for the most part, and give the associations a more rapid turnover of their money and greater flexibility in their loan portfolio.

Probably the greatest increase in flexibility for the savings associations has come from the rather sudden opening of the big secondary markets in mortgages. In 1969–1970 these thrift institutions had little opportunity to sell the mortgages they held in exchange for cash that they badly needed to take care of new loan commitments. This situation has changed somewhat. In 1971 the Federal Home Loan Mortgage Corporation (inevitably acquiring the nickname of "Freddie Mac") entered the market for conventional mortgage loans under the direction of the FHLB. Now the savings associations have a new entity for raising capital through the sale of bonds to the general public and can use this capital to buy mortgage loans from the member associations. There has been considerable variation in the individual policies of savings associations utilizing this new market for loans. Some have simply refused to sell any of their loans, while others have arranged to sell off most of their newer loans, holding only the servicing contracts in house.

Another organization that stepped into the market for conventional loans was the Federal National Mortgage Association, which in February, 1972, made its first purchase of loans other than FHA- and VA-underwritten loans. Under Chapter 5 of this text, the Federal National Mortgage Association—FNMA, or better known as "Fannie Mae"—is more fully discussed. This organization utilizes an offering procedure that it calls the "Free Market System" by which approved mortgage lenders periodically offer to sell to Fannie Mae blocks of mortgage loans at prices that float competitively with the market for long-term money.

As the rules were being changed to improve the ability of the savings associations to furnish capital for a growing need for mortgage money, the commercial bankers cast a strong competitive eye on the advantages enjoyed by the associations. Principally these have been: (1) government authorization to pay a higher rate of interest on savings deposits than commercial banks were allowed, and (2) the deferment of income tax liability on undistributed profits. In the tight money market of 1973, the banking authorities reduced one of these advantages a bit by allowing commercial banks to increase the rate of interest they could pay on their savings deposits by ½%, while permitting savings associations to raise their rates by only ¼%. The commercial bankers continue to seek a comparable tax advantage on the income from their own savings deposits.

The results of the changes as sketched above have been to open greater resources for mortgage lending purposes. The effort continues at many levels of our thrift and banking systems. The precise rules and limits will continue to be altered and improved as the need arises and as new ways are found to meet the ever-growing need for mortgage money.

Lending Limits of Savings Associations

The lending powers of both federal- and state-chartered associations are limited by their respective regulatory agencies. Federal charters have dollar limitations on the amount that can be loaned on any one property. In 1971 the maximum amount permitted on a 90% loan was raised to $45,000. The "90%" means the amount of the loan in relation to the value of the property, and the value of the property is determined by the appraised value or selling price, whichever is lower. At the same time the 90% limit was raised, the maximum ratio was also increased to 95% of the value. However, the 95% loans were restricted to a maximum of $36,000, and any loan over 90% must include the addition of mortgage default insurance to protect the lender. It was this requirement that caused the tremendous increase in the sale of private mortgage insurance all over the country, which is discussed in greater detail in the next chapter.

While state regulatory agencies exercise their own authority over lending limits, many choose to follow the guidelines established by the Federal Home Loan Bank Board for its member associations. As pointed out earlier, a large number of state-chartered associations have joined the Federal Home Loan Bank system, since it is much less confusing to follow a sound national policy when possible.

There are fewer dollar limits on the amount of money that may be loaned at ratios of 80% or less because the risk exposure of the lending institution is much lower. Some states have simply removed all dollar limits for their own chartered institutions, depending on the prudent judgment of the associations' lending officers to establish their own limitations.

Another limitation on loans is that no one borrower may have more than 5% of the association's assets outstanding. Loans to officers and directors are usually permitted but are always subject to the special scrutiny of banking examiners.

A major consideration of most savings associations in establishing their own limits and guidelines within the legal limitations is the pattern established for the purchase of loans in the secondary market. Both the Federal Home Loan Mortgage Corporation and the Federal National Mortgage Association have limiting requirements. The ability to sell a block of mortgage loans to either of these organizations at some future date gives an association's portfolio of loans a much greater flexibility. In addition to maximum dollar limitations for various types of loans, the secondary market purchasers are also concerned with the forms used for the note and mortgage instruments. Limitations also apply to the types of loans—the secondary market is not as strong for 95% loans as for the lower ratio loans. The market for resort, weekend, or second homes is not as good as for primary houses.

In the matter of geographical limits, some states still confine their thrift institutions to property loans within a maximum of 50 miles from an association's offices. Federal guidelines, which did limit member associations to loans within a radius of 100 miles, were recently expanded to permit loans within 100 miles of the lending institution's agent, which could be an authorized servicing office. Savings associations are restricted in the amount of money they can invest out of state. The long-time limit at 5% of their assets that could be invested out of state was raised several years ago to 10% and applies only to conventional loans. There is no limit on the amount of money any one institution can invest out of state in FHA- or VA-underwritten loans.

The need for making mortgage loans outside a local geographic area falls primarily on the large savings associations in the big eastern cities, in Chicago, and in some of the cash-heavy midwestern cities, and even in some of the smaller communities with good business activity but not a commensurate residential growth. It is these cash-surplus associations, which provide much of the mortgage money for the growing sections of the country, that have generally been short of lendable funds.

Table of Mortgage Activity

Table 4–1 gives the dollar volume of mortgage loans made by savings associations since 1965 showing amounts going into new home construction loans and amounts for home purchases. Also, the amount invested in conventional loans is detailed along with the amount for VA and FHA type loans. Note the substantial fluctuation in the amount of new loans made each year; i.e., 1972 shows over twice the amount of money going into loans as does 1970.

Conclusion. Looking at the large numbers of savings associations in the country, it should be noted that the great majority are relatively small in assets—under $25 million—and restrict their lending to their local areas. These associations are usually active, enthusiastic participants in the local community programs and take considerable pride in using their available funds to promote growth in their own area.

MUTUAL SAVINGS BANKS

Because the origins of mutual savings banks are so similar to that of savings and loan associations, they are included in the category of thrift institutions: savings and loan associations were organized for the specific purpose of savings intended for home ownership; mutual savings banks were organized simply to encourage saving with no specific usage in mind.

This latter type of bank exists only in the northeastern 18 states, with 75% of the total assets located in just two states—New York and Massachusetts. All are state-chartered, and all are mutually owned as the name implies. However, the depositor-owners have almost no voice in management.

TABLE 4–1

Mortgage Activity of Savings and Loan Associations
(In millions of dollars)

Period	Loans made			Loans outstanding (end of period)			
	Total [1]	New home construction	Home purchase	Total [2]	FHA-insured [3]	VA-guaranteed [3]	Conventional
1965	24,192	6,013	10,830	110,306	5,145	6,398	98,763
1966	16,924	3,653	7,828	114,427	5,269	6,157	103,001
1967	20,122	4,243	9,604	121,805	5,791	6,351	109,663
1968	21,983	4,916	11,215	130,802	6,658	7,012	117,132
1969	21,847	4,757	11,254	140,347	7,917	7,658	124,772
1970	21,383	4,150	10,237	150,331	10,178	8,494	131,659
1971	39,472	6,835	18,811	174,385	13,798	10,848	149,739
1972	51,408	8,553	26,615	206,387	29,391	......	176,996
1972–Dec. ...	4,591	667	2,167	206,387	15,639	13,764	176,964
1973–Jan. ...	3,702	590	1,970	208,132	29,581		178,551
Feb. ..	3,710	614	2,019	210,260	29,751		180,509
Mar. ..	4,990	887	2,685	213,259	30,045		183,214
Apr. ..	4,989	886	2,762	216,250	30,182		186,068
May ..	5,477	931	3,141	219,500	30,296		189,204
June ..	5,738	903	3,469	222,801	30,381		192,420
July ..	5,059	851	3,079	225,490	30,270		195,220
Aug. ..	4,971	801	3,059	228,006	30,268		197,738
Sept. ..	3,177	572	1,838	229,413	30,632		198,781
Oct. ..	2,788	532	1,548	230,425	30,328		200,097
Nov.r .	2,311	449	1,366	231,319	30,295		201,024
Dec. ..	2,505	417	1,336	232,322	30,274		202,048

[1] Includes loans for repairs, additions and alterations, refinancing, etc., not shown separately.

[2] Includes shares pledged against mortgage loans; beginning 1966, also includes junior liens and real estate sold on contract; beginning 1967, also includes downward structural adjustment for change in universe; and beginning 1973, excludes participation certificates guaranteed by the FHLMC and certain other related items.

[3] Beginning 1973, data for these groups available only on a combined basis.

Source: Federal Reserve Bank

As presently organized, the mutual savings banks elect their first board of trustees. Subsequent vacancies are filled by the board itself, thus creating a self-perpetuating management.

Mutual savings banks are an outgrowth of a banking method originally popular with new citizens of foreign birth who did not understand or place much confidence in the pieces of paper used as checks. They felt more comfortable dealing in cash. Consequently, the savings banks provided a convenient depository for a savings account and/or cashing pay checks. There was no real need in the beginning for checking account service, and these banks still do not handle this type of demand deposit.

Mutual savings banks, as controlled by the state regulatory bodies, may belong to the Federal Deposit Insurance Corporation (the same as commercial banks) or to one of several state agencies that provide similar account deposit insurance. These insurance agencies also exercise authority as to types of investments, limits on amounts for each, and require certain accounting procedures to be followed. They also run periodic examinations of the banks' records to assure standards are being met.

Investment Policies of Mutual Savings Banks

Mutual savings banks have a wider choice of investments than savings associations. Where the associations are substantially limited to residential mortgages, the savings banks can buy bonds and can make personal or educational loans and other consumer-type loans. It is interesting to note that despite the latitude available for investments by this type of institution, the loan portfolios of all savings banks have shown a steady increase in percentage of mortgage loans since World War II. In the period immediately following that war, savings banks held approximately 30% of their investments in mortgage loans. An explanation of this relatively low percentage is suggested by the fact that foreclosures accompanying the depression had left an unfavorable mark on mortgage loans, which was followed by the decreased building volume during the war years of 1941 through 1946, and these factors had correspondingly encouraged heavy investments in government securities. By 1960, however, the investments in mortgages had jumped to a little over 70% of the total loans negotiated and by 1970 had moved above 75%. What accounts for this strong growth of investments in mortgages, which has more than doubled since the 1940s? The following four reasons can be cited, three of which are also keys to the growth of all mortgage lending:

1.   The end of World War II brought a selling off of government bonds, depressing the yield from them as compared to mortgages.

2.   Changes in the banking laws of the largest states controlling Mutual Savings Banks permitted them to make out-of-state loans.

3.   The housing industry expanded following World War II, greatly increasing the demand for mortgage money.

4.   Mortgage lenders' attitudes generally changed toward acceptance of FHA and VA commitments, now considering them to be sound and valued procedures.

The impact of mutual savings banks on our mortgage money market is far greater than the rather regionalized base of their home offices would indicate. With the new authority to make out-of-state investments, the savings banks located in areas of heavy deposits relative to loan demands for housing have been able to profitably channel money to the cash-short growth areas of the south, southwest, and west. The movement of this money to out-of-state investments has mostly been handled through agreements with mortgage bankers and other savings institutions and will be more fully detailed in Chapter 6 on mortgage banking. The savings banks use both an immediate purchase procedure of buying large blocks of loans on a wholesale basis and a forward commitment method, which is a sales and service type of agreement with an agent, such as a mortgage banker, to accept a block of loans of a specific type at an agreed interest rate over the next four to nine months.

Table of Mutual Savings Bank Mortgage Investments

Table 4–2 below shows the larger proportion of FHA and VA type loans handled by the mutual savings banks compared

TABLE 4–2

Mutual Savings Bank Holdings
(in millions)

| Period | Total | Residential | | | Other non-farm | Farm |
		FHA-insured	VA-guaranteed	Conventional		
1965	40,096	13,791	11,408	14,897	4,469	52
1966	42,242	14,500	11,471	16,272	5,041	53
1967	44,641	15,074	11,795	17,772	5,732	117
1968	46,748	15,569	12,033	19,146	6,592	117
1969	48,682	15,862	12,166	20,654	7,342	114
1970	49,937	16,087	12,008	21,842	7,893	119
1971	53,027	16,141	12,074	24,812	8,901	50
1972	57,140	16,013	12,622	28,505	10,354	62
1972–I	53,733	16,184	12,144	25,405	9,195	50
II	54,758	16,256	12,325	26,178	9,586	60
III	55,889	16,130	12,463	27,296	9,951	61
IV	57,140	16,013	12,622	28,505	10,354	62
1973–Ir	58,169	. . . . .	. . . . .	. . . . .	10,683	68
II	59,397	. . . . .	. . . . .	. . . . .	11,178	59
III	r60,305	. . . . .	. . . . .	. . . . .	11,670	59

Source: Federal Reserve Bank

with the conventional loans. The federally underwritten loans can be placed anywhere in the country without the geographical limitations associated with conventional loans. It is this type of lending that has made the mutual savings banks an important source to all areas of the country.

COMMERCIAL BANKS

The largest of all lenders with the greatest total cash resources are the commercial banks. But in total investments they seldom carry over 10 to 12% of their portfolio in long-term mortgage loans. Before the Depression of the 1930s, commercial banks held a much larger proportion of their deposits in savings accounts, also called *time deposits,* as opposed to the demand deposits or checking accounts. After World War II, the growth of thrift institutions accounted for the greater portion of savings increases. The thrift institutions were permitted to pay a higher interest rate on their deposits, which fostered the movement away from the commercial banks. Being unable to compete for the longer term savings money, the commercial banks concentrated their efforts on the short-term loans they could make with their demand deposits.

In many smaller communities and rural areas, the commercial bank still represents the main source of all money, including mortgage money for farm loans. The banks make the longer term property loans in direct relation to the amount of savings deposits they hold. In the larger urban areas, most commercial banks refuse to make real estate loans for long terms, except, perhaps, as an accommodation to a good commercial customer or for some other appropriate reason such as a civic improvement. Even then the term of such a loan would be in the 5-to-15-year bracket rather than 20 to 30 years. During the 1970s, the patterns may be changing as banking regulations tend to reduce the former competitive advantages of the thrift institutions and make long-term investments more attractive for the commercial banks.

Regulation of Commercial Banks, State and National

Commercial banks can operate under either state charters or national charters. The distinction to the public lies in the use of the word *national* in the name of the bank.

State-chartered banks operate under the authority of a state banking board or commission, and the rules have considerable variety. State charters in the past have granted greater leeway than national charters within which to make loans in regard to the types of loans, the terms of the loans, the amount of the loan in relation to the collateral offered as security, and the dollar amount of the loan in relation to the bank's assets.

State banks can, and often do, become members of the Federal Reserve System and insure their deposits with the FDIC. If so, they become subject to the regulations and the audits of both the federal and state authorities. Some of the advantages of membership in the Federal Reserve System, such as the right to pass on a fully collateralized loan to the Federal Reserve Bank at the current discount rate of interest, become of less importance when the Federal Reserve Board adopts policies to restrict the ability of their member banks to make loans. At such times, state-chartered banks sometimes find it more profitable for them to simply withdraw from the Federal Reserve System. These withdrawals have the tendency to reduce the effectiveness of policies laid down by the Federal Reserve and may some day bring legislation to place all commercial banks under a single controlling agency.

The present trend in state regulatory agencies is to follow the patterns for investments, accounting procedures, and loan limitations as established by the Comptroller of the Currency, who governs the national banks. This prevents overlaps and confusion within the banking community.

National banks, chartered and supervised by the Comptroller of the Currency, must also submit to some control by the Board of Governors of the Federal Reserve Bank and to the requirements of the Federal Deposit Insurance Corporation. National banks have always been more restrictive in making real estate loans than state-chartered banks, a situation that stems in part from the different origins of the two types of banks. Prior to 1820, national banks were not even permitted to make mortgage loans. The rules have, of course, changed and will continue to change as to the term, amount, and ratio of different types of loans.

Real Estate Investments of Commercial Banks

In any type of loan, an obvious restriction is the size of the bank and its capitalization. There are over 15,000 commercial banks in the United States with resources averaging $25 million. The range in size is from less than $1 million in deposits to over $10 billion. Regulations limit any single loan of a bank to a percent of its total assets or not to exceed the capitalization (the equity interest) of the bank. In addition, each bank will establish guidelines for its own loans based on its size, which will also include loan minimums. For example, a huge bank such as Chase Manhattan of New York will not consider some categories of loans, such as oil production loans, for less than $1 million, whereas a small local bank could not touch a $1 million loan but can make money on a personal loan for a thousand dollars.

Within their individual limitations, all commercial banks make real estate loans of some form or another. These loans can be generally classified in the following three categories:

1. Direct mortgage loans
2. Construction loans
3. Mortgage warehouse line of credit

Direct Mortgage Loans. While all commercial banks are now legally authorized to make loans using real estate as collateral, the incentives to make such loans vary considerably. Smaller rural banks are still the only source of such loans in many areas. In medium-sized towns and cities, the banks often use their capacity to make long-term loans as an attraction for other business. In large urban areas, the commercial banks find more profitable use for their money in short-term loans that give the portfolio more liquidity. But there are short-term mortgage loans that do attract commercial bank investments.

Some city banks will make short-term loans—3 to 5 years—on raw land for a developer. These are usually limited to 65% of the land value and carry higher interest rates than, say, a home loan. Another type of short-term mortgage loan would be on a building fully leased with a fast pay-out assigned to the bank. Service stations can be handled with mortgage loans for up to 15 years, which are secured by a major oil company lease agreement.

Commercial banks often have customers or associated lending firms that are capable of making long-term loans and can lend assistance in accommodating a customer through referrals. A few banks have established real estate investment trusts, discussed later in this chapter, to provide long-term money for their customers outside of the bank's immediate deposits.

Another possible source of mortgage money under the control of most commercial banks is that held by their trust departments. In this field the bank acts as the manager of a trust and would not be investing deposits subject to demand withdrawals, nor would it be subject to the same banking regulations affecting deposits. However, most trusts are guided by the terms under which the money is placed in the bank's care, and the type of investment permitted may be restricted. Trust funds are usually held for specified terms and, as such, make a good source for mortgage money if the trust allows.

Construction Loans. Construction loans are a special form of real estate loan that will be discussed in greater detail in Chapter 11 on loan analysis, but should be noted here as one principal type of mortgage loan offered by some commercial banks. Because of the high risk and specialized construction knowledge required for these loans, not all commercial banks are qualified to handle them. The loans are short-term, generally 6 to 18 months, and return high rates of interest, such as one to five points over the prime rate. Prime is the rate charged by banks to their most credit-worthy customers.

Mortgage Warehouse Line of Credit. With many of the larger commercial banks, the warehousing of mortgage loans for other lenders comprises a major portion of their real estate credit lines. The purpose is to provide immediate cash for a customer such as a mortgage banker, to fund his loans at closing. After establishing a line of credit with the bank, the mortgage banker is able to pledge a note and mortgage obtained from his borrower as security for the cash to fund the loan. Since the mortgage company will be continually adding to the number of loans pledged with the commercial bank, and then periodically shipping groups of these loans on out to permanent investors, the practice has acquired the name of *warehousing.*

The credit lines can run from $1 to $10 million, depending on the strength of the mortgage company. Sale of these loans out of warehouse is usually made in blocks of $250,000 upward to $3 million. A warehouse line of credit will cost the mortgage company for money so borrowed on an interest rate based on the prime rate, or perhaps 1% (one point) over prime with a term of 6 to 18 months. Warehousing as a mortgage company procedure is more fully covered in Chapter 6.

Table of Mortgage Loan Activity

Table 4–3 indicates a sizeable investment in mortgage loans by the commercial banks. It shows almost half as much money as all the savings association loans that have requirements to make mortgage loans. What is not indicated in the table is the length of time that the loans are being held. A

TABLE 4–3

Mortgage Loans Held by Banks
(In millions of dollars)

End of period	Commercial bank holdings [1]							
		Residential						
	Total	Total	FHA-in-sured	VA-guar-anteed	Con-ven-tional	Other non-farm	Farm	Total
1965	49,675	32,387	7,702	2,688	21,997	14,377	2,911	44,617
1966	54,380	34,876	7,544	2,599	24,733	16,366	3,138	47,337
1967	59,019	37,642	7,709	2,696	27,237	17,931	3,446	50,490
1968	65,696	41,433	7,926	2,708	30,800	20,505	3,758	53,456
1969	70,705	44,573	7,960	2,663	33,950	22,113	4,019	56,138
1970	73,275	45,640	7,919	2,589	35,131	23,284	4,351	57,948
1971	82,515	52,004	8,310	3,980	40,714	26,306	4,205	61,978
1972	99,314	62,782	8,495	3,203	51,084	31,751	4,781	67,556
1972–I	85,614	53,937	8,360	2,999	42,578	27,353	4,324	62,978
II ...	90,114	56,782	8,477	3,141	45,163	28,785	4,547	64,404
III ..	95,048	59,976	8,515	3,118	48,343	30,415	4,657	65,901
IV ..	99,314	62,782	8,495	3,203	51,084	31,751	4,781	67,556
1973–I[r] ...	103,548	65,236	....	....	.....	33,342	4,970	68,920
II ...	109,114	68,650	8,482	3,211	56,957	35,224	5,240	70,634
III ..	114,414	71,852	....	....	.....	37,070	5,492	72,034

[1] Includes loans held by nondeposit trust companies but not bank trust depts.

Note. Second and fourth quarters, FDIC series for all commercial and mutual savings banks in the United States and possessions. First and third quarters, estimates based on special F.R. interpolations.

Source: Federal Reserve Bank

warehouse line of credit to a mortgage company could be limited to six months, but it is a mortgage loan for classification purposes and would show on the report above as such. Construction loans fall into the same category—mortgage loans but for short terms.

LIFE INSURANCE COMPANIES

Life insurance companies rank fifth in the nation's total investments by sources, and they have long had a substantial interest in real estate financing—both as an investment in the ownership or equity position and in the making of direct mortgage loans. At one time, life insurance companies equaled the total investments of savings associations in the amounts of their mortgage loans. But life insurance companies were not organized primarily for the purpose of providing mortgage money, as were the savings associations. Their primary interest in using their substantial investment funds has been to provide the highest yield possible commensurate with the safety of their policyholders' money. And this has dictated some flexibility in the movement of their investments from time to time for better returns.

Casualty insurance companies—those that handle fire coverage, automobile insurance, and a host of other types of hazard insurance—have tremendous premium incomes but are not required to maintain the larger permanent reserves demanded for the life insurance companies. Therefore, casualty companies hold their reserves in short-term investments due to the need for liquidity to pay claims. They negotiate practically no mortgage loans and are not a source for our consideration.

Like all sources of mortgage money, the life insurance companies must possess a predictable or controllable cash inflow and outflow with a large pool retained for investment. These companies fully meet this requirement because they have established the need for life insurance protection as a way of life and thus continue to enjoy steady growth of their premium income. The reserves held to assure a policyholder that his contract will be honored upon his reaching a specified age, or upon his death, provide a multibillion dollar pool of investment capital that also produces a continuing, and until recently, an untaxed profit for the life insurance company to reinvest.

The outflow of cash is about as predictable as the inflow. What many would consider an uncertain problem is the payment of death benefits; but carefully compiled mortality tables show quite accurately the average rates of death, and on the large number of policyholders that insurance companies deal with, the payment of benefits for any period is readily calculable. Smaller companies usually reinsure their life insurance contracts with the large companies, and even larger companies will spread the risk of a large policy with several other insurance companies.

One of the least predictable outflows of cash for an insurance company comes from the right of a policyholder to borrow up to the amount of the cash value of his policy at a rather low rate of interest. Repayment of such a loan carries a first claim on the insurance proceeds and is a secure investment for the company. But a sudden demand by policyholders for cash can strain a life company's resources and force liquidation of some other portion of its investment portfolio. Demands for loans by policyholders follow money cycles; for example, in periods of tight money, more policyholders seek the relatively lower cost policy loans.

In the United States there are over 1900 life insurance companies and a few from Canada selling policy contracts. They range in size from a very few million in assets to the multibillion-dollar giants that have become household words, such as Prudential, Metropolitan Life, and Equitable.

Regulation of Life Insurance Companies

All insurance companies are under the control of state regulatory bodies. There are no federal charters for insurance. Consequently, the life insurance companies are required to adhere to policies that do vary from state to state, but all the regulations are directed toward protecting the investing public.

The state regulations usually set limits on the types of investment that are permissible, the percent of total portfolio that may be kept in stock, or bonds, or mortgage loans, or the amount of liquidity that must be maintained for each policy dollar outstanding; and most states establish limits on the maximum amount of any one loan or any one property. Some states have limited their own chartered insurance companies to investments within their own states, and others have placed limits on out-of-state companies selling insurance within their state, unless proportional investments are made within the state. Restrictive investment policies based on geography are giving way to regulations designed more toward the safeguarding of the policyholder's dollar.

For the most part, state regulations and governing commissions are well conceived and show good intentions to foster sound investment policies. But not all states are able to administer regulations and to police the actual operations as well as a legislature may have intended. Some state insurance boards have been created with substantial investigative capacity but little real authority to correct an abuse if it is discovered. Over the years there have been a few spectacular failures that might have been prevented. Fortunately, the very great majority of life insurance companies are soundly managed and are far more cautious with their policyholders' money than the state might require. Loan applications are carefully scrutinized and objectively judged. A few companies will even refuse to permit their own sales representatives to present a loan application from an individual who also wishes to buy life insurance—the loan underwriters want no pressure exerted on their judgment from the sales personnel!

Investment Policies

The normal pressure on life insurance companies to seek maximum yield from their investments, commensurate with the safety of the money, increased with the introduction of variable annuity policies. This type of life insurance provided for increases in dividends or in the total value of the policy based on the yields from the company's investments. The policy is an effort to compete with the growing interest of mutual funds as a personal investment. Whereas in the past, insurance companies moved their investments from, say, stocks and bonds into mortgage loans or other forms of securities, or vice versa, in order to achieve the highest yields, the pressure increased to do something more.

Many company investment managers had watched the real estate projects that they had made possible with mortgage loans at interest rates of 4% or 5% grow in value as land escalated in the fifties and sixties, while the insurance company earned only a nominal interest rate in return. Thereafter, the larger companies with greater resources in personnel began to direct their money and their talents into outright ownership and development of real estate as an investment procedure. During periods of scarce money, insurance companies, as well as other lenders, found they could increase yields by demanding a part of the equity interest —the so-called piece-of-the-action stipulation. One way companies have used to protect their investments from inflationary trends is to calculate debt service based on current market rentals for income properties, then take, perhaps, a quarter of any rental income increases that are made.

Another method commonly used by insurance companies expanding their real estate investments is to join with an experienced development company as a partner. Metropolitan Life Insurance Company of New York City joins with such developers as Trammel Crow of Dallas to acquire land and build multimillion-dollar urban projects, such as the Allen Center in Houston projected at a half-billion dollars. Business Men's Assurance of Kansas City, in addition to making some direct mortgage loans, joins with developers as partners for large commercial ventures, builds housing projects for resale to owners, and builds hotels and motels for the purpose of leasing them to qualified operators such as the Marriott Hotel chain. Prudential uses real estate affiliates to build large urban complexes such as the $150 million residential and commercial complex in the Detroit suburb of Southfield. A few states, fearing the movement of the insurance giants into too much ownership of properties, have enacted restrictive laws to limit the trend; i.e., Texas does not permit an insurance company to own an apartment building except as acquired through foreclosure.

Life insurance companies have in the past maintained their own lending offices in selected locations, and a few still do. Lately, the trend has been more toward working through correspondents or loan representatives. In the handling of direct mortgage loans, the companies can and do make forward commitments to mortgage bankers for specific classes of home loans. Many of the smaller- and medium-sized companies find home loans in their operating territory to be both profitable investments and beneficial to their own company growth.

For the individual borrower, there is little access to an insurance company for a loan such as can be found by walking into a savings and loan office. This is possible with some of the smaller insurance companies, but the larger ones must deal in larger loans or blocks of smaller loans. The volume of money that a company such as Northwestern Mutual Life of Milwaukee must handle with over $6 billion in real estate loans outstanding, makes it impractical to deal directly on, say, a $30,000 house loan.

The investment portfolios of life insurance companies will continue to be influenced by the need for greater yields. Long-term mortgage loans are sound investments for the companies and should always be of interest to them when the yields are competitive with other forms of investment. But yield and security alone are not the only goals; there is also a desire to maintain a particular balance with a company's overall investments. Thus, a higher return from one type of investment would not attract all of a company's money at that time. Looking ahead, it is not likely that states will enact more restrictive legislation to direct an insurance company's investments so as to press more money into the mortgage lending field.

Table of Mortgage Activity of Life Insurance Companies

Table 4–4 shows a pattern of investment that indicates no substantial increase in life insurance companies holdings of

TABLE 4-4

Mortgage Activity of Life Insurance Companies (In millions of dollars)

Period	Loans acquired						Loans outstanding (end of period)					
	Total	Nonfarm Total	Nonfarm FHA-insured	Nonfarm VA-guaranteed	Nonfarm Other¹	Farm	Total	Nonfarm Total	Nonfarm FHA-insured	Nonfarm VA-guaranteed	Nonfarm Other	Farm
1945	976	.....	.....	.....	.....	.....	6,637	5,860	1,394	.....	4,466	766
1964	10,433	9,386	1,812	674	6,900	1,047	55,152	50,848	11,484	6,403	32,961	4,304
1965	11,137	9,988	1,738	553	7,697	1,149	60,013	55,190	12,068	6,286	36,836	4,823
1966	10,217	9,223	1,300	467	7,456	994	64,609	59,369	12,351	6,201	40,817	5,240
1967	8,470	7,633	757	444	6,432	837	67,516	61,947	12,161	6,122	43,664	5,569
1968	7,925	7,153	733	346	6,074	772	69,973	64,172	11,961	5,954	46,257	5,801
1969	7,531	6,991	594	220	6,177	540	72,027	66,254	11,715	5,701	48,838	5,773
1970	7,181	6,867	386	88	6,393	314	74,375	68,726	11,419	5,394	51,913	5,649
1971	7,573	7,070	322	101	6,647	503	75,496	69,895	10,767	5,004	54,124	5,601
1972	8,696	7,996	331	182	7,483	700	76,948	71,270	9,962	4,660	56,648	5,678
Dec.	786	730	25	10	695	56	75,904	70,266	10,017	4,681	55,568	5,638
1972–Nov.	1,890	1,784	23	17	1,744	106	76,948	71,270	9,962	4,660	56,648	5,678
1973–Jan.	711	649	16	20	613	62	77,481	71,856	9,901	4,630	57,325	5,625
Feb.	603	542	27	24	491	61	77,510	71,892	9,806	4,613	57,473	5,618
Mar.	670	573	37	24	512	97	77,587	71,953	9,735	4,594	57,624	5,634
Apr.	702	624	20	22	582	78	77,258	71,611	9,708	4,572	57,331	5,647
May	744	694	22	21	651	80	77,400	71,721	9,627	4,549	57,545	5,679
June	1,101	1,009	24	27	958	92	77,914	72,187	9,544	4,524	58,119	5,727
July	933	849	26	19	804	84	78,243	72,474	9,464	4,496	58,514	5,769
Aug.	1,034	947	11	20	916	87	78,657	72,839	9,388	4,471	58,980	5,818
Sept.	944	862	23	17	822	82	79,040	73,182	9,330	4,447	59,405	5,858
Oct.	972	899	13	18	868	73	79,516	73,619	9,270	4,428	59,921	5,897
Nov.	1,146	1,051	25	15	1,011	95	79,549	73,619	9,233	4,428	60,614	5,930

¹ Includes mortgage loans secured by land on which oil drilling or extracting operations are in process.

Source: Federal Reserve Bank

mortgage loans over the past few years. The amount invested each year in new loans acquired has actually been declining while other lenders have followed a growth pattern. In reading this table it should be kept in mind that the figures reflect loans outstanding on real estate and do not show the ownership of properties held by life insurance companies. The ownership, or equity interests, are usually reported as real estate holdings, or property investments, to distinguish them from direct mortgage loans.

FEDERAL AND STATE GOVERNMENTS

In addition to the private sources of money discussed so far, several federal and state government agencies provide funds for making direct mortgage loans or purchasing them from other lenders.

A few states have established housing agencies with authority to make direct mortgage loans to assist home buyers, and many more are seeking ways to encourage more lendable funds in their states. Money for this purpose is raised by the sale of bonds and with the assistance of various programs developed by the Department of Housing and Urban Development. All states have pension funds and most have specialized trust funds of some kind. These are increasingly being utilized to provide capital for development within the state and to improve housing for its people.

Another type of mortgage money that is available in some states is that, when authorized, a municipality may issue a tax-exempt type of bond for the purpose of financing industrial growth. One of the more common methods used is for the municipality to establish an industrial park by the purchase of suitable land. Sites for new plants are then sold or leased to acceptable companies, and the municipality will provide the mortgage money for building a new plant.

The federal government has felt a need to assist the people in their living and housing requirements and has long maintained programs of direct loans for such purposes. While a number of agencies provide financing and direct grants of money to assist farmers and ranchers, small businesses, minority businesses, disaster victims, and displaced families, the three most active agencies making direct loans based on real estate mortgages are the Federal Land Bank, the Farmers Home Administration, and the Government National Mortgage Association, discussed below.

Federal Land Bank

Established in 1916 to provide funds to farmers and ranchers —funds that were not always available in the private sector —the Federal Land Banks have provided many billions of dollars for the purchase and improvement of farms and ranches. The system operates through 12 regional offices and smaller district offices somewhat similar to our Federal Reserve organization. At quarterly intervals during the year, the system will sell its own Federal Land Bank bonds, which are secured by the mortgages on properties they finance. These are not government-guaranteed bonds and cannot be classed as *governments*. They are called *agency* bonds because the Federal Land Bank is one of many federal agencies authorized to issue its own bonds and sell them on the open market. The proceeds of each bond sale are allocated to the various regions, as may be required, and are then made available to qualified borrowers.

The Federal Land Bank evaluates a loan application much the same as a private bank and has no real social motivation other than that its money is restricted to loans for farms or ranches. The borrower need not live on the land but must be able to mortgage the property and to show a record of productivity with that land or a previous record of experience. Loans are limited to 80% of the Bank's own appraisal and up to a maximum term of 33 years.

The interest rate for these loans is adjusted periodically but is normally held under open market rates. The main reason for the lower rate is that the Federal Land Bank calculates its rates based on an *average* cost of its money as determined from the periodic sale of agency bonds. And the Bank, as an agency of the federal government, is not seeking a profit for an investor with its operations.

Farmers Home Administration

As a part of the efforts of the Roosevelt administration to revitalize the economy from the depths of the Depression, a separate agency was established in 1934 to make direct loans to farmers for land and housing known as the Farmers Home Administration. The hope of using the initials "FmHA" to minimize confusion with the initials of the Federal Housing Administration has not been very successful.

The Farmers Home Administration has, in addition to its economic help, a social guideline to direct its lending. Limitations are placed on the maximum amount that can be loaned, presently at $20,000, and the interest rate is held under the current market rates similar to the Federal Land Bank method. Properties used as collateral must be outside of urban areas (city limits), or in towns of less than 10,000 population.

The main qualifying difference in a Farmers Home Administration loan, besides the location of the property, is that the borrower must show a need for the housing and a limited income record. Currently the income limitation is $9000. This amount is calculated by adjusting the total income with a deduction allowance of $500 per year for each minor child; i.e., a family could have an income of $11,500 per year but with five children, the adjusted income would be reduced to $9000 and thus they would qualify for a loan.

To give some idea of the size of the FmHA program, the fiscal year of 1973 produced a record breaking 195,572 loans for a total amount of $1.4 billion.

Government National Mortgage Association

This is a newer agency of the federal government under the Department of Housing and Urban Development (HUD), created in 1968 to carry a portion of the financing chores previously handled by the Federal National Mortgage Association. The Government National Mortgage Association, GNMA or "Ginnie Mae," sells bonds, as do other federal agencies, to raise funds for direct mortgage loans. This agency also has authority to borrow money from the United States Treasury when authorized for specific purposes. And it is the agency that handles direct subsidies for housing programs as appropriated by Congress. GNMA has used its authority to guarantee blocks of mortgages in order to attract more private capital into the mortgage lending field. The impact of this government agency is far broader than the capacity to make some direct loans, and as such, the organization and programs will be discussed in greater detail in Chapter 8.

Federal National Mortgage Association

FNMA (Fannie Mae) should no longer be considered as a source of money under the direction of the federal government as it has been publicly owned and listed on the New York Stock Exchange since 1970. However, as a quasi-public organization it still has strong ties to the federal government and a commitment to various government programs. The bonds it sells to finance its purchases of residential mortgage loans are still classed in the financial community as "agency" issues. With its Free Market System of handling mortgage loan offerings from approved lenders throughout the country, FNMA provides an interesting guide to the fluctuations in mortgage interest rates. As a major factor in the secondary markets, buying and selling mortgage loans, the FNMA organization and methods will be more fully covered in Chapter 5.

Federal Housing Administration and Veterans Administration

The FHA and VA are included in this chapter under Sources of Mortgage Money only to dispel the thought that they are. Neither agency makes loans as a continuing practice. The VA does actually make loans in special circumstances. What these two agencies do, in the case of the FHA, is to issue an insurance policy protecting the lender against a default by the borrower; and in the case of the VA, to issue a certificate guaranteeing a specific portion of a loan to enable a veteran to acquire housing without a down payment if he desires. Both agencies are of sufficient importance in real estate finance to warrant separate coverage, which will be found in Chapter 8.

LESSER SOURCES

Pension and Trust Funds

The purpose of a *pension* fund is to accumulate cash and hold it in such a manner that will assure an annual or monthly payment to an individual worker upon retirement or upon reaching a certain age. The purpose of a *trust* fund is to protect an asset over a period of time so as to achieve a specified purpose. While the reasons for creating a trust fund are different from that of a pension fund, the manner in which both funds are held and the need for delivering the assets upon maturity give both a similarity insofar as their possible use as sources of mortgage money.

Both pension and trust fund administrators are guided by the cardinal rule of security for the asset. No pressure exists for them to achieve maximum yields, nor do state or federal laws yet exercise much control over the type of investments they may make. A good administrator is obligated to protect the body of the assets and make sure the funds can be delivered when pledged to do so. Consequently, these assets have tended to be invested in high-grade stocks and bonds, which represent minimum risk and a ready market when they have to be sold for cash. Lately, some of this money is finding its way into the long-term mortgage market as the yields are good and the security is generally acceptable.

As sources of mortgage money, both pension and trust funds represent a near ideal situation in the predictability of inflow and outflow of funds that are needed for any long-term investment. The inflow of cash is easily determined by the agreements establishing the fund, and the outflow is an integral part of that agreement.

Pension Funds. Pension funds date back nearly one hundred years, but only recently have they become a factor in real estate financing. The quarter century from 1945 to 1970 showed tremendous growth in corporate pension funds, both insured and noninsured, along with federal, state, and local government pension funds, union funds, and funds of fraternal groups. As recently as 1940, pension funds totaled only $2.4 billion. By 1970 the amount increased to $137 billion with a projection of $215 billion by 1980. The number of employees covered under these plans has increased in the same period from 4.3 million to 30.5 million persons.

Pension funds can be divided into insured or uninsured plans. The insured pension plans are those offered by most large insurance companies. The employer, perhaps with a participating contribution from the employee, pays the premium directly to the insurance company, who is responsible for making future pay-outs to the employee when due. There is usually the added protection of life insurance coverage, and the insurance carrier is obligated to invest the premium payments just as with any other insurance policy.

The majority of pension funds fall into the uninsured category. Under this procedure the company establishes its own fund for its employees' benefit and usually exercises some control over the management of it. It is this uninsured class of funds, largely unregulated, that has caused some abuses and failures and has attracted public scrutiny. Therefore, the federal government has been developing procedures to establish more controls over these unregulated funds. Legislation recently enacted provides requirements for proper funding, investment guidelines, and a form of insurance protection as a means of providing greater security for an employee's stake in his pension.

So far the government has not set a mandatory requirement of any percentage of investments for mortgage loans, to guide the pension funds. Rather the effort has been directed toward making mortgage investment more attractive for the funds. The Government National Mortgage Associations "pass-through" mortgage-backed securities are one good example of the government effort in this direction. The mortgage-backed security is actually a certificate of guarantee by the United States government applicable to a specific block of mortgage loans, which have in turn been underwritten by the FHA, VA, or the Farmers Home Administration. GNMA reviews packages of such mortgages (the minimum amount has been $2 million) presented to them by mortgage bankers or others, and if found to be in good order, it issues a separate guarantee for each complete package—hence, the descriptive name of *pass-through security*. For a pension fund the GNMA mortgage-backed security has three special advantages:

1. The pay-back of both principal and interest is passed directly to the investor on a monthly basis.

2. All of the mortgages involved are federally underwritten and give an attractive yield.

3. The GNMA guarantee certificate can be traded on the market in the same way as stocks and bonds.

Trust Funds. Because trust funds are a practical means of accomplishing a person's objectives in spite of death, and because they hold a means of reducing tax liabilities in estate planning, the usage has grown substantially, and the accumulated assets in the hands of trust administrators have multiplied. Trust funds are usually specific in the purpose to be accomplished and provide guidelines and restrictions as to the ways in which the assets may be invested. Since these funds are essentially a form of private property, there is not much public interest in control or regulation of investments other than for the tax angles involved.

What motivates trust fund administrators is the security of the investment and a fair return. The growing size of the accumulated funds and the near absolute control on withdrawals make long-term mortgage loans practical investments. Mortgage-backed securities, the growing flexibility of the secondary market, the advantages of private mortgage insurance, and the attractive yields over the long term have all added to the appeal of mortgage loans for trust funds. While many funds are administered by competent individuals who may not have expertise in mortgage loans, a growing number of trusts are handled by commercial banks whose trust departments have access to men of broad experience in this type of loan.

Individuals

The earliest lenders were wealthy individuals. In today's market the terms of mortgage loans are much too lengthy for most individuals to undertake. With a few exceptions, almost all primary mortgage lending by individuals has a motive other than as an investment to earn a return of interest. Some individuals make mortgage loans to assist a member of their family or perhaps a valued employee or associate. By far the largest investment by individuals in mortgage loans stems from a seller accepting a second mortgage as a partial payment for his house or land. The motive is to make a sale rather than an investment. In some areas, such as California, second and even third mortgages are sold to brokers or other individuals at substantial discounts, which increases the yields sufficiently to make an attractive investment.

As investors, individuals come under no specific regulations as to how they must lend money. A mortgage loan must comply with the real estate laws governing such transactions plus the usury laws that limit the amount of interest that can be charged.

Individuals can make mortgage loans on any type of property: residential or commercial, raw land, or development work. Some mortgage companies represent individuals who want to make investments in certain types of property.

With the escalating land values of the late sixties and seventies, urban areas have seen the acreage surrounding them sold on seller-financed deals. In this procedure the raw land is sold by an individual at a fair market price with a small down payment plus interest payments only on the unpaid balance for the next five or ten years. A mortgage is held by the seller until full payment has been made, which makes it in effect a mortgage loan.

Due to the lack of regulation, there is no sound statistical basis for establishing the actual volume of mortgage loans held by individuals.

Real Estate Investment Trusts (REIT)

A relatively new source of mortgage money was encouraged in 1960 when Congress passed the Real Estate Investment Trust Act. The purpose of the Act was to provide more capital to satisfy the growing demand for long-term mortgage money by opening the field to the individual small investor. In order to encourage a person to buy stock in a corporation that qualified itself as a real estate investment trust, Congress exempted the corporation from income taxes, provided that at least 90% of the income is distributed each year as dividends. Also, the income must be derived from real property investments to qualify for the tax exemption. The dividends are taxable to the investor.

The idea was not enthusiastically received at first, but by 1970 many investment trust issues were placed on the market and sold very well. The trusts are formed primarily by leading banks and insurance companies, and most are traded on the nation's stock exchanges. A few of the well-known companies operating in this field are Massachusetts Mutual Mortgage, Northwestern Mutual Life Mortgage, Associated Mortgage Investors, Bank American Realty, Equitable Life Mortgage, MONY Mortgage, Mortgage Trust of America, and many others.

With relative freedom to select their investments, the investment trusts have focused on the higher yield construction and development loans. These interim loans have led to permanent loans on the same or other properties, often with the participation of another major lender. The trust corporation may borrow money from other sources to reinvest in its development projects, and thus can earn an interest differential on the borrowed funds in addition to its own invested funds.

The yield to the stockholder has generally been a solid 6% to 7½% return plus a steady, if sometimes slow, growth in stock value as the trust properties appreciate. With 90% of the income paid out in dividends each year, there is no real opportunity for reinvestment of the profits.

Most of the trusts are controlled by a board of trustees responsible for the integrity of the fund. Actual management of the investment portfolio is contracted to a professional money-management team. The management company is paid a fee for its services, usually about 1% of the total assets per year. The managers are all experienced lending officers who have worked with or are well known to the sponsoring bank or insurance company.

Miscellaneous Other Sources

In different parts of the country various types of companies and institutions have established themselves as a source of mortgage funds, usually limiting the geographic area in which they will loan money. In the following paragraphs the most important of these sources are identified.

Mortgage Bankers. While the great majority of mortgage banking companies operate as a service industry handling funds for other major sources of money, a few of the larger companies have generated their own funds for lending through the sale of mortgage bonds. In the pre-Depression days of the 1920s, the sale of mortgage bonds was quite popular, but the Depression brought many of these issues and their sponsoring companies into collapse.

As the industry has reestablished itself, the sale of mortgage bonds to investors has started to grow again. In the hands of the established mortgage bankers, these funds have provided another source of money for both residential and commercial loans.

Title Companies. Because of the close association and considerable knowledge of the industry carried by the title companies, a few of them have developed direct loan departments or subsidiary companies handling loans. These affiliated companies act both as primary sources in lending their own funds or those raised from the sale of mortgage bonds, and as correspondents or agents for other major lenders.

Endowment Funds, Universities, Colleges, Hospitals. As a group, endowment funds prefer to maintain their assets in high-grade stocks and bonds that have a good record for security, are considered to be more liquid, and, most important, require less administrative attention than a portfolio of mortgage loans. However, many endowments are passed on in the form of land and other real property, and these have required more expertise in the mortgage loan field. The endowment funds can and do assist in the development of their own land by experienced developers, and they are increasing their activities in mortgage lending with such encouragements as the GNMA mortgage-backed security.

Foundations. Foundations have been established primarily by corporations or by wealthy families as a means of continuing charitable or other purposes through the use of income earned from the foundations' investments. The attitude of foundations toward mortgage lending is somewhat similar to that of the endowment funds. They are primarily interested in investing in high-grade stocks and bonds, but are not adverse to mortgage loans, particularly if a purpose of special interest to the foundation can be served.

Foundations have been under substantial legal attack as to their tax obligations and sometimes for the controversial use of their tax-free funds. However, they do represent a limited pool of investment capital that can be used in the mortgage market.

Fraternal, Benevolent, and Religious Associations. Over the years some fraternal, benevolent, and religious organizations have accumulated substantial pools of investment money, which are generally little known and very seldom advertised. The administration of these funds is usually handled on a sound economic basis with security of the loan of more importance than the yield. Some of these organizations limit their lending to their own members and will provide low-cost loans to qualified members in good standing.

SECONDARY
MARKETS

Prior to the 1940s, mortgage lenders were not able to sell their loans easily and their investment portfolios lacked liquidity; that is, the mortgage loans could not readily be converted to cash. Unlike other forms of capital investment, such as stocks and bonds, there is no national market as yet organized to trade in mortgage loans. Of course, one of the major reasons is the past lack of any common denominator by which mortgage loans could be compared. The evaluation of a mortgage loan has necessarily required some knowledge of the geographic area of the property used as collateral. This has made trading in loans difficult.

ORIGINS OF SECONDARY MARKET

To make a loan more salable, other means are needed to provide some standardization and a method to protect the secondary lender. The government has succeeded in doing just this with its insured FHA programs and guarantees of VA loans. In this type of loan, the government agencies have established certain standard forms and procedures that are known and accepted by the lenders. And most important, the government agencies provide that necessary common denominator of protection to the lender in the individual insurance commitment.

However, even this was not always the case. When the FHA was initially established, the government effort was not accepted at face value by private investors, and it became necessary to establish a market for government-underwritten loans. Thus the Federal National Mortgage Association was born, and with it the first step toward creating a national market for mortgage loans, or what has become known as the *secondary market.*

The precise delineation between the primary and secondary markets for mortgage loans is difficult to draw as there is an overlap. The clearest line can be made at the origination of the loan, which would be the primary lender. Any lender who buys, or takes, a mortgage loan that he did not originate is considered to be the secondary market.

PROCEDURES USED IN SECONDARY MARKET

Now note the difference in terminology at this point. The originator of a loan speaks to his customers, who are the *borrowers,* in terms of *loaning money,* and he expresses the cost of the borrowed money as interest plus *points* of discount and fees. Once the originator closes the loan to the borrower, the note and mortgage instrument become marketable paper that can be assigned—and the terminology changes. The mortgage note is now a salable commodity and is negotiated as such. The originator of the loan becomes a *seller,* and the large lending institutions that deal in the secondary market for mortgage loans are called *purchasers.* When a mortgage loan is thus offered for sale, the potential purchaser is interested in only one attribute for loans of similar types, size, and quality, and that is the *net yield* to him.

Pricing Loans to Adjust Yields

Since the interest and discount on the loan or loans held by the originator have a previously established rate, the only way a seller can change the yield to a purchaser is to adjust the price of the loan. For example, if the mortgage note is for $10,000 at 7% interest, the yield would be 7%. If the seller must offer a higher yield than 7% in order to attract a purchaser, he must sell the loan for less than $10,000, that is, discount the face value in order to increase the yield. By selling the $10,000 loan for, say $9500, the purchaser is putting up less cash, but still collects the originally agreed interest and principal reduction applicable to the $10,000 loan at 7%, hence, a greater return or yield for the $9500.

The principal balance due on an existing mortgage loan normally changes each month, so therefore the price is quoted as a percentage figure. One hundred is, of course, par. If we were quoting the $10,000 loan mentioned above to sell for $9500, the quotation would simply be "95." This indicates a 5% reduction in whatever the principal balance due on the mortgage note may be, or a 5-point discount.

In times of falling interest rates, a loan calling for a higher than current market interest can sell for a premium—at say 102% or even 104% of its face value. An example of prices and yields that are used in the secondary market follows:

TABLE 5–1

Price Yield Table Calculated at 7% Interest
for Term of 30 Years

Price	Discount	Yield if prepaid 8 yrs.	Yield if prepaid 10 yrs.	Yield if prepaid 12 yrs.	To maturity
102	+2 (Premium)	6.66	6.71	6.74	6.81
100	0	7.00	7.00	7.00	7.00
96	4	7.70	7.61	7.54	7.41
92	8	8.44	8.24	8.12	7.85

A simple reading of the table shows that the length of time a loan is outstanding has a direct effect on the yield for that loan. Since loans vary considerably in the time for payoff, it is necessary to use some standard. Records of loan payoffs indicate a steadily decreasing length of time due largely to the increased moving that families do. Most mortgage loans are simply refinanced with each sale or after several sales. The average life of a 30-year loan is now under nine years. For simplification, most lenders use a ten-year term to calculate the actual yield.

Growth Factors of Secondary Market

The strongest impetus toward establishing a truly national market for mortgage loans must be credited to (1) the Federal National Mortgage Association, (2) the growth of private mortgage insurance fostered by the 1971 change in banking regulations, and (3) establishment of the Federal Home Loan Mortgage Corp. In order to examine the background and growth of FNMA, the succeeding portion of this chapter is devoted to the organization and operations of this quasi-private corporation.

FEDERAL NATIONAL MORTGAGE ASSOCIATION

Origin and Purpose of FNMA

By 1938, it had become obvious that private lenders were not looking with much favor on the four-year-old FHA concept of government insured commitments to assist a credit-worthy but cash-short family in buying a home. Consequently, on February 10, 1938, the National Mortgage Association of Washington was formed as a subsidiary of the Reconstruction Finance Corporation, then changed on April 5, 1938, to the Federal National Mortgage Association, referred to as FNMA, or Fannie Mae. The ground work had been laid by Congress under Title III of the original FHA Authorization Act.

The basic aims of the Federal National Mortgage Association as determined by the chartering act and subsequent revisions to 1968 included:

1. Establishing a market for the purchase and sale of first mortgages.
2. Providing special assistance on certain residential mort-

gages and housing programs as designated by the President
and by Congress.

3. Managing and liquidating the mortgage portfolio in an
orderly manner with minimum adverse effect on the market
and minimum loss to the government.

Money needed for the purchase of mortgages was derived
from the sale of notes and debentures to private investors.
While these FNMA obligations were subject to the approval
of the Secretary of the Treasury, they were not guaranteed
by the government. Some additional capital was raised by
the requirement to purchase FNMA stock in the amount of
one-half of 1% of every commitment sold. Operating money
was raised through certain fees charged on the purchase of
mortgages and through part of the discounts taken.

The initial concept of FNMA embodied the idea that it
would serve as a secondary market primarily for buying and
selling first mortgages, but over the years the portfolio
steadily increased as selling of loans lagged behind. Congress
has, from time to time, ordered Fannie Mae to make mortgage purchases to stimulate a lagging economy or to assist
in financing new government lending programs as stipulated
in the FNMA purposes outlined previously, since these programs were not readily acceptable to private investors as
mortgage investments.

Finally, FNMA was charged with the task of management
and liquidation, including the handling and disposition of
the substantial accumulation of first mortgages in such a
manner as not to upset the capital market or cause a loss to
the government.

FNMA as Private Corporation

A major change was made in the FNMA establishment when
it was transformed into a "private corporation with a public
purpose" by Act of Congress in September, 1968. Roughly,
the FNMA entity was partitioned by this Act in such a way
that the first of its three functions—that of maintaining a
secondary market, with FNMA as a private corporation—was
retained. The other two functions—special assistance pro-

grams and management and liquidation of mortgages—were transferred to a newly formed body corporate without capital stock known as the Government National Mortgage Association (GNMA or Ginnie Mae), designed to operate as a part of the Department of Housing and Urban Development.

The Federal National Mortgage Association began its private corporate life in September, 1968, but was not fully transformed until May 21, 1970. At that time the HUD secretary, George Romney, appeared at the annual stock-holders meeting, concurred with the finding that at least one-third of the outstanding stock was owned by persons or firms in housing-related industries, and approved the new directors for the corporation.

Relationship with Government

Actually, the "private corporation with a public purpose" is a concept rather than a matter of statute. It is a congressional recognition of the need for continuing a close relationship between FNMA and the government, backing up the latter's efforts to limit the peaks and valleys in the flow of mortgage funds so as to stabilize and increase the supply of housing.

This FNMA-government relationship is unique and has been developed by a number of rules, chartering stipulations, and organization methods, such as:

1. Five of FNMA's 15 directors are appointed by the President of the United States.

2. The HUD Secretary is given regulatory authority to set Fannie Mae's debt limit and its ratio of debt to capital.

3. The HUD Secretary may require that a reasonable portion of the mortgages purchased be related to the national goal to provide adequate housing for low- and moderate-income families.

4. The Secretary of the Treasury has been given authority to buy FNMA debt obligations up to $2.25 billion, which greatly enhances its credit position.

5. While FNMA is a private corporation and its debts are not obligations of the government, by its chartering act, FNMA obligations are lawful investments for fiduciary, trust, and public funds under the control of the federal government.

It might be well to note that this special relationship with the government did much to provide the funds needed for housing in the 1969–1970 financial squeeze when private capital was not readily available. The mortgage portfolio of FNMA, since it was partitioned in 1968, increased from approximately $7 billion to $18 billion by 1972, which vividly underlines the support it gave to our housing programs.

The year 1970 for FNMA marked not only its conversion to a private corporation and its continuing successful support of the mortgage market but also flagged several milestones with its listing on the nation's major stock exchanges, the first public offering of stock, and the issuing of the first $1 billion in mortgage-backed bonds supported by the credit of the United States; and procedures were begun to buy conventional mortgages. Also on July 24, 1970, FNMA was given authority to buy conventional home mortgages—in the past it had been restricted to only government-insured or government-guaranteed commitments.

FNMA Standardization of Mortgage Forms

The initial draft of a standard form mortgage instrument was widely circulated within the industry for guidance and comments, including the need to work with the Federal Home Loan Bank System, which provides support to our savings and loan institutions. Considerable protests were raised, and some law suits filed by organized consumer groups against what was termed the "lender-oriented" form, and some revisions were made. The standard forms finally agreed upon modifying several provisions, such as allowing interest to be paid on an escrow account if mutually agreed between borrower and lender, dropping the prepayment penalty clause, and allowing the borrower a voice in the settlement of insurance claims. It is important to remember that the primary goal was to attract more private capital into the mortgage market, not to appease consumer groups. Several of these approved forms are reproduced in Chapter 3.

FNMA Purchase of Conventional Loans

On February 14, 1972, the first purchase of conventional loans was made through the free market system. Separate approval of sellers was required for the conventional loan program, and only a very few mortgagees were approved in the beginning. Unlike the FHA/VA type of loans that hold a government commitment as an ultimate recourse, the conventional loans look only to the borrowers and depend heavily on the careful underwriting analysis of the seller to produce sound loans. The purchase of conventional loans by FNMA has been slow in times of plentiful money as the private sources become more competitive. Under such competitive conditions, the rates offered by FNMA, which reflect an average from all sections of the country, are higher than can be found in the competitive big city areas. When money tightens up, the interest rates increase, and many lenders are forced to withdraw from the market for lack of funds. In such times, as in 1969–1970 and in 1973, FNMA's purchases increase sharply. The rates reflected by the national offerings are more stable than those found in most of the high loan-demand growth areas.

Operations

The Federal National Mortgage Association operates from its headquarters in Washington, D.C., with five regional offices in Dallas, Atlanta, Los Angeles, Chicago, and Philadelphia. The regional offices have authority to negotiate loan purchases within their areas and serve as bases for all regional operations.

In order to sell a loan commitment to FNMA, it is first necessary to qualify as an approved seller. Most mortgage companies, some savings and loan associations, and some insurance companies have found it beneficial to be able to do business with FNMA. An approval by the FHA and the VA have been normal prerequisites but do not in themselves qualify a mortgagee for FNMA—a complete file on the capitalization, background, and experience of the qualifying company and its key personnel is required.

All companies doing business with FNMA automatically become stockholders, as one of the requirements is that the seller purchase stock with the one-half of 1% commitment fee on each commitment. And the stock must be retained by the mortgagee at one-quarter of 1% of its total loans being serviced for FNMA.

FNMA—Purchases of Loan Commitments

The Federal National Mortgage Association buys mortgage loans in several ways. The most commonly used method is the "Free Market System." From its headquarters in Washington, D.C., Fannie Mae establishes *offer dates*—biweekly for FHA/VA and monthly for conventional-type loans. Approved sellers are asked to submit their offerings for money requirements, usually for loans they expect to make over the next four months, on these offer dates. The offerings are of two types:

1. The *competitive* offering, normally limited to a maximum of $3 million, must specify the yield that the seller of the loans will pay to FNMA. No commitment fee is required with the offer, but it must be paid if the offer is accepted. It is from this range of specified yields offered that FNMA decides what it will purchase and how low a yield it can accept under existing market conditions. From the range of accepted yields, the weighted average yield is computed.

2. The *noncompetitive* offerings are limited to $200,000 per seller at any one sale and do not specify a yield. These noncompetitive offerings are funded initially from the available funds at that particular sale and are then automatically assigned the weighted average yield as determined by the accepted competitive offers. It is from these noncompetitive offerings that many smaller mortgage companies obtain their assurance of available funds and are able to determine precisely what discount must be charged in order to cover the yield for that commitment of funds.

Both types of offerings are made by telephone to the Washington office using the seller's code number for identification. On the day following each offer date, an announcement is made of the acceptable offers giving the range of yields and the new weighted average yield. In the next few pages, there are copies of actual notices covering several weeks of announcements and results of the free market system. You will note that the conditions vary somewhat with each auction as to the length of commitment, eligible mortgages, method of submittal, and money available. Each notice also publishes the results of the previous auction. Table 5-2 shows the movement in the amount of offers and the yields as handled by FNMA during the period from April 30, 1973 to September 17, 1973. In this five month span yields climbed sharply reflecting the reduced availability of mortgage money.

Other Methods Used by FNMA

There are other methods used by FNMA to purchase mortgage loans. One is the "immediate purchase contract," or IPC. Under this procedure a specific mortgage, such as a multifamily project or a block of single-family house mortgages, is offered for immediate sale and delivery to FNMA. The price is subject to negotiation. No commitment fee is required, but the usual half-point funding fee and the stock purchase are required.

Another method, formerly called the "advance commitment contract," is now called the "stand-by commitment." With this plan, a mortgage banker can go to FNMA at the time his client, the borrower, receives a feasibility letter from the FHA and buy a commitment to cover the funding requirements at a firm price with delivery of the mortgage in up to two years time. The commitment costs one point, payable upon issuance. Delivery of the mortgage is *not* mandatory, and if the mortgage banker can find a lower cost source for the permanent financing before the permanent loan is closed, he is free to forfeit his commitment fee to FNMA and use the alternate source.

FNMA—Sale of Loans

As a secondary market operation, FNMA must also sell some of its mortgage notes from time to time as conditions permit. Large insurance companies and savings associations are prime customers and deal in multimillion dollar blocks of loans. To improve and broaden its sales, FNMA established the auction technique in 1968 and has found it gives a more

FEDERAL NATIONAL MORTGAGE ASSOCIATION
2001 Bryan Tower, Suite 1200
Dallas, Texas 75201

December 18, 1973

NOTICE   FNMA No. FMS-CHM 26-73

TO   : ALL FNMA CONVENTIONAL SELLERS

SUBJECT: Free Market System - Conventionals
          Notice of Available Commitment Funds

Federal National Mortgage Association announces that during the following
Offer Period the amount set forth below will be available to purchase
eligible conventional home mortgages.

The offer of a Seller for the Offer Date identified herein may not exceed
the applicable maximum set forth below:

Offer Date: Monday, January 14, 1974, between the hours of 9 a.m.
             and 3 p.m., Washington, DC, time - Dial (202) 293-7500.

          Available Funds   NO LIMIT ESTABLISHED
          Competitive Seller's Maximum $3,000,000
          Noncompetitive Seller's Maximum   100,000

This auction will be conducted under the same general rules which have been
established for FMS-Conventional auctions as stated in the FNMA Conventional
Selling Contract Supplement.

Results of FMS-CHM Auction of December 17, 1973:

Type of Contract	Total Offers Received *	Total Offers Accepted *	Yield Range	Weighted Average Yield – Accepted Offers
4-month	$51.4	$32.2	8.762 - 9.000	8.821

* In Millions

The home loan convertible standby commitment yield required is 9.150.
Sellers maximum convertible standby commitment activity per week (Monday
through Friday) will be limited to $2 million.

NOTE: The next Conventional auction will be held in four weeks, January 14, 1974.

Hughes A. King
Regional Vice President

Figure 5–1

113

FEDERAL NATIONAL MORTGAGE ASSOCIATION

January 15, 1974

NOTICE   FNMA No. FMS-CHM 1-74

TO   : ALL FNMA CONVENTIONAL SELLERS

SUBJECT: Free Market System – Conventionals
         Notice of Available Commitment Funds

Federal National Mortgage Association announces that during the following
Offer Period the amount set forth below will be available to purchase
eligible conventional home mortgages.

The offer of a Seller for the Offer Date identified herein may not exceed
the applicable maximum set forth below:

Offer Date: Monday, February 11, 1974, between the hours of 9 a.m.
            and 3 p.m., Washington, DC, time – Dial (202) 293-7500.

Available Funds	NO LIMIT ESTABLISHED
Competitive Seller's Maximum	$3,000,000
Noncompetitive Seller's Maximum	200,000

This auction will be conducted under the same general rules which have been
established for FMS-Conventional auctions as stated in the FNMA Conventional
Selling Contract Supplement.

Results of FMS-CHM Auction of January 14, 1974:

Type of Contract	Total Offers Received *	Total Offers Accepted *	Yield Range	Weighted Average Yield – Accepted Offers
4-month	$48.9	$34.5	8.742 - 9.000	8.774

* In Millions

The home loan convertible standby commitment yield required is 9.150.
Sellers maximum convertible standby commitment activity per week (Monday
through Friday) will be limited to $2 million.

NOTE: The next Conventional auction will be held in four weeks, February 11,
1974.

Beginning February 11, 1974, the noncompetitive seller's maximum will be
increased to $200,000.

Hughes A. King
Regional Vice President

2001 Bryan Tower, Dallas, Texas 75201

Figure 5–2

114

FEDERAL NATIONAL MORTGAGE ASSOCIATION
2001 Bryan Tower, Suite 1200
Dallas, Texas 75201

December 18, 1973

NOTICE   FNMA No. FMS-FHA/VA 26-73

TO   : ALL FNMA SELLERS

SUBJECT: Free Market System - FHA/VA
          Notice of Available Commitment Funds

Federal National Mortgage Association announces that during the following Offer Period
the amount set forth below will be available to purchase eligible FHA/VA home mortgages.

The offer of a Seller for the Offer Date identified herein may not exceed the applicable
maximum set forth below:

Offer Date: Monday, January 14, 1974, between the hours of 9 a.m. and 3 p.m.,
             Washington, DC, time - Dial (202) 293-7500.

          Available Funds   NO LIMIT ESTABLISHED
          Competitive Seller's Maximum $3,000,000
          Noncompetitive Seller's Maximum   200,000

This auction will be conducted under the same general rules which have been established
for the FMS-FHA/VA auctions as stated in the FNMA Selling Agreement (Supplement).

Results of FMS-FHA/VA Auction of December 17, 1973:

Type of Contract	Total Offers Received *	Total Offers Accepted *	Yield Range	Weighted Average Yield - Accepted Offers
4-month	$38.6	$36.2	8.713 - 8.908	8.775

* In Millions

The home loan convertible standby commitment yield required is 9.000. Sellers maximum
convertible standby commitment activity per week (Monday through Friday) will be
limited to $2 million.

Project mortgage requirements through the next Offer Date as specified above are as
follows:

Project immediate purchase yield required is 8.780; this yield converts to a price of
84.14 for 7% mortgages, 90.77 for 7 3/4% mortgages, or 97.50 for 8 1/2% mortgages.

Project standby yield required is 9.301; this yield converts to a price of 80.17 for
7% mortgages, 86.53 for 7 3/4% mortgages, or 93.00 for 8 1/2% mortgages.

Required percentage of financing charge in construction loans as referred to in
Section 309.05(b) of the FNMA Selling Agreement (Supplement) is 1.41% for 7% loans,
0.70% for 7 3/4% loans, and 0.0% for 8 1/2% loans.

NOTE: The next FHA/VA auction will be held in four weeks, January 14, 1974.

Hughes A. King
Regional Vice President

Figure 5-3

FEDERAL NATIONAL MORTGAGE ASSOCIATION

January 15, 1974

NOTICE   FNMA No. FMS-FHA/VA 1-74

TO   : ALL FNMA SELLERS

SUBJECT: Free Market System - FHA/VA
          Notice of Available Commitment Funds

Federal National Mortgage Association announces that during the following Offer Period the amount set forth below will be available to purchase eligible FHA/VA home mortgages.

The offer of a Seller for the Offer Date identified herein may not exceed the applicable maximum set forth below:

Offer Date: Monday, February 11, 1974, between the hours of 9 a.m. and 3 p.m., Washington, DC, time - Dial (202) 293-7500.

Available Funds	NO LIMIT ESTABLISHED
Competitive Seller's Maximum	$3,000,000
Noncompetitive Seller's Maximum	200,000

This auction will be conducted under the same general rules which have been established for the FMS-FHA/VA auctions as stated in the FNMA Selling Agreement (Supplement).

Results of FMS-FHA/VA Auction of January 14, 1974:

Type of Contract	Total Offers Received *	Total Offers Accepted *	Yield Range	Weighted Average Yield - Accepted Offers
4-month	$40.2	$35.6	8.640 - 8.806	8.706

* In Millions

The home loan convertible standby commitment yield required is 9.000. Sellers maximum convertible standby commitment activity per week (Monday through Friday) will be limited to $2 million.

2001 Bryan Tower, Dallas, Texas 75201

Figure 5–4a

116

TO: ALL FNMA SELLERS   January 15, 1974

Project mortgage requirements through the next Offer Date as specified above
are as follows:

Project immediate purchase yield required is 8.697; this yield converts to a
price of 84.80 for 7% mortgages, 91.47 for 7 3/4% mortgages, or 98.25 for
8 1/2% mortgages.

Project standby yield required is 9.211; this yield converts to a price of
80.83 for 7% mortgages, 87.24 for 7 3/4% mortgages, or 93.75 for 8 1/2%
mortgages.

The required percentage of financing charge in construction loans as referred
to in Section 309.05(b) of the FNMA Selling Agreement (Supplement) is 1.41%
for 7% loans, 0.70% for 7 3/4% loans, and 0.0% for 8 1/2% loans.

NOTE: The next FHA/VA auction will be held in four weeks, February 11, 1974.

Hughes A. King
Regional Vice President

Figure 5–4b

TABLE 5-2

Federal National Mortgage Association—Free Market System
Details of Recent FHA/VA and Conventional Auctions
(dollars in millions)

1973 Date	FHA/VA			CONVENTIONAL		
	Offers Rec'd/Accept.	Aver. Yield/Price	Yield/Price Range	Offers Rec'd/Accept.	Aver. Yield	Yield Range
4/30	$261.2-$185.9	7.915 (93.38)	8.174-7.899 (91.62) (93.49)	$128.9-$88.2	8.233	8.449-8.200
5/14	$258.3-$187.7	7.963 (93.05)	8.195-7.938 (91.48) (93.23)	$117.6-$84.4	8.314	8.529-8.256
5/29	$212.4-$140.0	8.001 (92.79)	8.063-7.978 (92.37) (92.95)	$113.3-$74.0	8.388	8.529-8.327
6/11	$184.5-$142.2	8.040 (92.53)	8.138-8.015 (91.86) (92.70)	$110.1-$74.1	8.442	8.529-8.401
6/25	$199.3-$118.7	8.094 (92.16)	8.192-8.060 (91.50) (92.39)	$95.0-$69.4	8.512	8.774-8.500
7/9	$539.3-$244.8	8.382 (90.23)	8.985-8.309 (86.37) (90.72)	$108.4-$72.5	8.673	8.770-8.610
7/23	$351.4-$181.4	8.538 (89.21)	8.715-8.465 (88.07) (89.69)	$119.0-$61.7	8.791	8.877-8.752
8/6	$458.5-$201.9	8.713 (88.08)	8.676-8.900 (88.32) (86.90)	$154.3-$77.4	8.981	9.250-8.905
8/20 *	$525.0-$223.8	8.949 (91.69)	9.119-8.907 (90.59) (91.97)	$171.3-$77.2	9.265	9.500-9.195
9/4 **	$551.0-$288.9	9.271 (94.70)	9.598-9.198 (92.57) (95.19)	$118.6-$61.5	9.525	9.755-9.500
9/17 **	$138.1-$107.9	9.371 (94.04)	9.688-9.201 (92.00) (95.17)	$48.6-$46.8	9.676	9.822-9.550

* FHA/VA at 7¾%
** FHA/VA at 8½%

accurate indication of the mortgage market. This system proved itself by helping to remove some of the uncertainty about the true state of the mortgage market in the period following the increases in the FHA/VA interest rates in 1968 and the later reductions in these rates during 1970–1971.

FEDERAL HOME LOAN MORTGAGE CORPORATION

The credit crunch of 1969–1970 highlighted a problem within the savings associations during periods of tight money. Many depositors simply withdrew their money for investments of higher yields than the fixed rates offered on savings accounts. The outflow of cash could easily exceed the repayments of loans outstanding and make any new loans impossible for an association to make. The Federal Home Loan Bank could not provide sufficient capital to give all the relief that might be needed with loans to members, so an additional agency was created. This was the Federal Home Loan Mortgage Corporation, which worked under the FHLBB and was able to sell bonds on the open market to provide additional funds with which to *purchase* mortgages from member savings associations.

When a seller (the savings association) wishes to turn some of its existing portfolio of mortgages to FHLMC for cash, it does so by making an offer to the purchaser (FHLMC) as per the forms reproduced as Figures 5–5 and 5–6. In this procedure, the seller must state a price at which he will sell the listed mortgages—the price being stated as a percentage (to three decimal places in this instance) of the aggregate balance due on the mortgages presented for sale. As explained more fully earlier in this chapter, the price at which the mortgages are offered is expected to be adjusted so as to make the yield to the purchaser commensurate with the existing market for long-term money. FHLMC periodically publishes the current acceptable yield. Herein lies the problem—mortgages taken at earlier, lower rates than the present market, become salable only with substantial discounts off the balance due. In a period of rising interest rates, the seller might be placed in the position of taking

FHLMC Form 1

OVER-THE-COUNTER PURCHASE CONTRACT
(Conventional Home Mortgages)

To FHLMC:

Sale: The undersigned Seller hereby offers to sell the mortgages listed in the attached Schedule (or others substituted therefore) in the aggregate outstanding principal amount and on the terms stated below, in accordance with the Master Selling Agreement Conventional, the Invitation in response to which this offer was submitted ("the applicable Invitation"), and the Sellers Guide Conventional, as in effect on the date of this offer, all of which are incorporated in full herein by reference.

Servicing: The undersigned Seller hereby agrees to service all mortgages sold hereunder, in accordance with the Servicing Agreement, the Servicers Guide as in effect on the date of this offer, and the applicable Invitation, all of which are incorporated in full herein by reference; or ☐ [check if applicable] substitute Servicer is offered per attached FHLMC Form 4.

1. Aggregate Principal Balance: $ _____

2. Price: _____%
           (TO 3 DECIMAL PLACES)

Seller's FHLBB Docket No.
or FDIC Certificate No.: _____

SELLER _____

Date of Offer: _____ , 19 _____

ADDRESS _____

(SEAL, if legally required for execution of contracts by Seller)

By _____
        AUTHORIZED REPRESENTATIVE

Offer Hereby Accepted by FHLMC:

Federal Home Loan Mortgage Corporation

Date of Acceptance: _____

Purchase Contract No.: _____

Required
Delivery Date _____

By _____
       AUTHORIZED REPRESENTATIVE

Seller's FHLMC Seller/
Servicer No.: _____

or ☐ Offer Declined by FHLMC

Date of Declination: _____

FHLMC-1 2/72

Figure 5–5

FHLMC Form 1

SCHEDULE OF MORTGAGES

	Borrower's Name	Property Address	Approximate Current Principal Balance
1.			
2.			
3.			
4.			
5.			
6.			
7.			
8.			
9.			
10.			
11.			
12.			
13.			
14.			
15.			
16.			
17.			
18.			
19.			
20.			
21.			
22.			
23.			
24.			
25.			
	TOTAL		$ _____

FHLMC-1 2/72 (REVERSE)

Figure 5–6

a considerable loss in liquidating a portion of his mortgage portfolio.

The possibility of selling a block of mortgages at a loss would be weighed against the advantage of having some additional cash on hand to make new loans at the higher interest rates, earning the origination fees, and adding to the total amount of loans that the seller would be servicing. The seller might also be faced with the need for additional cash to provide funds for commitments made much earlier to a good customer, such as a developer or builder who has continued to send good business to that particular savings association.

The popular opinion that any agency representing a governmental operation is pumping out money for the benefit of banks or savings associations to use for loans should again be dispelled. There are some subsidy programs, but the beneficiaries are the people, such as those in lower income circumstances with living needs. The Federal Home Loan Mortgage Corporation is not a subsidy operation, and it is expected to raise money in the open market in competition with all other long- and short-term borrowers. Hence, it can only purchase mortgages from the offers presented that will meet the existing market requirements. It does provide an additional outlet for a savings association to achieve some needed liquidity, but always at a price.

POINTS AND DISCOUNTS

The use of points in discounting loans stems from the need to sell these loans in the secondary market. Hence, a closer examination of the methods and reasons is presented here.

The definition of "points" used in this text refers to the term as a unit of measurement. Thus, the word *point(s)* can be used to identify various fees, such as the origination fee for processing a loan; or it may be used to refer to the costs of private mortgage insurance; or it can be used in reference to the discount. A point is simply 1% of the loan amount.

The word *point*, as used to express a discount, is the percentage that must be added or subtracted from the face value of a loan in order to increase, or decrease, the yield to a competitive amount. Discounts are increasingly being asked on conventional loans as a method or gimmick to obtain an increase in yield without showing an increase in interest rate. To the borrowing public, the expression is more closely associated with the fixed interest loans underwritten by the FHA and VA. In financial circles, a discount is converted to a "price" for a loan in order to facilitate trading.

Because the FNMA free market system is the most widely publicized arena showing the movements of market yields from mortgage loans, a specific example will be used to illustrate the manner in which points are determined by most mortgage companies.

In this connection, *yield* is defined as the total amount of the interest and the discount taken together. *Yield* and *discount* are differentiated by the fact that discount is a lump sum retained by the lender at the time of making a loan, so it must be spread over the life of the loan to reflect its actual addition to the interest earned in any one year. While most FHA and VA supported loans are for a term of 30 years, the realistic life of the loan is approximately ten years. That is to say, within ten years, the average loan is paid off, usually by resale and refinancing. So FNMA uses the time span of ten years to determine the yield value of a discount. The free market system offerings are made in terms of yield and can be converted to a discount mathematically, or more easily, by means of a standard conversion table.

The following short table is an example of several typical yield figures and the process by which they are converted into discount points and prices according to a standard conversion table:

TABLE 5–3

For a yield amount	At interest rate	Price must be	Points to achieve
7.862	7%	93.75	6¼
8.044	7%	92.50	7½

The mortgage banking industry is able to use the FNMA free market system yields as solid criteria from which to base its own handling of individual mortgage loans. Based on the above figures and the knowledge that, say, the last yield quoted was 8.04%, the conservative lender for a home loan would ask a discount between 7½ to 8 points for a good loan in excess of $18,000. He would ask perhaps another one-half point for a smaller $12,000 to $18,000 loan and a full extra point for any loan under $12,000. Some variation in these points exists due to competitive pressures, but the market for money remains the controlling factor. The loan originator using the FNMA yields as a guide to trends would be watching for an upward or downward movement to further guide his decision as to what discount he might need in order to be making loans at a price, or yield, at which they could be sold.

It should be borne in mind that the normal brokerage fee of 1 to 1½ points is not to be confused with the charge for discount points. Charges for discounts, on the whole, are passed on by the mortgage company to the ultimate lender. The brokerage, or finance fee, is the remuneration earned by the mortgage company for soliciting, processing, and arranging the funding of the loan. Another term for this charge is *origination fee*.

PRIVATE MORTGAGE INSURANCE

One of the essential elements needed to facilitate free trading in mortgage loans is some standard of reliability. The fact that home loans and other property loans are so local in their nature has prevented many investors from moving very far geographically to invest in conventional mortgages. The FHA and VA proved that investors would cross state lines and assist the cash-short growth areas of the country if they had some assurance of protection against the problems incurred in foreclosing a remote property.

The idea of providing insurance against a default in mortgage payments must be credited to the federal programs instigated by the FHA in 1933. It was some years later, during the 1950s, that several entrepreneurs began testing the market for the same type of insurance sold by private insurance companies. Progress was slow at first, and the independents did not really take hold in the mortgage industry until 1971. In the year the regulatory authorities expanded lending limits for conventional residential loans that called for default insurance coverage. Savings and loan associations were permitted to make loans up to 95% of appraised value, compared to 90% previously, provided that the higher ratio loans were insured. The result was a tremendous growth in private mortgage insurance.

One major insuring company, MGIC, based in Milwaukee, increased its loan coverage volume to $2.8 billion in 1971 and then to $7.5 billion in 1972 with about 40% of the coverage in 95% loans. The private sector topped the FHA coverage in that year, which in itself amounted to $4.5 billion.

Undoubtedly, adding to the boom in private mortgage insurance, often identified as PMI, was the unfortunate series of abuses revealed in connection with certain FHA home loan transactions occurring in isolated instances in the East and Midwest. In an effort to correct these problems and prevent a recurrence, subsequent new and stringent regulations were imposed and rigidly enforced to a point where it became difficult to sell a house through the FHA programs. Although most of the requirements were later modified, the private mortgage insurance had found its niche and proved its value.

Consider, for example, that under a given set of circumstances, a prospective borrower needing a loan of over $21,000 can actually obtain a smaller down payment through private mortgage insurance procedures than through the FHA. Also, it may cost the borrower less overall, with the transaction completed more quickly and involving a minimum of red tape.

What is private mortgage insurance and how does it work? Since it is a fairly new development in general usage, there has been some confusion regarding the facts. Basically, private mortgage insurance covers the top 25% of the loan against default. Whereas the FHA insures the total amount of its loan commitment, private mortgage insurance companies limit their exposure to the top portion of the loan, which, of course, is the most risky end.

What they are insuring against is an actual default on the mortgage payments. They are not immediately concerned with the borrower's life, the destruction of the property by fire, or with other hazards. Consequently, the insuring company must make an evaluation of the risk involved with the borrower, the reliability of his credit record, and the value of the property in question, should foreclosure become necessary.

There are only a few companies capable of selling this type of specialized insurance coverage, and they all work through loan originators: the mortgage companies, savings and loan associations, commercial banks, and other lending institutions. The loan originator must first qualify himself with the insurance company as an acceptable lender. The insurance carrier normally requires that each mortgage loan undergo evaluation by its own underwriting group before a certificate of coverage is issued. A request for coverage includes submitting (1) a property appraisal made by a professional appraiser approved by the insurance company, (2) a copy of the loan application, (3) a credit report on the borrower, (4) several verifications, and (5) any other data helpful in analyzing the loan. Once the necessary documents and information have been submitted, processing of the application tends to move quickly and is usually completed within 24 hours.

The essence of the insurance certificate is that in case the mortgage loan is defaulted and taken through foreclosure, the insurance company will pay off up to 25% of the loan. This means an exposure for the lender of 71.25% of the value on a 95% loan, and 67.5% on a 90% loan. The advantage to the lender is obvious in reducing his risk to a more practical level wherein full recovery might be made even through an early foreclosure proceeding. The advantage to the borrower lies in his being able to borrow a larger percentage of the value than previously obtainable in terms of a conventional loan. Now, for instance, a family might buy a $37,500 house for as little as $1,750 down—a down payment previously available only to a veteran qualifying on a VA guarantee requiring no down payment at all.

In actual operation it has been the practice of at least one insurance carrier, MGIC, to take over the property itself in a foreclosure proceeding and pay off the lender in full, thus relieving him of any further management problems. This is the same procedure that is commonly used by the Veterans Administration in similar circumstances and has given much greater acceptance to its guarantee programs. No lender is interested in spending the time and money necessary to take a property through foreclosure, manage and protect it, and make suitable disposition to another user. Mortgage insurance greatly reduces this possibility and has attracted many small investors into conventional mortgage loans.

The cost of mortgage insurance is paid for by the borrower, the same as under the FHA. While the FHA has only one plan for payment—½% annually on the declining balance— private insurors have a variety of methods to offer. This causes some problems in trying to quote loan costs as the insurance rates vary with 80%, 90%, and 95% loan-to-value ratios. The insuring companies also offer single payment plans for different terms of years, such as five years, seven years, or ten years. Most originators have attempted to reduce this confusion by offering only one or two plans for payment. A common practice is to offer two alternatives—a single payment plan at closing, or a monthly payment plan. On a 95% loan the single payment cost is 2½% of the loan amount and provides coverage for ten years; for a 90% loan this payment drops to 2%. On extended payments, the 95% loan insurance costs 1% at closing plus ¼% annually for up to ten years, while on a 90% loan the initial cost drops to ½% at closing with the same ¼% annually for the remainder of the term. These rates are subject to change.

Conventional loans are usually quoted without discount points, as the full cost is represented in the interest. Using only the interest rate, a current quote might be "8% + 1 + mortgage insurance." The one point would be the origination fee or finance fee, as some prefer to call it. To reduce the mortgage insurance cost to a quotation requires knowing which of the payment plans offered will be used by the borrower. Some companies simply add the initial premium cost to the origination fee and then quote the extended payment plan as an increase in the interest cost.

MORTGAGE COMPANIES

HISTORICAL BACKGROUND

From its origin as a brokerage-type service arranging loans, the mortgage banking industry has grown to a major business, handling well over half the mortgage loans in this country. As early as 1914, the men in this business formed a trade organization, known as the Farm Mortgage Bankers Association, indicating the original emphasis placed on farm loans. The name was changed to its present title of Mortgage Bankers Association of America in 1923, and it now has members from every state and a large permanent staff.

The Association serves as a communications and information center for the industry. Educational programs are sponsored to keep the many persons employed by mortgage bankers up-to-date on an ever-changing business. And a constant effort is being made to improve the methods and procedures of the industry.

In the early years of this century, mortgage bankers arranged for the sale of their own bonds and used these funds to buy small home and farm mortgages. Because of the thrift-conscious nature of the earlier farmers and home owners, mortgages were amazingly free of defaults and provided a widely used medium of investment.

The 1920s brought an increase in mortgage company financing of income properties such as office buildings, apartments, and hotels, perhaps with the firm conviction that a mortgage loan was as secure as gold. And the mortgage companies even referred to the small denomination bonds that they sold to the general public for mortgage financing as "gold bonds."

However, the Depression, beginning in October 1929, and triggered by the collapse of prices on the nation's largest stock exchange, showed up many basic weaknesses in the mortgage loan system. In the next two to three years most of the mortgage companies that had issued their own bonds, as well as those that had guaranteed bonds for other development companies, were faced with massive foreclosures, unable to meet their obligations, and were forced into bankruptcy.

From these ruins has arisen a far more enlightened and professionally sound industry—one that today not only arranges for permanent financing of all types of mortgage loans, but also uses its own resources to fund the loans initially, sometimes handling the interim or construction financing, and finally servicing or administering the repayment of the loan for the permanent investor.

MORTGAGE BROKERS

There is a significant difference between the services offered by "loan brokers," and that offered by mortgage bankers working within the mortgage industry. Brokers limit their activity to serving as an intermediary between the client-borrower and the client-lender. While brokers are capable of handling all arrangements for the processing or "packaging" of the loan, they do no funding and have no facilities to service or administer a loan once it has been made. There are some loan-wise individuals who prefer to work on their own as brokers and carry their loan applications to a mortgage banker for verification and funding. They earn a portion of the normal one point finance fee plus an application fee.

Other types of mortgage brokers are companies operating on a national scale who primarily arrange purchases and sales of mortgage loans between originators and investors, or between investor and investor, and in so doing, greatly aid the free flow of mortgages across state lines in the private mortgage market. These brokers seldom originate a loan and do not service them. They are a part of the secondary market in some of their operations.

Occasionally, a mortgage banker, or even a savings association will broker a loan for a customer. Money may not be readily available through regular channels, or the loan request may be for something that the lender cannot handle with his own funds. The lender may then turn to other sources and earn a brokerage fee for handling the loan. This type of extra service is more commonly found in smaller communities.

The lines between a broker, a mortgage banker, and a lender are not always clearly drawn, as brokerage service may be handled by any one of them. Brokerage is essentially the service of processing the loan information for the borrower and arranging for a lender to make the loan. Good brokerage work is done by professionals who respect the confidential nature of the information they must obtain and who earn their fees by knowing which lenders are presently seeking certain types of loans.

MORTGAGE BANKERS

The "full-service" facility offered by the mortgage banker today developed from both the need for a new approach after the Depression collapse and from the desire of the Federal Housing Administration to conduct its programs in conjunction with private industry. The economic pressures of 1930–1931 had dried up lendable funds, construction had been halted, and many banks had closed their doors. The shortage of available funds made the mortgage banker an intermediary for the only remaining sources of cash—cash from insurance companies, from a few large savings banks, and from the Federal National Mortgage Corporation. And the growth of the FHA brought the need for more servicing or loan administration by the mortgage bankers. More than half the mortgage companies operating today were founded after World War II, and in the 1950s four-fifths of all federally underwritten loans held by life insurance companies, savings and loans, and FNMA were serviced by mortgage bankers. The upward trend has continued, and if the government ventures further into the field of real estate financing, it undoubtedly will move through the channels that it helped to create—channels that have helped the government programs to succeed, i.e., the mortgage banking industry.

Qualifications of a Mortgage Banker

At present there are no federal requirements regarding the qualifications or licensing of an individual or a company handling mortgage loans, and few states have established requirements. In most areas any individual meriting the confidence of a lending institution could assist in arranging a loan, thereby earning a fee for his services. In practice, however, most mortgage companies and lenders require more concrete proof of ability and integrity.

Some mortgage companies went into business initially to handle only conventional loans for various investor-clients, and not FHA or VA loans. Those companies that specialize in large commercial loans have no real need of approval from FHA, nor do they feel compelled to comply with its regulations. Most mortgage companies, however, feel that a prime requisite for successful loan negotiation is to hold an FHA-approved certificate. The reason for this is that the home loan market, previously dominated by the FHA, is considered to be the most solidly reliable field, the "bread and butter" field, so to speak. In addition, many institutional lenders use the FHA certification of approval as one method of determining the reliability of potential correspondents.

The FHA requires a minimum capitalization of $100,000 (a sum now considered small within the industry), plus relevant details on the background and qualifications of the officers, directors, stockholders, and owners who will control and set policies for the mortgage company. It also requires that offices be made available for serving the general public and that no other business be conducted in those offices. Once the FHA has issued its charter of acceptance, the mortgage company becomes an "approved mortgagee" within the circle of companies qualified to handle federally underwritten commitments. Only approved mortgagees may present loan applications to the FHA for insured commitments. And in turn, the FHA depends heavily on its approved list of mortgage companies to prepare each application properly so as to include the relevant data needed for expeditious processing. Thus the FHA can rely on all information and verifications, the security of any cash required to be escrowed, and the prompt payment of any fees to be collected because it has already carefully examined the company and its official personnel before issuing its approval. A deliberate violation of an FHA requirement could result in the cancellation of the mortgage company's qualifications as an approved mortgagee.

As will become apparent in later chapters, the powerful role of the FHA in real estate finance began diminishing in early 1971, accelerated by a tightening of regulations brought on by abuses caused by a few groups and individuals. At about this same time, private mortgage insurance business was boosted, and its activities became serious competition. Despite the fall from a dominant position, however, the FHA acceptance charter held by a company or institution remains an important credential of a mortgage company's qualifications to transact loans.

MORTGAGE COMPANY OPERATIONS

Although mortgage companies vary widely in their methods, the business organization common to most operates by means of three basic divisions:

1. Administration
2. Loan servicing
3. Loan acquisition

The administrative group supervises and directs all operations and usually seeks out and maintains contacts with its sources of money—the lending institutions. The development of stable, continuing relations with a group of investors is a source of pride with the mortgage companies. And there is always more than one investor, since it is not considered good business for either the mortgage company or the lender to maintain an exclusive arrangement. Lenders are in and out of the market as their particular needs fluctuate, while the mortgage company must maintain a rather steady supply of funds. The mortgage company officers must know which sources are available for loans and what particular type each lender prefers.

Loan servicing includes the record-keeping section that maintains the customers' or borrowers' accounts. Larger companies have converted much of this accounting to computerized methods for more efficient handling. One part of the records involves the escrow section, which holds the required insurance and tax deposits. Escrow personnel must maintain a continuous analysis of taxes and insurance costs for each property to assure the company that sufficient money will be available when needed to pay the taxes and insurance premiums and to signal action should a default occur. In larger companies a collection department could be a separate group.

The loan acquisition group, the division best known to outsiders, consists of the loan representatives or supervisors who make the contacts with potential borrowers, real estate agents, banks, accountants, and others in order to seek out the best loans and to handle the actual application for a loan. A loan processor usually works with one of these representatives to maintain the files and to help collect the information required on both the property and the borrower in putting together the complete loan package.

Loan Package

Basically, a loan package is all of the data needed to properly evaluate the property and to analyze the borrower as a credit risk. It is the information assembled by the mortgage banker to substantiate a loan. Following is a list of the ordinary requirements that a loan representative would assemble in preparing a house loan package.

Information required on the property:

1. Earnest money contract on the sale, which should provide proper legal names of seller and purchaser, legal description of the property, and any special terms.

2. An appraisal by a qualified person.

3. A land survey by a registered surveyor.

4. A title opinion from the title company who will issue the title insurance.

Information required on the borrower (mortgagor):

1. Information questionnaire covering legal names, marital status, address, children, employment (for both husband and wife), assets and liabilities, and income and expenses (including fixed payments).

2. Verifications of employment.

3. Verifications of assets and debts.

4. Credit report from accepted agency.

5. Letters of explanation if unusual circumstances are involved.

The mortgage company then adds to this assemblage a covering letter or a report (FHA and VA have a special analysis form). The pertinent details are summarized with an analysis of the borrower's income, subtracting calculable living expenses and installment or monthly payments already committed, to show the cash available for debt retirement. Lenders each have varying requirements as to how this analysis should be presented, and the mortgage company is expected to know precisely what is needed.

For larger loans, the same general information is required but in much greater depth. Usually this borrower is a corporation or partnership, and the loan package would require complete company information, financial statements, and corporate resolutions, if applicable. If the loan involves a project to be constructed, the package must include complete plans and specifications plus an assurance of the contractor's capability. A completion bond is required of the contractor under FHA procedures but is not always used in conventional financing. There is a growing list of certifications needed, such as the status with labor unions, nondiscrimination pledges, impact on the neighborhood statements, and new pollution standards. Any special participation agreements required by the lender must be worked out in advance of the loan commitment.

A loan package assembled for initial closing under FHA procedure with multifamily projects includes 30 to 40 separate instruments, with all plans and data, and is often assembled under the guidance of an attorney who has specialized in such requirements and can knowledgeably represent the sponsor to the FHA and its attorneys at the closing.

MONEY COMMITMENTS

There are a number of ways for money to be promised or committed to a loan. The nomenclature for basic procedures may differ in some parts of the country, but the intent and purpose are similar and can be classed under the following categories of commitments:

Money Commitments, Forward (Sales and Servicing Contracts)

Since most mortgage bankers represent various institutional investors, some form of understanding or agreement is used to spell out the terms. Such an agreement between a lender and a mortgage company is called a "sales and servicing contract." The agreement recites the type of loan and conditions under which the lender will accept a loan, and also states the services that must be provided by the mortgage company along with the fees charged for these services.

The lender, by terms of the agreement, offers to provide a specified amount of money to the mortgage company for certain classes of loans at a fixed interest rate. The mortgage company is allowed a service charge for handling collections, providing the escrow services, paying taxes and insurance, and for representing the lender if problems occur during the transaction. This service charge, which varies from one-tenth of 1% to one-half of 1% of the loan depending on the amount of servicing required, is a direct addition (add-on) to the interest rate. For example, presuming that a lender, such as an eastern savings and loan association, agrees to accept a mortgage company's loans for an interest rate of 7½%, and the mortgage company requires ⅜% for servicing the loan, then the quotation submitted by the mortgage company to the borrower would be an interest rate of 7⅞%. In the example above, the 7½% rate is referred to as *net* to the lender. The lender then sets up a time limit during which the mortgage company may exercise its rights under the commitment, which usually extends from three to six months. This type of commitment is termed a *forward* commitment, and depending on the relationship between the mortgage company and the lender, it is not unusual for the lender to require a commitment fee.

The commitment fee, when required, is usually 1% (or one point) of the total commitment payable upon issuance of the agreement by the lender. Generally this fee is refundable when the commitment is fully used. However, if the mortgage company does not use the full amount of the commitment, it may be required to forfeit a portion of the fee. For example, if a mutual bank makes a $1 million commitment to the M Mortgage Company for four months and the mortgage company deposits $10,000 as a commitment fee, then at the end of the four months term if only $750,000 of acceptable loans have been made, the mortgage company may have to forfeit the unfulfilled portion of the fee, or $2500.

Under the forward commitment procedure, a mortgage company may be allowed to submit loans one at a time to the prime lender, but since this is a burdensome procedure, most agreements call for a minimum amount, say $250,000, in a group of loans at any one time. Unless the mortgage company has considerable capital of its own, it will resort to a warehouse line of credit with a local commercial bank to carry the loans until the minimum shipping package has been reached.

Money Commitments, Immediate

Another method employed, and one that accounts for the greatest volume of commitment money, is the immediate or direct purchase of loans from the mortgage company by an institutional lender. Under this procedure the mortgage company funds large volumes of loans with their own capital and credit lines and periodically offers the loans in multi-million dollar blocks to the institutional investor. Immediate delivery usually means within 90 days.

A lender with surplus money to invest will tend to accept a lower net interest rate on a large block of loans where it is possible to make an immediate purchase. In this manner the lender's money is earning interest sooner. Under a forward commitment procedure, the lender may be reluctant to tie up his money for future months since interest rates may change.

The large blocks of loans available by means of immediate purchase procedures are of greater interest to the big investors who must move their money in wholesale lots. Most large investors will not undertake a purchase of less than $1 million in loan totals from any single mortgage company.

Mortgage companies are generally able to retain the servicing contracts for residential loans when they are passed on to the institutional lenders regardless of the type of commitment—forward or immediate purchase. The amount of the servicing fee is determined in advance with the forward commitment but can vary somewhat with an immediate purchase commitment. With the latter, the servicing fee to be earned by the mortgage company would amount to whatever the differential is between the interest rate at which the loan was made to the borrower and the net rate acceptable to the secondary lender.

In the large commercial loans, the servicing may be passed on to the secondary lender, or a fee for this service may be negotiated with the mortgage company. Federally chartered thrift institutions and many state regulations require an authorized servicing agent of the lender to be located within 100 miles of the property mortgaged.

Money Commitments, Future

While some of the terms used to describe the various types of money commitments are not always consistent in various parts of the country, the difference between a forward commitment, which is meant for an agreement to lend money as may be required over a given period of time, and a future commitment is the most confusing. The future commitment applies to an agreement to make a specific loan on or before a specific date. It is this type of commitment that is used in making a permanent loan for a building yet to be constructed.

A future commitment almost always costs a nonrefundable commitment fee, which is negotiable. Normally it will run one to two points. The reason for the fee is that the lender is agreeing to have money available for a loan, perhaps one or two years from the date of commitment, and usually at a fixed rate of interest, and the lender feels entitled to a fee for this promise to deliver. As interest rates have become more volatile, future commitments are tending to be tied to a leading indicator of the capital market rather than held to a fixed rate.

It might be well to recall here that the long-term capital market fluctuates far more slowly than the short-term money market. The long-term investor is more interested in the *average* return on his total investments and thus can accept small increases and decreases in the periodic new investments. The movement of rates, upward or downward, affects only a small portion of the overall portfolio at any one time. These investments over or under the average return are the *marginal* investments.

Money Commitments, Take-Out or Stand-by

A take-out or stand-by commitment is actually a back-up promise to make a loan. It is more popular in periods of tight money and can be applied to any kind of a loan on a projected building, residential property, or income property. It is a commitment that is really not intended to be utilized but is available if needed.

An example of a take-out commitment in operation would be an apartment builder wanting to build in a tight money situation. In this instance a large city may appear to be overbuilt with apartment units and with decreasing occupancy. Let us assume that the major lenders have withdrawn from further apartment loans in the entire city for the time being. However, the builder owns a piece of land in an area of the city that is growing and that shows a real need for more apartment units. In such a case the builder might seek stand-by financing in the form of a take-out commitment from a mortgage company, a real estate investment trust, or another type of lender. A take-out commitment is issued at a higher than market interest rate and lasts for a longer term than the average construction loan commitment. The builder may be allowed three to five years to exercise his rights. To obtain this type of commitment, the builder must pay from two to four points in cash at the time the commitment letter is issued. This assurance of a permanent loan, even though it is at uneconomical rates, is used as a back-up to obtain a construction loan.

The real idea of the take-out commitment is to enable a builder to proceed with the construction of a building, giving him perhaps a year to achieve good occupancy, and with a proven income he can then obtain a more reasonable permanent loan and simply drop the higher cost take-out commitment. The builder would, of course, forfeit his initial commitment fee. The idea has worked well when everything clicks and the market analysis has proved accurate. It has also caused some disasters when it hasn't worked.

The idea of take-out commitments has moved into the field of house construction loans as a better protection to the construction lender than a plain speculative house loan. A commitment for residential house loans would be made at 80% of the appraised value of the finished house (usually the same amount as the construction loan itself), to be exercised within one year and at a cost of one point, payable when issued. Sometimes the mortgage company that issues the take-out will allow a portion of the commitment fee to apply on the origination fee if the mortgage company also handles the home buyer's permanent loan. Unlike a take-out commitment for a commercial project, the take-out on a house loan is used to help the issuing mortgage company to secure the *permanent* loan when the house is sold. The borrower then would be the new house buyer.

Money Commitments, Permanent

The permanent loan is the final mortgage loan with repayment extended over many years. It can be made as a future commitment or immediate. Conventional loans are made for a period of time extending to 30 years, while some federally underwritten loans extend to terms up to 40 years.

Commercial projects should have a permanent loan commitment (or a valid take-out loan commitment as per above), before a construction loan will be released. The construction lender wants to know how he will be repaid when the building is completed. Only a few builders are financially strong enough to give this assurance without a permanent loan commitment to support them. If a builder is capable of handling the construction costs with his own resources, it is far easier for him to obtain permanent financing upon completion of the project when the building can be inspected and the income potential more easily ascertained. Such a strong builder would also save paying a commitment fee that would be necessary if the permanent financing is handled as a future commitment rather than immediate.

The permanent loan for a single-family residence is made to the buyer, which may be in the form of a future commitment made prior to actual construction, or more commonly, as an immediate commitment for an existing house.

WAREHOUSING OF MORTGAGE LOANS

In order to accumulate the volume of mortgages needed to satisfy a forward commitment or to work with immediate sales of blocks of mortgage loans, the mortgagee (mortgage company) must use its own cash to make the initial funding of a loan at closing. Or, as most mortgage companies do, it borrows short-term money at a local commercial bank to provide the cash.

As mentioned in Chapter 4 on commercial banks, warehouse lines are established by mortgage companies on a fully secured basis; that is, each loan advanced by the commercial bank is secured by a note and mortgage assigned to the bank by the mortgage company.

While the credit-worthiness and capabilities of the mortgage banking company will have been fully cleared by the commercial bank before a line of credit is established, there is still a concern as to what will become of the accumulated loans as interest rates fluctuate. If the commercial bank accepts, say $1 million in home loans, which were made at a 7¼% interest rate, and the rate then begins to climb upward to 8%, can the loans be sold without a loss? The answer, of course, is negative unless the loans have previously been committed, or unless the mortgage banker is willing to discount the loans, taking the substantial loss himself.

Under these conditions, the smaller mortgage companies seek to protect themselves and their warehouse line with a forward commitment. As discussed earlier in this chapter, the commitment by a permanent lending source to accept a fixed amount of certain types of loans over a period of four to six months not only assures the mortgage company of its sale of loans but provides assurance to the commercial bank that the loans in warehouse will be liquidated at an established price.

It is by means of this assurance to the smaller mortgage companies, and to some of the giants, that the Federal National Mortgage Association has played such a dramatic role. If a smaller mortgage company is simply unable to find any lenders willing to furnish a forward commitment because they themselves are short of cash, the mortgage company can then turn to FNMA and acquire, for example, a $200,000 commitment under the free market system procedure by making a noncompetitive offering (see Chapter 5), and accepting the weighted average yield.

The large mortgage companies are capable of playing a

different game with their warehouse lines. In the multimillion dollar business of handling large blocks of residential loans and some commercial loans, the commercial banks know that their large mortgage company customers are quite capable of selling big blocks of loans and absorbing substantial losses, if necessary, in an adverse market. Medium to large mortgage companies may have lines of credit at one or more banks totaling from $10 million to $100 million. As the mortgage company makes loans each day and places them in the warehouse line one or more of the company's officers will be watching the secondary market and discussing possible loan sales with the larger lenders. This procedure is somewhat like a speculation game, for when the market is right the mortgage company may sell off $10 or $20 million in loans at a price that provides a slight additional profit to the mortgage company. In these large volumes, a very slight movement of loan prices has a tremendous effect on the gain (or loss) in the sale.

In view of all this shifting around of the actual note and mortgage, what happens then to the person who borrowed the money to buy a house? He is relatively unaffected and in most cases is not knowledgeable of the movement of his note. This is due to the fact that the responsibility for the proper servicing of the loan is normally held by the originator of the loan who handles the collections and escrows the necessary tax and insurance money in his own name, although as an agent for the holder of the note. The originator earns a service fee for this work and provides a continuity to the borrower who continues to make his monthly payments to the same office.

OTHER SOURCES OF INCOME FOR MORTGAGE COMPANIES

Mortgage companies often furnish other services in addition to their mortgage loan work, and these are usually affiliated with the building industry. The more common of these activities are:

Insurance. The sale of hazard insurance is closely associated with mortgage financing and is often handled by the mortgage company or an affiliated agency.

Appraising. Most mortgage companies have qualified appraisers on their staffs as a service to both their customers and their lenders.

Real Estate Sales. Since many mortgage company loan representatives are also qualified real estate brokers, the sale of real estate is an easy step. However, this represents direct competition to some of the mortgage company's best customers—the other real estate brokers—and is not practical in many cases.

Construction. Some mortgage companies have developed very competent construction divisions and will build both residential housing and commercial buildings for their own use as investments or for sales to others.

Land Development. One of the methods used to move a step ahead of the competition is for a mortgage company to buy land for subdivision development and make the lots available to builders. In this manner the mortgage company can usually retain a first refusal look at all loans and other services that may be required in the new development.

THE FUTURE OF MORTGAGE COMPANIES

Mortgage companies have reached their present high position in the lending field by performing two principal services: (1) a service to borrowers in processing sometimes difficult and tricky loan applications and making sure the funds are available to them at closing, and (2) a service to lenders who are too large and remote to undertake processing of smaller individual loans. The method used by mortgage companies is to actively solicit loan applications through personal contact, through sales and service to the real estate industry, and through the home buyers. But the key to their continuing success lies more in their ability to find lenders willing to work with them and to provide the money for the loans, rather than on their proven sales ability. In periods of tight money, the smaller mortgage company can easily find itself short of funds and dependent on the higher cost sources, which could be mainly the Federal National Mortgage Association. As savings associations continue to grow and spread through their branches into the smaller communities, some have become more aggressive and sales-minded in their approach to lending. The increase in activity of the secondary market and the growing acceptance by savings associations to sell some of their loans have fostered an increase in competition. Mortgage companies without direct affiliation to actual sources of money will find it increasingly hard to compete in a fluctuating market. Many have recognized the trend and are broadening their field of activities into other related businesses, and/or are taking steps to acquire, or be acquired by, a bank, a bank holding corporation, or a savings association.

PROPERTY
IDENTIFICATION

PROPERTY APPRAISALS

One of the major factors controlling the actual amount of a real estate loan is the appraised value. In the not too distant past a loan officer or other official of a lending institution would determine property value based only on his own knowledge and experience in the area. Only in the past few decades has the skill of the professional appraiser been recognized as a valuable addition to the proper analysis of a mortgage loan.

Today, we have two highly professional organizations, both headquartered in Chicago, that qualify members after careful consideration of their educational background, their practical experience in the field, and their passing of extensive tests in this subject. These are:

1. The American Institute of Real Estate Appraisers, which was organized under, and requires an applicant to be a member of, the National Association of Real Estate Boards. The Institute issues two basic designations—Residential Member (RM) and Member Appraisers Institute (MAI). The MAI designation is considered by many experts to be tops in the field.

2. The Society of Real Estate Appraisers, de-

veloped primarily from the savings and loan group of staff appraisers, also grants two designations—Senior Residential Appraiser (SRA) and the highest designation, Senior Real Estate Analyst (SREA).

Definition of an Appraisal

An appraisal may be defined as an estimate of the value of an adequately described property as of a specific date, which is supported by an analysis of relevant data. An appraisal is an evaluation of ownership rights. Appraisals can be delivered in three forms: (1) a letter form that touches the high points, (2) a form report such as the one used by the FHA, or (3) a narrative form that goes into considerable analytical detail to substantiate the findings.

Principles of Appraising

How do appraisers approach their problems? What are they looking for in determining values? What analytical details should lenders or borrowers expect to find in written appraisals?

Principles of Appraiser's Analysis. First, let us look at the broad theory behind a professional appraiser's analysis. There are certain principles that guide their thinking in evaluating property. Most important among these are the following:

1. *Supply and demand.* The same theory underlying all economic practice is that scarcity influences supply and that what people want controls the demand.
2. *Substitution.* The value of replaceable property will tend to coincide with the value of an equally desirable substitute property.
3. *Highest and best use.* It is the use of the land at the time of the appraisal that will provide the greatest net return. This requires the proper balance of the four agents of production (labor, coordination, capital, and land) to provide the maximum return for the land used.
4. *Contribution.* This principle applies to the amount of value

added by an improvement, such as an elevator in a three-story building, or the value added to a building lot by increasing the depth of that lot.

5. *Conformity.* To achieve maximum value the land use must conform to the surrounding area. An over-improvement, such as a $100,000 house built in a neighborhood of $30,000 homes, will lower the value of the larger house.

6. *Anticipation.* Since value is considered to be the worth of all present and future benefits resulting from property ownership, the anticipation of future benefits has to be evaluated.

The Narrative Type Appraisal

With the theory of the appraisal principles as a background to guide the analysis, the appraiser presents his information in a logical sequence. The narrative report, which is the most comprehensive form of appraisal, uses the following pattern and guidelines:

Description of the Property. The property should be defined in accurate legal wording, and the precise rights of ownership must be considered. The rights may be a leasehold interest, mineral rights, surface rights, or the full value of all the land and buildings thereon.

The Date and Purpose of the Appraisal. Appraisals can be made for times other than the present, such as when needed to settle an earlier legal dispute. The date of the appraised value must be clearly shown. Also, the purpose of the appraisal should be stated as it will influence the dominant approach to value. In professional appraisals there is no such thing as a buyer's or seller's value—this is not a "purpose" as identified here. An example of purpose would be to estimate value for an insurance settlement, which would involve a cost approach to value as claims are adjusted on the basis of cost. If the purpose is a condemnation action, the most relevant approach would be the market value.

The Background Data. While the standard form and simple letter report will not provide any economic background data, the narrative report discloses the economic information as clues to value. An overall study of the market region, which may be as large as an entire state, is made. The focus is then brought down to the local area—the town or the portion of a city where the property is located. From there the analysis narrows to the specific neighborhood and then to the actual site under appraisal.

The Approaches to Value. Appraisers use three common approaches to determine value (a) cost, (b) market, and (c) income. All approaches should be used wherever possible, and all should reach approximately similar values, although these values are seldom the same. In certain appraisals, only one approach may be practical, such as valuing a city hall building for insurance purposes. In this analysis only a cost approach would be practical as there is not much buying or selling of city halls to provide market data, nor is there a true income from the building itself to provide figures for an income approach. A single-family residence may appear to lack any income for analysis, but certain neighborhoods have sufficient houses being rented to provide enough data to reach an income approach conclusion. The three approaches to value are discussed in greater detail later in this chapter.

Qualifying Conditions. If in the analysis of the property, the appraiser discovers any material factors that will affect the property's value, these can be reported as further substantiation of the conclusion.

Estimate of Value. This is the real conclusion of the study, the figure most people turn to first when handed a finished appraisal. Each of the approaches to value will result in a firm dollar valuation for that approach. Then, it is the purpose of this estimate to explain why one of the approaches to value is favored over the others. For example, with an income property such as a motel, the value judgment would rest most heavily on the income analysis. The final conclusion is a single value for the property and represents the considered knowledge and experience of the appraiser making the report.

Certification of the Appraiser and His Qualifications. The professional appraiser certifies to his opinion by signature, and he disclaims any financial interest in the property being appraised that could influence a truly objective conclusion. A recitation of the appraiser's educational background, of his standing within his profession as indicated by his professional ratings, and of his previous experience such as appraisals he has made and for whom, serves to substantiate the quality of the appraisal for the underwriting officer.

Addendum. Depending on the need for clarification, the appraisal will include maps of the area under consideration with the site pointed out, plus the location of comparable properties referred to in the analysis. Charts may be used to indicate such things as the variables in a market analysis. Photos of the actual property are usually mandatory.

Three Approaches to Property Values

In order to understand more clearly the use of the three approaches to value, which is the essence of an appraisal, each is discussed below.

Property Value as Determined by Cost Approach. The cost approach is developed as the sum of the building reproduction costs, less depreciation, plus land value. The reproduction costs can be developed the same way a builder would prepare a bid proposal by listing every item of material, labor, field burden, and administrative overhead. Reproduction cost estimates have been simplified in active urban areas through compilation of many cost experiences converted to a cost per square foot figure. The offices of active appraisers collect such data in depth for reference.

Depreciation, by definition, detracts from the value and must be deducted from the reproduction costs. Depreciation consists of three separate types:

1. *Physical deterioration.* The wear and tear of the actual building—this is the type most commonly associated with the word *depreciation.* Examples would be the need for repaint-

ing, a worn-out roof needing new shingles, and rotting window casements. These are "curable" items and under the breakdown method should be deducted from value as a rehabilitation cost. All other items of physical deterioration are "incurable," that is, not economically feasible to repair. An illustration would be the aging of the foundations or of the walls, and this kind of deterioration should be charged off as a certain portion of the usable life of the building. Another method of handling physical deterioration, in contrast to the breakdown method, is the engineering or observed method wherein each major component of the building is listed, and a percent of its full life is charged off. This method recognizes that each major component of a building may have a different life and the percentage of depreciation would vary at any point in time.

2. *Functional obsolescence.* Equally as important as physical deterioration is that category of loss in value resulting from poor basic design, inadequate facilities, or outdated equipment. These elements, too, can be curable or incurable. An example of incurable functional obsolescence would be a two-bedroom, one-bath house, which was very popular at the end of World War II, but now is a hard item to sell in today's more demanding market. There could be an excess of walls or partitions in an office building, which would cost money to remove and modernize, but would be curable. Lack of air conditioning in a hotel or office building is another example of curable functional obsolescence.

3. *Economic obsolescence.* The third type of depreciation has a more elusive quality and really is not in the building at all. Economic obsolescence is that set of factors outside and surrounding the property that affect the value, requiring the determination of the plus or minus effect of these forces. Some are very obvious influences—a new freeway bypassing an existing service station, the construction of an undesirable industry in an area adjacent to residential property, or the bridging of a stream to open new land for development. The more difficult problem is ascertaining economic impact of the long-term rise or fall of a specific neighborhood. While land owners are able to exercise some voice in protest or encouragement of these outside forces, for the most part what is done with neighboring properties is not controllable and is not curable. And it will always be a force that will affect the value of an individual property.

The last factor to be considered under the cost approach is the value of the land. Lately, almost all land has been marked by a steady appreciation in value. But economic factors can adversely affect land value as well as favorably influence it. Normally, land value can be determined through an examination of recent sales of similarly located properties —the same basic method as used under a market approach to value. However, there are sometimes specific reasons for changes in the appraised value of land. Buildings can and do deteriorate, while the land itself can continue to increase in value due to the same outside factors noted in economic obsolescence above. For example, as urban areas expand, certain intersections become more and more valuable, new throughways and freeways concentrate greater flows of traffic, and huge shopping centers add to the value of all surrounding land. As the suburban sprawl moves outward, former farm land increases in value when it is converted into residential subdivisions; or, as another example, in some older sections of a city the land can become more valuable than the building. The building itself may represent such poor usage of the land that it becomes a liability to the property value, and its removal costs can be deducted from the stated value of the land. It is these fluctuations in land value that bring cost-analysis into step with market evaluation.

Property Value as Determined by Market Approach. Also known as a sales-comparison approach, the value by market approach is determined by prices paid for similar properties. Since no two properties are ever precisely comparable, much of the analysis under this method concerns itself with the detailing of major characteristics and whether these add to or subtract from the value of the property. These details of comparison cover items such as date of sale, location of property, size of lot, type of materials used in construction, and many other factors that the appraiser considers relevant.

The market approach represents one of the most important analyses, as the true worth of any property is the actual amount for which it can be sold. And to this end, accurate information on the present market is essential.

Some confusion does exist in the use of sales prices and

asking prices. The appraiser is primarily concerned with completed sales and with sales uncomplicated by extraneous pressures such as forced sales, estate disposals, or transfers within a family. The asking or offering price is considered by most to represent a ceiling or maximum value for the property, and appraisers usually recognize the inherent inaccuracy of an asking price, especially one set by homeowners. This figure is often arrived at by adding the original purchase price, plus the full cost of all improvements that have been made, plus the selling commission, plus the owner's amateur notion of general market appreciation. But every so often an owner actually receives such a sales price from a willing buyer, and this makes the professional feel a bit foolish!

Property Value as Determined by Income Approach. Because the income approach looks at the actual return per dollar invested, it is the most important method for any investment property.

When a man buys an investment property he normally expects to recover, or "recapture" in appraisal terminology, his money with a profit. He does this from two sources: (1) the annual earnings (excess income over all costs) and (2) the proceeds from a resale at the end of the term of ownership, called *reversion.*

Thus, value of property by the income approach is derived by capitalizing the present worth of an income stream for a certain number of years plus a lump sum reversion at the end of the stream.

Capitalization is achieved by dividing the stabilized income by the rate of return to equal value; i.e.,

$$\frac{\text{Income}}{\text{Rate of return}} = \text{Value}$$

$$\frac{16{,}000}{.08} = \$200{,}000$$

or a reciprocal method,

$$\frac{100}{8} = 12.5 \qquad 12.5 \times 16{,}000 = \$200{,}000$$

Obviously there are many variables to consider in achieving the rather simple illustration above. The income itself is a projection of what the property can reasonably be expected to produce. The rate of return can and should be a composite rate reflecting perhaps one or two mortgage notes to be assumed plus the expected return on the equity investment. One can readily see the importance an appraiser must place in the selection of a rate of return—since a slight variation in this figure produces a wide variation in the calculated value.

The value of the reversion is a calculated estimate of the property's value 15, 20, or 30 years from now. It requires good knowledge and experience to support a realistic figure of this kind.

SURVEYS

One of the recurring problems in passing land titles and in making sure that a lender is actually receiving a mortgage on the proper land is the identification of that land. Improper identification of the property to be mortgaged, through field error or typographical error, will invalidate the mortgage instrument. A survey is an accurate measurement of the property, not a legal description of it.

An example of an error in property description occurred in a motel loan several years ago. In this case, the property described in the mortgage was identified by the perimeter of the building, rather than by the boundaries of the land on which the building stood. The parking areas surrounding the building, which provided the only access to the premises, were not included in the mortgage indenture. When it became necessary to foreclose, the mortgagee learned that he did not have access to the property!

A survey for our purposes is the physical measurement of a specific piece of property certified by a professionally registered surveyor. In processing a mortgage loan, no lender will accept any measurements other than a professional's, as it is a precise business and the loan package requires an accurate description of the land being mortgaged.

When a licensed surveyor defines a piece of property, it is customary to drive stakes or iron rods into the ground at the corners and to "flag" them with colored ribbons. It is not unusual for a lending officer to physically walk the land, checking the corner markers, and thus satisfying himself as to the shape of the parcel, and whether or not there might be any encroachments that would infringe on the mortgage lien. However, the prime responsibility to determine encroachments belong to the surveyor, which is one of the reasons why a survey is necessary.

LEGAL DESCRIPTIONS

A completed survey is a map showing each boundary line of the property with its precise length and direction. A survey should not be confused with the legal description of a piece of land. A legal description describes property in words, while a survey describes by illustration. Legal descriptions are most commonly found in the following three forms.

Lot and Block. The best known type of legal description is that found in incorporated areas that have established procedures for land development. A subdivider, in obtaining city approval to build streets and connect utilities, submits a master survey of the entire block of land, showing how the subdivision is broken into *lots,* which are then numbered and grouped into *blocks* for easier identification. Once the subdivision plan is accepted, it is recorded in the county offices and becomes a readily available legal reference to any lot in the plan.

For lending purposes, where the need is to identify a specific property over a period of 30 or even 40 years, the recorded subdivision plat is a much better method than a street address. Street names change and numbers can be altered, but the lot and block numbers remain secure because they are recorded. It may be argued that a street address gives a much better picture of where a property lies in discussing various houses or properties, but such identification is not sufficiently accurate to be acceptable to a lender. The common method of clearly identifying property in real estate transactions is, first, to give the legal description, followed by a phrase such as "also known as," and then to provide the street address. To illustrate, a property identification might be spelled out as, "Lot 6, Block 9, Nottingham Addition, Harris County, Texas, also known as 1234 Ashford Lane, Houston, Harris County, Texas."

Metes and Bounds. When recorded plats are not available for identification of land (and sometimes when plats *are* available), it becomes necessary to use an exact survey of the boundary lines for complete identification. This might be true of a recorded lot that has a stream or river as one boundary—the precise boundary being subject to change through erosion or realignment.

The method used is to define a starting corner with proper references to other marking lines, then note the direction in degrees and the distance to the next marking corner, and so on around the perimeter of the property back to the starting point. These descriptions can be quite lengthy and involved. An example of the wording used to describe several boundary lines might be: ". . . and thence along said Smith Street south 61 degrees 32 minutes 18 seconds west 948 and 25/100 feet; thence continuing along said Smith Street south 64 degrees 45 minutes 51 seconds west 162 and 80/100 feet to the point of beginning."

It is obvious that considerable accuracy is required to figure the necessary directions down to a second of a degree and to measure the distances over highly variable and often rough terrain in order to close the boundaries properly. Such a description is acceptable only if certified by a registered surveyor.

In some rural areas, land is identified in the form of metes and bounds by the use of monuments. A "monument" may be something tangible such as a river, a tree, rocks, fences, or streets; or intangible such as a survey line from an adjoining property. Physical monuments such as these are subject to destruction, removal, or shifting, and do not provide lasting identifications for long-term loans.

Geodetic or Government Survey. As long ago as 1785, the federal government adopted a measurement system for land based on survey lines running north and south, called *meridians,* and those running east and west, called *base lines.* The system eventually applied to 30 western states with the exception of Texas. A number of prime meridians and base lines were established. Then the surveyors divided the areas between the intersections into squares, called *checks,* which were 24 miles on each side. These checks were further divided into 16 squares, each measuring 6 miles by 6 miles, called *townships.* The townships were then divided into square mile units (36 to a township), called *sections,* which amounted to 640 acres each. These sections were then divided into halves, quarters, or such portions as were needed to describe individual land holdings. An example is shown in the diagram below.

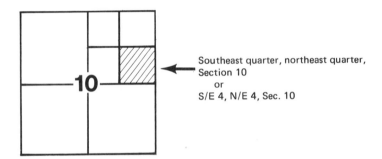

Southeast quarter, northeast quarter, Section 10
or
S/E 4, N/E 4, Sec. 10

During the growth years of our country, much of our western land was laid out in this fashion by contract survey crews. Marking stakes were duly placed to identify the corners, and these stakes are frequently used today. The fact that many of the surveys accumulated errors, including the failure to close lines, has created some confusion that concerns principally the oil and mining companies today who are attempting to identify leases, and ranchers claiming property lines against a neighbor.

However, these faulty descriptions have not constituted a

serious problem for lending institutions. Land described, for example, as "Section 16, 31 north, Range 16 east, New Mexico Prime Meridian," could effectively handle a farm or ranch loan, and a minor inaccuracy in describing such a tract would not undermine the basic security of the collateral.

In pledging property where there is the possibility or probability that some slight inaccuracy has occurred as to the exact amount of land involved, it is customary to use a qualifying term such as "comprising 640 acres, more or less." Any variation in property size should be considered in the light of what might be termed "reasonable." A few acres out of line among 640 acres would not matter a great deal, but a few feet in a downtown city property could well be of critical importance.

FEDERAL GOVERNMENT PROGRAMS

FEDERAL HOUSING ADMINISTRATION (HUD INSURING OFFICE)

The Federal Housing Administration was one of several score agencies spawned during the Depression to help resolve the economic problems that plagued this nation. It is one of the very few that has survived, and it has proved its value over four decades of operations.

The reasons for which the FHA was formed in 1934 are still valid today, although the area of operations has expanded tremendously from the initial assistance program for home buyers. The purposes for the FHA are (1) to encourage wider home ownership, (2) to improve housing standards, and (3) to create a better method of financing mortgage loans. All of these aims have been realized, perhaps even beyond the original hopes, without making a single loan, but by the sound use of government credit to insure mortgage loans. From its initial widespread rejection by many private lenders, a government-insured commitment now is readily salable to a wealth of investors. Even in the tightest of money markets, from 1968 through 1970, there was always funding available for a government-insured loan!

161

When the FHA stepped into the housing picture in 1934, houses had been financed for 50% to 60% of their sales price on a first mortgage of three to five years, with a second mortgage and even a third mortgage at increasingly higher interest rates. By offering to insure a single large loan up to 80% of value (an extremely high rate in those days), the FHA was able to insist that the down payment be made in cash, permit no secondary financing, and command a moderate interest rate. The loans were for long terms—up to 20 years at first—and were fully amortized over the life of the loan. Equal monthly payments were charged for principal and interest. Escrow accounts were established for hazard insurance and for taxes, to collect one-twelfth of the yearly cost each month. Each of these monthly payments also included a fee of ½% of the unpaid balance annually to cover the cost of mortgage default insurance. Most of these features were later incorporated into the loan guarantee program of the Veterans Administration and have now become normal procedure for conventional loans as well. While none of these ideas actually originated with the FHA, this agency gave them wide usage for the first time and thus brought about a sweeping reform in the field of residential financing.

Time brought the need for changes in some of the requirements. By 1963 the down payment for a house loan had been reduced to 3% on the first $15,000, 10% on the next $5000, and 25% on any balance over $20,000. Under the latest set of regulations (March, 1970), the widely used Title II, Section 203(b), the Home Mortgage Insurance program calls for a 3% down payment on the first $15,000, 10% on the next $10,000, and 20% on any balance up to the maximum of $33,000 for a single-family house loan. Thus, an FHA estimate of property value in the amount of $28,000 would require a down payment in the amount of $2050 ($450 as 3% of the first $15,000, $1000 as 10% of the next $10,000, and $600 as 20% of the balance over $25,000, or of $3000, to cover the total value of $28,000. A major addition to the newest rules is the inclusion of "closing costs" (not prepaid items) as a part of the house cost and added to the FHA estimate of property value for the calculation of down payments. The FHA has recently added a special program to Section 203(b), that if the mortgagor is a veteran, it will permit a 100% insured commitment for the first $15,000 plus closing costs, with lesser down payment requirements on larger amounts. The term of these loans has now been extended to 30 years and can go to 35 years if the house was constructed under FHA inspection procedures.

Meanwhile, the well-controlled or stabilized interest rate had succumbed in the early 1950s to the practice of discounting government-insured loans in order to keep pace with the increasing yields available in the conventional money market. This rise in interest costs followed the 1951 Federal Reserve withdrawal of support in the government bond market.

As the FHA gained strength in its housing assistance, more Titles and Sections were added to its program. While the FHA has over 50 different programs to offer in its portfolio of assistance to home loans, improvement loans, and multifamily project loans, our concern is primarily with loans for single-family residences. Under the assistance programs for home loans, the FHA has special help for servicemen, civilian employees of the armed services, and disaster victims, as well as programs in experimental housing, urban renewal, and condominium housing. Our text will be directed at the most popular of these programs, which are as follows:

1. Title II, Section 203(b)—Home Mortgage Insurance

2. Title II, Section 221(d)(2)—Home Mortgage Insurance for Low and Moderate Income

3. Title II, Section 235—Home Ownership for Lower Income Families

4. Title II, Section 237—Home Mortgage Insurance for Special Credit Risks

All programs are implemented by the issuance of a Certificate of Insurance, which protects the lender against default. The differences between the programs are based on the qualifications of the individual who needs the help. There may be lower cash requirements and, in certain cases, an actual subsidy of interest costs. Also, the property must meet certain parameters to qualify for an insured commitment.

Until several years ago, the FHA had been required to analyze each loan on the basis of its economic feasibility and to limit its insured commitments to only those families who presented a reasonable credit risk. The care with which the FHA has exercised its authority over the years is indicated by the fact that it has, in the past, returned over two-thirds of its insurance fees to the Federal Treasury.

In the past few years Congress has seen fit to recognize a growing social need for housing and has introduced a number of new programs through the FHA which are based not only on economic feasibility but also on a family's need for housing. This country has long supported various types of public housing built by government agencies and rented to lower income families for well-below market rents. Public housing of this sort has not worked out very successfully, and in 1965 Congress altered the direction of the program to place the problem in the hands of private business. Money previously allocated to support public housing was now to be used to subsidize the private developer with the expectation that he could do a more effective and efficient job. And the programs to activate these social objectives have been channeled through the FHA with the first funding for such a project as far back as 1966.

In January 1973, the Secretary of HUD announced a suspension of all government-subsidized housing programs pending a reevaluation. Abuses and profiteering had been uncovered in some areas, and the Nixon administration felt a better method of giving assistance might be found. Meanwhile, a reduction in spending would be more helpful.

On the following pages are illustrated the standard FHA Form 2800 used to apply for a property appraisal and commitment for mortgage insurance, and Form 2900 used in applying for credit approval of the borrower. The proper completion of both of these forms is required in all four of the housing programs considered in this text—they are the only forms needed to qualify a property and a buyer for 203(b) and 221(d)(2), with an additional form needed to qualify an applicant under 235 and 237. Although the latter

FHA MORTGAGEE NO. *(Please Verify)*	U.S. DEPARTMENT OF HOUSING AND URBAN DEVELOPMENT FEDERAL HOUSING ADMINISTRATION	FHA CASE NO.

MORTGAGEE'S APPLICATION FOR PROPERTY APPRAISAL AND COMMITMENT FOR MORTGAGE INSURANCE UNDER THE NATIONAL HOUSING ACT	PROPERTY ADDRESS

☐ SEC. 203(b)   ☐ SEC. _____

MORTGAGEE Name and Address including ZIP Code *(Please Type)*
(Please locate address within corner marks)

This form is a request for an appraisal and a commitment to insure a loan on an individual property.

We cannot process incomplete applications.
Rejecting them is costly.
Please help by giving us well prepared applications.
Keep all entries within alloted spaces.

Telephone No.

EXISTING HOUSE	Name of Occupant *(or person to call if unoccupied)*	Tel. No.	Key Encl. ☐ *(If unfurnished)*

Mon. & Yr. Completed   ☐ Never Occup. ☐ Vacant   Occupied by ☐ Owner ☐ Tenant at $_____ Per Mo. ☐ Furn. ☐ Unfurn.

PROPOSED SUBSTAN. REHAB. UNDER CONSTR.	Builder's Name & Address Including ZIP Code	Tel. No.	Model Identification

Plans: ☐ First Subm.   Prob. Repeat Cases ☐ Yes ☐ No   ☐ Prev. Proc. as FHA Case No.

DESCRIPTION						
☐ Detached	☐ Wood siding	___ Stories	___ Bedrooms	☐ Store Rm.	Mineral Rights Reserved	Type of Heating
☐ Semi-det.	☐ Wood shingle	☐ Split Foyer	___ Liv. room	☐ Util. Rm.	☐ No ☐ Yes *(Explain)*	
☐ Row	☐ Asb. shingle	☐ Bi-Level	___ Din. room	☐ Garage	Util-ities: Public Comm. Individual	☐ Cent. Air Cond.
☐ Frame	☐ Fiber board	☐ Split Level	___ Kitchen	☐ Carport	Water ☐ ☐ ☐	☐ Wall Air Cond.
☐ Masonry	☐ Brick or stone	☐ Full Basement	___ No. rms.	No cars	Gas ☐ ☐ ☐	Type of Paving (Str.)
☐ Concrete	☐ Stuc. or c. blk.	___ % Basement		☐ Built-in	Elect. ☐ ☐ ☐	☐ None
Factory Fabricated	☐ Aluminum	☐ Slab on Gr.	___ Baths	☐ Attached	Underground Wiring	☐ Curb & Gutter
☐ Yes 2.☐ No	☐ Asph. siding	☐ Crawl Space	___ ½ Baths	☐ Detached	Sanitary: Sept. Cess tank Pool	☐ Sidewalk
		Living Units	% Non-res.		Sewer ☐ ☐ ☐	☐ Storm Sewer

EXTRA FEATURES	☐ Fireplace	☐ Rec. Room	☐ Sw. Pool	☐ Enclosed Porch	☐ Breezeway	☐ Fence
	☐ Extra Fire Pl.	☐ Expand Attic	☐ Fin. Attic			

SPEC. ASSESS. Prepayable $_____ Non-Prepay.$_____   LOT _____ x _____   ☐ Irr. ☐ Acres _____ Sq. Ft.

Int.___% Ann. Pay.$_____ Unpd. Bal. $_____ Rem. Term ___Yrs.   GENERAL LOCATION:

ANN. R. EST. TAXES $	ANN. FIRE INS. $	SALE PRICE $

EQUAL OPPORTUNITY IN HOUSING

Federal laws and regulations prohibit discrimination because of race, color, religion, or national origin in the sale or rental of residential property. Numerous state statutes and local ordinances also prohibit such discrimination. In addition, section 805 of the Civil Rights Act of 1968 prohibits discriminatory practices in connection with the financing of housing.

If FHA finds there is noncompliance with any applicable antidiscrimination laws or regulations, it may discontinue FHA business with the violator.

LEGAL DESCRIPTION   *(Attach one page if necessary)*

SHOW BELOW: Shape, location, distance from nearest intersection and street names. Mark N at NORTH point.

Please consider the following TITLE EXCEPTIONS in value:

Please consider the following
Equipment in value:

LEASEHOLD   Ground Rent *(Per Yr)* $ Lease is: ☐ 99 years   ☐ Renewable   ☐ FHA Approved   Expires

BUILDER/SELLER'S AGREEMENT: All Houses: The undersigned agrees to deliver to the purchaser FHA's statement of appraised value. Proposed Construction: The undersigned agrees, upon sale or conveyance of title within one year from date of initial occupancy, to deliver to the purchaser FHA Form 2544, warranting that the house is constructed in substantial conformity with the plans and specifications on which FHA based its value and to furnish FHA a conformed copy with the purchaser's receipt thereon that the original warranty was delivered to him. All Houses: In consideration of the issuance of the commitment requested by this application, I (we) hereby agree that any deposit or downpayment made in connection with the purchase of the property described above, whether received by the undersigned or an agent of the undersigned, shall upon receipt be deposited in escrow or in trust or in a special account which is not subject to the claims of my creditors and where it will be maintained until it has been disbursed for the benefit of the purchaser or otherwise disposed of in accordance with the terms of the contract of sale.

Signature ☐ Mortgagee ☐ Builder ☐ Seller ☐ Other   19

MORTGAGEE'S CERTIFICATE: The undersigned mortgagee certifies that to the best of its knowledge all statements made in this application and the supporting documents are true, correct and complete.

Signature/Title of Mortgagee Officer: 19

WARNING: Section 1010 of Title 18, U.S.C., provides: "Whoever, for the purpose of . . . influencing such Administration . . . makes, passes, utters, or publishes any statement, knowing the same to be false . . . shall be fined not more than $5,000 or imprisoned not more than two years, or both."

FHA FORM NO. 2800-1 Rev 10/71   FHA COPY - FILE IN CASE BINDER

Figure 8-1

two programs have been suspended, the procedures do provide guidelines that can be expected to influence future programs.

Form 2800—Application for Property Appraisal. In practice, Form 2800 is prepared by the mortgagee in cooperation with the real estate broker and the seller. Access to the house must be arranged for the FHA appraiser to make his evaluation and determine what, if any, parts of the structure and equipment must be inspected by a registered craftsman. The appraiser makes his report directly to the FHA, citing repair and reconditioning requirements, and a valuation when the requirements are satisfied.

At this point, under a recently introduced experimental procedure, the FHA furnishes all the appraisal information to the mortgagee *except* the actual valuation. By this method the FHA is attempting to reduce the use of its agency as an appraisal facility and to minimize the accusations of setting prices on houses, which is not its business. However, if a bona fide earnest money contract is submitted with Form 2800 showing a sales price, the FHA will release all data, including its valuation and the insured commitment amount. The FHA appraisers are expected to consider the actual sales price in making their evaluation and have some leeway in trying to agree with the price contracted for. This is the procedure more commonly used in conventional lending wherein an appraisal is sought *after* the price has been agreed upon—and the FHA is following that practice.

Certifications. Because of the discovery of some abuses in handling practices, primarily in the New York area in early 1972, the FHA added a number of extra requirements to prevent the sale of deteriorated houses as sound property, and to eliminate speculative profiteering at the expense of an uninformed buyer. The initial rules were somewhat of an overreaction to the problems, as the great majority of the FHA offices, mortgagees, brokers, and sellers had always abided by the guidelines established. Furthermore, the extra cost in time and money forced many sellers out of the FHA market and deprived deserving people of the assistance they needed to buy homes.

The many requirements for having all plumbing, electrical wiring, heating, air conditioning, and roofs inspected, repaired, and warranted were reduced to only such items as were specified by the FHA appraiser and were applicable to existing homes only. And further, the FHA agreed to pay for the first inspection themselves. A list of approved inspecting contractors is available for this purpose, and the fee is fixed by the FHA.

On the following pages are some reproductions of the certifications that may be required to be made, which are limited to plumbing, heating, air conditioning, roofing, and electrical wiring. The warranty is reduced to the condition as of the date of inspection—not for future operations. However, if problems are discovered in the facility, repairs must be accomplished and a further inspection made before FHA approval can be given. Any work so required is at the expense of the seller.

In practice, the FHA tries to condition their appraisals upon the repair of all deficiencies that are in evidence and to virtually eliminate the necessity for these certifications. The repairs that may be called for are spelled out under the commitment requirements attached to Form 2800–6 (Statement of Appraised Value), which is returned to the mortgagee.

Form 2900—Application for Mortgagor Approval. On page 172 is the FHA Form 2900 used to identify the buyer-borrower as to his family, employment, income, assets, and liabilities. With this information in hand, the mortgagee can then determine the borrower's income in relation to future monthly payments and his assets available for closing costs. The information needed to determine the applicant's qualifications is taken from the borrower by the mortgagee's representative. Verifications of bank balances and employment are needed.

Most of the form is self-explanatory as to the information requested. There are several guidelines used in determining actual qualifications. But the rules cannot cover all of the

PLUMBING

Contractor's Name: FHA Case No. _____

Address:

▱ First inspection at HUD expense. Check box 1 or 4 as appropriate.

▱ Subsequent inspection (if necessary) at Seller's expense. Check box 1 and box 2 or 3 as appropriate.

A qualified plumber employed by this firm has carefully inspected the plumbing system of the dwelling located at:

_____

▱ 1. The inspection reveals that:

      (a) The plumbing system is consistent with the code enforcement standards applicable to this jurisdiction.

      (b) All fixtures operate properly.

      (c) The piping appears to be in sound condition.

      (d) The water heater functions satisfactorily, and is equipped with properly installed temperature and pressure relief valve.

▱ 2. The following repairs were considered necessary and have been completed in a workmanlike manner. (List repairs.)

▱ 3. The following equipment has been replaced, using good quality new material, installed in a workmanlike manner, and a written warranty (if appropriate) has been furnished the mortgagee for delivery to the purchaser of this property. (List equipment replaced.)

▱ 4. This inspection reveals the following deficiencies requiring correction:

I certify that I am authorized to sign this certification on behalf of _____
_____ and that, by the signature hereinafter made,
_____ is duly bound under the terms and conditions of the
certification.

I further certify that I have no interest, present or prospective in the property, buyer, seller, broker, mortgagee or any other party involved in the transaction. Only the condition of the system as of this date is warranted by this inspection.

Date: _____   EMPLOYER'S ID #_____

                                           or

Signature:_____

                                    SOCIAL SECURITY NO._____

Title: _____

WARNING

Section 1010 of Title 18, U.S.C, "Federal Housing Administration transactions," provides: "Whoever, for the purpose of -- influencing in any way the action of such Administration -- makes, passes, utters, or publishes any statement, knowing the same to be false -- shall be fined not more than $5,000 or imprisoned not more than two years, or both." Other Federal Statutes provide severe penalties for any fraud as intentional misrepresentation made for the purpose of influencing the issuance of any guaranty or insurance or the making of any loan by the Administrator for Veterans Affairs.

                                          Val. #101

Figure 8-2

HEATING AND AIR CONDITIONING

Contractor's Name: FHA Case No._____

Address:

☐ First inspection at HUD expense. Check box 1 or 4 as appropriate.

☐ Subsequent inspection (if necessary) at Seller's expense. Check box 1
   and box 2 or 3 as appropriate.

A qualified mechanic employed by this firm has carefully inspected the heating
and air conditioning system of the dwelling located at:

_____

☐ 1. This inspection reveals that the heating and air conditioning system
        is functioning properly and is capable of furnishing adequate service
        for this dwelling.

☐ 2. The following repairs were considered necessary and were completed in
        a workmanlike manner. (List repairs.)

☐ 3. The following new equipment was considered necessary, and was installed
        in a workmanlike manner. A written warranty (if appropriate) has been
        furnished the mortgagee for delivery to the purchaser of this property.
        (List equipment replaced.)

☐ 4. This inspection reveals the following deficiencies required correction:

I certify that I am authorized to sign this certification on behalf of:
_____ and that, by the signature hereinafter
made, _____ is duly bound under the terms and
conditions of the certification.

I further certify that I have no interest, present or prospective, in the property,
buyer, seller, broker, mortgagee or other party involved in the transaction. Only
the condition of the system as of this date is warranted by this inspection.

Date: _____   Employer's I.B.#_____

Signature: _____   or

Title: _____   SOCIAL SECURITY #_____

WARNING

Section 1010 of Title 18, U.S.C., "Federal Housing Administration transactions,"
provides: "Whoever, for the purpose of -- influencing in any way the action of
such Administration -- makes, passes, utters, or publishes any statement, knowing
the same to be false -- shall be fined not more than $5,000 or imprisoned not more
than two years, or both." Other Federal Statutes provide severe penalties for any
fraud as intentional misrepresentation made for the purpose of influencing the
issuance of any guaranty or insurance or the making of any loan by the Administrator for Veterans Affairs.

                                        Val.#104

Figure 8-3

<u>ROOFING</u>

Contractor's Name: FHA Case No._____

Address:

[/]   First inspection at HUD expense. Check box 1 or 4 as appropriate.

[/]   Subsequent inspection (if necessary) at Seller's expense. Check box 1 and box 2 or 3 as appropriate.

A qualified roofer employed by this firm has inspected the roof of the dwelling located at:

_____

[/]   1.   This inspection reveals that the roof and roof covering is in satisfactory condition with no evidence of leaks.

[/]   2.   The following repairs were considered necessary and have been completed in a workmanlike manner. (List repairs made.)

[/]   3.   This dwelling has been re-roofed using the following material:

         The roofing was applied in a workmanlike manner and a written warranty has been furnished the mortgagee for delivery to the purchaser of this property.

[/]   4.   This inspection reveals the following deficiencies requiring correction:

I certify that I am authorized to sign this certification on behalf of _____
_____ and that, by the signature hereinafter made,
_____ is duly bound under the terms and conditions of the
certification.

I further certify that I have no interest, present or prospective, in the property, buyer, seller, broker, mortgagee or other party involved in the transaction. Only the condition of the system as of this date is warranted by this inspection.

Date:_____   EMPLOYER'S ID #_____

Signature: _____   OR

Title: _____   SOCIAL SECURITY #_____

Figure 8—4

<u>ELECTRICAL</u>

Contractor's Name: FHA Case No._____

Address:

[ ]   First inspection at HUD expense. Check box 1 or 4 as appropriate.

[ ]   Subsequent inspection (if necessary) at Seller's expense. Check box 1 and
      box 2 or 3 as appropriate.

A qualified electrician employed by this firm has inspected the electrical system
of the dwelling located at:

_____

[ ]   1.   This inspection reveals that this system is consistent with the code
           enforcement standards applicable to this jurisdiction; that all visible
           wiring is properly installed and is in good condition, and that the
           service is adequate for the connected load.

[ ]   2.   The following repairs were considered necessary and have been completed
           in a workmanlike manner. (List repairs made.)

[ ]   3.   The following equipment has been replaced using good quality new
           material, installed in a workmanlike manner, in accordance with the
           local code, and a written warranty (if appropriate) has been furnished
           the mortgagee for delivery to the purchaser of this property. (List
           equipment replaced.)

[ ]   4.   This inspection reveals the following deficiencies requiring correction:

I certify that I am authorized to sign this certification on behalf of _____
_____ and that, by the signature hereinafter made,
_____ is duly bound under the terms and conditions of
the certification.

I further certify that I have no interest, present or prospective, in the property,
buyer, seller, broker, mortgagee or any other party involved in the transaction.
Only the condition of the system as of this date is warranted by this inspection.

Date: _____   Employer's I.D.#_____

Signature: _____   or

Title: _____   Social Security #_____

WARNING

Section 1010 of Title 18, U.S.C., "Federal Housing Administration transactions,"
provides: "Whoever, for the purpose of -- influencing in any way the action of
such Administration -- makes, passes, utters, or publishes any statement, knowing
the same to be false -- shall be fined not more than $5,000 or imprisoned not more
than two years, or both." Other Federal Statutes provide severe penalties for any
fraud as intentional misrepresentation made for the purpose of influencing the
issuance of any guaranty or insurance or the making of any loan by the Administrator for Veterans Affairs.

Val.#103

Figure 8-5

Form Approved
OMB No. 63–R1062

U. S. DEPARTMENT OF HOUSING AND URBAN DEVELOPMENT FEDERAL HOUSING ADMINISTRATION	2. FHA Case No.

1.

MORTGAGEE'S APPLICATION FOR MORTGAGOR APPROVAL AND COMMITMENT FOR MORTGAGE INSURANCE UNDER THE NATIONAL HOUSING ACT

☐ SEC. 203(b) ☐ SEC.

3. PROPERTY ADDRESS

4. MORTGAGORS:

Husband_____ Age ____

Wife _____ Age ____

Address _____

Married	Yrs.	No. of Dependents		Ages	

Co-Mortgagor(s) _____ Age(s)_____

(Check One)
☐ White *(Non-Minority)*   ☐ American Indian   ☐ Spanish American
☐ Negro / Black   ☐ Oriental   ☐ Other Minority

5. MORTGAGEE - Name, Address & Zip Code   *(Please Type)*

(Please locate address within corner marks)

6.
MORTGAGE APPLIED FOR →

Mortgage Amount	Interest Rate	No. of Months	Monthly Payment Principal & Interest
$	%		$

7.

PURPOSE OF LOAN: . . .   ☐ Finance Constr. on Own Land   ☐ Finance Purchase   ☐ Refinance Exist. Loan   ☐ Finance Impr. to Exist. Prop.   ☐ Other

MORTGAGOR WILL BE: .   ☐ Occupant   ☐ Landlord   ☐ Builder   ☐ Escrow Commit. Mortgagor

8. EMPLOYMENT

Husband's occupation_____

Employer's name & address_____

_____years employed_____

Wife's occupation_____

Employer's name & address_____

_____years employed_____

9. MONTHLY INCOME

Husband's base pay . . . . $_____

Other Earnings (explain) . . . . _____

Wife's base pay . . . . _____

Other Earnings (explain) . . . . _____

Gross Income, Real Estate . . . . _____

Other (explain). . . . . _____

TOTAL $_____

10. PREVIOUS MONTHLY HOUSING EXPENSE

Mortgage payment or rent . . . .$_____

Fire Insurance. . . . . _____

Taxes, special assessments . . . . _____

Maintenance . . . . _____

Heat & Utilities. . . . . _____

Other (explain) . . . . _____

TOTAL $_____

11. PREVIOUS MONTHLY FIXED CHARGES

Federal, State & Local income taxes . . . . $_____

Prem. for$_____Life Insurance . . . . . . _____

Social Security & Retirement Payments . . . . _____

Installment account payments. . . . . _____

Operating Expenses, other Real Estate . . . . _____

Other (explain) . . . . _____

TOTAL $_____

12. ASSETS FOR CLOSING

Cash accounts_____ $_____

Marketable securities _____

Other (explain)_____ _____

OTHER ASSETS   (A) TOTAL $_____

Cash deposit on purchase . . . . _____

Other (explain)_____ _____

_____ _____

_____ _____

(B) TOTAL $_____

13. LIABILITIES

	Monthly Payt.	Unpd. Bal.
Automobile. . . . . $	$	
Debts, other Real Estate.		
Life Insurance Loans		
Notes payable.		
Credit Union		
Retail accounts.		
TOTAL $		$

14. FUTURE MONTHLY PAYMENTS

(a) Principal & Interest. . . . . $_____

(b) FHA Mortgage Insurance Premium . . . . _____

(c) Ground rent (Leasehold only) . . . . _____

(d) TOTAL DEBT SERVICE (a+b+c). . . . . _____

(e) Fire Insurance . . . . _____

(f) Taxes, special assessments . . . . _____

(g) TOTAL MTG. PAYT. (d+e+f) . . . . _____

(h) Maintenance . . . . _____

(i) Heat & utilities . . . . _____

(j) TOTAL HSG. EXPENSE (g+h+i) . . . . _____

(k) Other recurring charges (explain) . . . . _____

(l) TOTAL FIXED PAYT. (j+k). . . . . $_____

15. SETTLEMENT REQUIREMENTS

(a) Existing debt (Refinancing only) . . . . $_____

(b) Sale price (Realty only) . . . . _____

(c) Repairs & Improvements . . . . _____

(d) Closing Costs . . . . _____

(e) TOTAL (a+b+c+d) . . . . _____

(f) Mortgage amount . . . . _____

(g) Mortgagor's required investment(e−f) . . . . _____

(h) Prepayable expenses . . . . _____

(i) Non-realty & other items . . . . _____

(j) TOTAL REQUIREMENTS (g+h+i) . . . . _____

(k) Amt. pd. ☐ cash ☐ Other (explain) . . . . _____

(l) Amt. to be pd. ☐ cash ☐ Other (explain) . . . . _____

(m) Tot. assets available for closing (12A) . . . . $_____

16. Do you own other Real Estate ☐ Yes ☐ No   Is it to be sold ☐ Yes ☐ No   FHA mortgage ☐ Yes ☐ No   Sales Price $_____   Orig-Mtg. Amt $_____

Unpaid Bal. $_____   Address_____   Lender_____

17. MORTGAGOR'S CERTIFICATE-- I ☐ have ☐ have not received a copy of the FHA Statement of Value (FHA Form 2800-6) or Veterans Administration Certificate of Reasonable Value (VA Form 26-1843) showing the estimated value of the property described in this application. Have you sold a property within the last 2 years which had an FHA mortgage?☐ Yes ☐ No. If "Yes" was the mortgage paid in full? ☐ Yes ☐ No. If "No" give FHA Case Number

_____, buyer's name_____, property address_____, date of transfer_____,

lender's name and address_____original mortgage amount $_____,

unpaid balance when sold $_____. Did buyer intend to occupy? ☐ Yes ☐ No.Have you ever been obligated on a home loan, home improvement loan or a mobile home which resulted in foreclosure, transfer of title in lieu of foreclosure, or judgement?☐ Yes ☐ No. If "Yes" attach statement giving full details including date, property address, name and address of lender, FHA or VA Case Number, if any, and reasons for the action. If dwelling to be covered by this mortgage is to be rented, is it a part of, adjacent or contiguous to any project, subdivison, or group of rental properties involving eight or more dwelling units in which you have any financial interest? ☐ Yes ☐ No ☐Not to be rented. If "Yes" give details. Do you own four or more dwelling units with mortgages insured under any title of the National Housing Act? ☐ Yes ☐ No. If "Yes" submit FHA Form 2561. The Mortgagor certifies that all information in this application is given for the purpose of obtaining a loan to be insured under the National Housing Act and is true and complete to the best of his knowledge and belief. Verification may be obtained from any source named herein.

Signature(s)_____   Date_____ 19___

18. MORTGAGEE'S CERTIFICATE- The mortgagee certifies that all information in this application is true and complete to the best of its knowledge and belief. Signature_____   Date:_____ 19___

WARNING: Section 1010 of Title 18, U. S. C., "Federal Housing Administration transactions," provides: "Whoever, for the purpose of . . .influencing in any way the action of such Administration . . .makes, passes, utters, or publishes any statement, knowing the same to be false . . .shall be fined not more than$5,000 or imprisoned not more than two years, or both."

FHA FORM NO. 2900-1 Rev. 10/71   FHA COPY - FILE IN CASE BINDER

Figure 8–6

variations to be found in the different applicants, and in the final analysis, it is the experienced judgment of the FHA underwriting department that must weigh the factors and make a decision. There are no computers—it is an individual human judgment. If the applicant feels a negative judgment has been made in error, the FHA will reopen the file to any new information that could be considered and make a new determination.

All the information submitted by the mortgagee and applicant is not always accepted at full value by the FHA, which is one reason a rejection can be misunderstood. Figure 8–7 is a copy of Form 2900–2, which is the credit analysis used by the FHA. The difference between Form 2900–1, which is the submittal form, and 2900–2, the analysis form, is primarily in the space provided to recalculate #9 (effective income), #14 (future monthly payments), and #15 (settlement requirements), plus the ratios and mortgagor rating near the bottom.

Effective Income (2900–2 #9). By the FHA rules, the mortgagor's effective income is the estimated amount of the mortgagor's earning capacity that is likely to prevail during the early period of the mortgage risk, that being approximately one-third of the term of the loan. Although the income reported is confirmed, there may be reasons why the total amount cannot logically be considered a sound basis for future house payments. When the income is temporary in character, or is not of an assured nature, such as child care, the FHA must reduce the stated effective income in its analysis. Also, the FHA deducts its estimate of federal income taxes to arrive at its own figure of net effective income.

This estimate of effective income does not attempt to evaluate the possibility of future decrease in income due to weakness of an employer or type of employment—that factor is rated under item #18 (stability of effective income).

More and more wives are taking jobs to help the family improve its standard of living, and in the lower income groups this becomes almost a necessity. The principal element of mortgage risk in allowing the income of working wives to be classified as effective income is the possibility

U. S. DEPARTMENT OF HOUSING AND URBAN DEVELOPMENT FEDERAL HOUSING ADMINISTRATION	2. FHA Case No. ▲

1. SPECIAL PROCESSING ▲
1. ☐ Veteran   2. ☐ Assistance Payment   4. ☐

CREDIT ANALYSIS PAGE
MORTGAGE TO BE INSURED UNDER   **2**
☐ SEC. 203(b) ☐ SEC.

5.

3. PROPERTY ADDRESS

4. MORTGAGORS:
Husband _____ Age ▲ ___
Wife _____ Age ▲ ___
Address _____

Married ▲ Yrs.   No. of Dependents ▲   Ages ▲
Co-Mortgagor(s) _____ Age(s) ▲
▲ *(Check One)*
1 ☐ White *(Non-Minority)*   3 ☐ American Indian   5 ☐ Spanish American
2 ☐ Negro / Black   4 ☐ Oriental   6 ☐ Other Minority

6. MORTGAGE APPLIED FOR →	Mortgage Amount $	Interest Rate %	No. of Months	Monthly Payment Principal & Interest $

7.
PURPOSE OF LOAN: . ▲   Finance Constr. ☐ on Own Land   Finance ☐ Purchase   Refinance ☐ Exist. Loan   Finance Impr. ☐ to Exist. Prop.   ☐ Other
MORTGAGOR WILL BE: ▲   ☐ Occupant   ☐ Landlord   ☐ Builder   ☐ Escrow Commit. Mortgagor

8. EMPLOYMENT	9. EFFECTIVE INCOME	MONTHLY INCOME
Husband's occupation _____	▲$ .... Husband's base pay	$ _____
Employer's name & address _____	.... Other Earnings	_____
_____	.... Wife's base pay	_____
_____ years employed _____	.... Other Earnings	_____
Wife's occupation _____	..... Income, other Real Estate	_____
Employer's name & address _____	.... Other	_____
_____	▲ .... TOTAL	▲$ _____
_____ years employed _____	..... Less Federal Income Tax	_____
	▲$ NET EFFECTIVE INCOME	

10. PREVIOUS MONTHLY HOUSING EXPENSE	11. PREVIOUS MONTHLY FIXED CHARGES
Mortgage payment or rent ....$ _____	Federal, State & Local income taxes .... $ _____
Fire Insurance ..... _____	Prem. for $ _____ Life Insurance _____
Taxes, special assessments .... _____	Social Security & Retirement Payments .... _____
Maintenance .... _____	Installment account payments .... _____
Heat & Utilities .... _____	Operating Expenses, other Real Estate .... _____
Other (explain) .... _____	Other (explain) .... _____
TOTAL $ _____	TOTAL $ _____

12. ASSETS FOR CLOSING	13. LIABILITIES	Monthly Payt.	Unpd. Bal.
Cash accounts _____ $ _____	Automobile .... $ _____	$ _____	
_____	Debts, other Real Estate		
Marketable securities _____	Life Insurance Loans		
Other (explain) _____	Notes payable		
OTHER ASSETS (A) TOTAL $ _____	Credit Union		
Cash deposit on purchase .... _____	Retail accounts		
Other (explain) _____	_____		
_____	_____		
(B) TOTAL $ _____	TOTAL $ _____	$ _____	

14. FUTURE MONTHLY PAYMENTS	15. SETTLEMENT REQUIREMENTS
(a) Principal & Interest .... $ _____ $ _____	(a) Existing debt (Refinancing only) . $ _____ $ _____
(b) FHA Mortgage Insurance Premium · _____	(b) Sale price (Realty only) .... _____ ▲ _____
(c) Ground rent (Leasehold only) ..... _____	(c) Repairs & Improvements .... _____
(d) TOTAL DEBT SERVICE (a+b+c).. _____	(d) Closing Costs .... _____ ▲ _____
(e) Fire Insurance .... _____	(e) TOTAL (a+b+c+d) .... _____ ▲ _____
(f) Taxes, special assessments ..... _____ ▲ _____	(f) Mortgage amount .... _____
(g) TOTAL MTG. PAYT. (d+e+f) ..... _____ ▲ _____	(g) Mortgagor's required investment(e-f) _____
(h) Maintenance .... _____ ▲ _____	(h) Prepayable expenses .... _____
(i) Heat & utilities .... _____	(i) Non-realty & other items .... _____
(j) TOTAL HSG. EXPENSE (g+h+i) ... _____ ▲ _____	(j) TOTAL REQUIREMENTS (g+h+i) .. _____
(k) Other recurring charges (explain) _____	(k) Amt. pd. ☐ cash ☐ Other (explain) _____
(l) TOTAL FIXED PAYT. (i+k) .... $ _____ ▲$ _____	(l) Amt. to be pd. ☐ cash ☐ Other (explain) _____
	(m) Tot. assets available for closing(12(A)) $ _____

16. Do you own other Real Estate ☐ Yes ☐ No   Is it to be sold ☐ Yes ☐ No   FHA mortgage ☐ Yes ☐ No   Sales Price $ _____   Orig-Mtg. Amt $ _____
Unpaid Bal. $ _____   Address _____   Lender _____

17. RATIOS: Loan to Value _____ % : Term to Remain. Econ. Life _____ % : Total Payt. to Rental Value _____ % : Debt Serv. to Rent Inc. _____ %

18. MORTGAGOR RATING _____
Credit Characteristics _____ Motivating Interest in Ownership _____ Importance of Monetary Interest _____
Adequacy of Available Assets _____ Stability of Effective Income _____ Adequacy of Effective Income _____

Remarks:

Examiner: _____   Reviewer: _____   Date: _____   19 _____

FHA FORM NO. 2900-2 Rev. 10/71   FHA COPY - FILE IN CASE BINDER

Figure 8–7

174

of its interruption by maternity leave. But the motivation would be to return to work, and so a wife's income is generally acceptable.

When the wife's income is established by length of employment and/or placement in a particular position for which she has had special training, her income is fully allowed. If the continuity of her income appears questionable and cannot be allowed, it is possible in some cases to consider her income as an offset to temporary nonrecurring obligations.

The FHA approaches other than base salary income in about the same way as do conventional lenders; i.e., overtime is not acceptable income unless supported by long experience with a reasonable expectation to continue; and commission or fee types of income are acceptable for an amount that can be stabilized over a longer period of time than would ordinarily be required. An owner of a business would be allowed the amount he withdraws as salary or withdrawals, providing this amount does not exceed actual earnings.

Money received for travel expenses cannot be considered as effective income, nor can contributions received, nor the payments received on principal in repayment of a capital investment. And in calculating Federal Income Tax, the FHA bases its estimate on the *effective* income rather than on the current income.

Future Monthly Payments (#2900–2 #14). The monthly payments for debt service, taxes, and insurance are added to reach the total mortgage payment [item #14(g)]. To this total is added the anticipated maintenance and the heat and utilities [items #14(h) and (i)]. These amounts are estimated by the FHA appraiser and reported in the valuation report returned to the mortgagee. Item #14(k) for other recurring charges includes such items as premiums on life insurance, compulsory contributions to retirement funds, payments on other loans or on real estate (that is, property not to be sold as a part of this transaction), and payments on installment accounts. The last item is not included if the debt is of a nonrecurring nature and will be paid off in less than a year. Car payments for someone who uses the car in his work would be considered a recurring payment.

Settlement Requirements (2900–2 #15). Each application must have an estimate of the net amount of cash needed to close the transaction. Basically, this is the difference between the sales price plus closing costs and the earnest money plus mortgage proceeds. As shown in Form 2900–2, the FHA reserves a separate column for its own calculations.

The sales price would be determined by the sales contract. If the seller agrees to pay any closing costs normally paid by the buyer, and if any nonrealty items such as furniture or a television set are included in the contract sales price, then these would be deducted to determine the actual sales price. The FHA does not insure loans on nonrealty items.

Repairs and improvements, #15(c), include the cost of any repairs or improvements proposed by the mortgagor plus the estimated costs of any additional repairs called for in the appraisal requirements to bring the property up to acceptable standards.

Under closing costs, #15(d), are included the items incidental to the acquisition and financing of the property. These would include the FHA examination fee, the mortgagee's initial service charge, the cost of mortgagee's title policy, charges for preparation of the mortgage documents, recording fees, and similar items. Closing costs do not include the prepaid items, which are the tax and insurance deposits.

The prepayable expenses, #15(h), are the deposits to cover unaccrued taxes, hazard insurance, and mortgage insurance. These are not considered part of the acquisition costs but must be included to determine the adequacy of available assets for settlement. The FHA has no set requirements as to the size of the deposits, which vary from one to three months of the yearly costs incurred, but it does insist that the mortgagee maintain a consistent policy. In the case of maintenance fees that are assessed on an annual basis, these too must be included in the prepaid deposits and collected monthly. This practice is becoming more common in townhouses.

Item #15(i), nonrealty and other items, is where the value of any furniture, appliances, etc., is added back in to show the actual total requirements needed for settlement. The mortgage amount, item #15(f), is calculated on the value of the realty only.

Items #15(k) and #15(l) reflect the amount of money or other value (such as a lot traded) already paid by the mortgagor and the amount to be paid at closing. For item #15(m), the amount shown from item #12(a), total current assets, is entered and used to determine adequacy in meeting the cash requirements. The so-called "sweat equity," the cost of actual work done on the property by the mortgagor, is acceptable to apply against closing costs, prepayment, or down payment, if it is reasonably valued.

In reviewing the credit analysis thus far, the settlement requirements must be met in full without resort to any secondary borrowing. If a recent loan appears in the record with the loan proceeds held in a bank account for obvious settlement purposes, the applicant will be rejected. On the income versus monthly payments relationship, the FHA has a general rule that total fixed obligations, item #14(1), should not exceed 50% of the net effective income (that is, FHA's calculated effective income); or the total housing expense, item #14(j), should not exceed 30% of the net effective income. As in many of these rules, this too is a guideline. If other factors of credit, such as assets available, manner of living, etc., add strength to the borrower, he still could be approved.

As a final guide to acceptance or rejection of the applicant, the FHA makes an extensive review of the many variables involved and produces an "evaluation of mortgagor risk." This is item #18 on the credit analysis and covers six features:

1. Credit characteristics
2. Motivating interest in ownership
3. Importance of monetary interests
4. Adequacy of available assets
5. Stability of effective income
6. Adequacy of effective income.

The scale of grading runs as follows: 1, Excellent; 2, Good; 3, Fair; 4, Poor, and 5, Reject. Grading is a matter of the underwriter's judgment based on the facts presented through the analysis outlined above in Form 2900–2. Often direct contact is made by the FHA with involved parties to clarify or enlarge on a particular item of information. If any of the six features rates a "reject," the applicant will be turned down. An explanation of the reasons may be noted under the "remarks" column by the examiner, for record purposes.

A review is always possible after a rejection if the mortgagee or applicant feels that a mistake has been made or if new information is available to cast further light on any problem area.

Section 203(b)—Home Mortgage Insurance

Home mortgage insurance under Section 203(b) is the oldest and still the basic program with which the FHA determines qualifications for insured commitments. This insurance can cover one- to four-family residences. The limit on the insurable amount is $33,000 for a one-family unit, $35,750 for two- or three-family units, and $41,250 for a four-family unit. If the buyer does not intend to live in the house, the maximum insurable amount is reduced to 85% of that available to an owner-occupant.

The amount of down payment required is 3% on the first $15,000 of the FHA estimate of property value and closing costs, 10% on the next $10,000, and 20% on any value over $25,000 up to maximum limits. If the buyer is a veteran, and this applies to a single-family unit only, then the down payment is reduced to zero for the first $15,000 of value, 10% for the next $10,000, and 15% for values over $25,000.

The term of the loan is for 30 years or three-quarters of the remaining economic life of the house as determined by the FHA appraiser, whichever is less. The 30-year term can be extended to 35 years if the mortgagor cannot qualify for 30-year term and if the property was constructed subject to FHA or VA inspection.

As an additional help to a buyer 60 years or older, the FHA permits borrowing of the down payment, settlement costs, and prepaid expenses from an approved corporation or individual. Under that age the buyer is expressly forbidden to borrow any of the cash requirements, as this would be considered secondary financing and cause for denial of insurance.

Section 221(d)(2)—Home Mortgage Insurance for Low and Moderate Income

This program is a modification of the same basic 203(b) plan with the exception of the cash requirements for closing. It also carries lower maximum loan limits. The requirements are intended as an additional assist in obtaining suitable housing for displaced families and for low- and moderate-income families. The maximum amount insurable is limited to $18,000 on a single-family house, or $21,000 if the house has four bedrooms and the family consists of five or more persons. There are other limits for two-, three-, and four-family units as well as higher limits in areas where cost levels require it.

The amount insured reflects the lower cash requirements. The rule states that for a low- or moderate-income family the insured commitment will be 100% of the FHA estimate of value and closing costs (prepays would be paid by the buyer), or 97% of the FHA estimate of value plus closing costs plus prepaid expenses—whichever of the two approaches gives the lesser loan commitment. If the family has been displaced, such as by freeway construction, urban renewal, or other acceptable criteria, a little larger loan commitment will be granted, thus reducing the cash required even more.

The net effect of the program, for example, would reduce the cash requirements on an $18,000 house from approximately $1000 under 203(b) to about $650 under 221(d)(2).

Section 235—Home Ownership for Lower Income Families

Section 235 is one of the newer subsidy programs to assist a lower income family to buy their own home. It is a program for people, not houses. There is no such thing as a "235 house." Any house built in accordance with FHA standard requirements is eligible under the program—except that it must sell for $18,000 or less. Or, if it is a four-bedroom house, it can sell for $24,000 to a family of five or more.

Since one of the expressed intentions of the 235 program was to spur much needed new housing, only a small portion of the allocated funds was made available for use in resale housing. Builders were expected to handle the greater part of this program and could, upon application, obtain a preliminary reservation for 235 funds from the FHA.

The basic requirement for qualification of a 235 subsidized interest payment for a potential home buyer is that his income must fall under a limit that is set at 135% of the rate used for public housing. On the following page is Form 3100, used to make application for a 235 subsidy payment. All family income is included under total annual income in these calculations, but the earnings of eligible minors are later deducted to arrive at the family's adjusted annual income. Also, to arrive at the adjusted annual income, a sum of 5% of the total annual income plus $300 for each eligible child is deducted from the annual income. For example, in Harris County, Texas, as of April 1971, a family of five could have no more than $7425 income (135% of public housing limits) plus $300 for each child in order to qualify. It is on the adjusted annual income that the amount of subsidy is based. The home buyer must agree to pay 20% of his *adjusted income* toward his house payment. The difference between this amount and the full mortgage payment is the subsidy paid by the government. But the subsidy cannot exceed the amount of the interest in excess of 1% per annum. Thus, the subsidy does not cover the principal payments. The subsidy money is paid directly to the mortgagee on a commitment for the 30-year life of the loan. However, the home owner, or mortgagor, must requalify his current income and adjust his subsidy payment annually.

The section 235 subsidy program was one of those suspended in January, 1973.

Section 237—Home Mortgage Insurance for Special Credit Risks

In order to assist families who have established a poor credit rating through bad money management or through circumstances beyond their control, this special program has been

FHA FORM NO. 3100 Rev. 11/70

Form Approved
Budget Bureau No. 63-R1209

U. S. DEPARTMENT OF HOUSING AND URBAN DEVELOPMENT
FEDERAL HOUSING ADMINISTRATION

Mortgagee's No.

A. FHA Case No.
▲

APPLICATION FOR HOME OWNERSHIP ASSISTANCE
UNDER SECTION 235 OF THE NATIONAL HOUSING ACT

C. Property Address:

B. Mortgagee-Name, Address and Zip Code *(Please Type)*

D. Mortgagor(s) Name(s):
Husband
or Head
Spouse
Co-Mortgagor(s)

▲ *(Check One)*

1 ☐ White *(Non-Minority)* 3 ☐ American Indian 5 ☐ Spanish American
2 ☐ Negro/Black 4 ☐ Oriental 6 ☐ Other Minority

E. EMPLOYMENT:

	(1) Occupation ▲	(2) Social Security No.	(3) Years Empl'd ▲	(4) Employer
Husband or Head				
Spouse				
Co-Mortgagor(s)				

F. HOUSEHOLD COMPOSITION AND ANNUAL INCOME:

					INCOME DURING LAST 12 MONTHS								Current Income	Expected Income	
Name	▲ Age	▲ Sex	Rela- tionship	Wages or Salary	▲RETIREMENT		▲ BENEFIT PAYMENTS			Total Last 12 Months *(sum of all entries)*			☐Wkly. ☐Mon. ☐Ann.	Next 12 Months	FHA Review
					1. Social Security	2. Other	1. Disa- bility	2. Unem- ployment	4. Welfare	Other					
1.			Husband or Head												
2.															
3.															
4.															
5.															
6.															
7.															
8. TOTAL ▲											(a)	(b)	(c)		

9. No. in Household ▲ _____

10. No. Eligible Minors ▲ _____ 12. No. of Dependents *(exclude spouse)* ▲ _____

11. No. Other Minors ▲ _____ 13. No. of Handicapped – – – – – – ▲ _____

	INCOME	FHA REVIEW
14. Total Annual Income *(F-8 (b) or (c))*– –▲	$	
(a) Less: 5 % of Tot. Ann. Inc. *(See Instr. 5)*		
(b) Less: Earnings of Eligible Minors _ _ _ _		
(c) Less: Eligible Minors *(F-10)* _____ x $ 300)		
15. Adjusted Annual Income – – – – – – – ▲	$	$
16. Adjusted Monthly Income *(15 ÷ 12)*– – –▲	$	$

H. HOME INSURANCE TRANSACTION: *(FROM FHA FORM NO. 2900)*

1. Sale Price – – – –▲ $_____ 4. Term in Months_____
2. Mortgage Amt.▲ $_____ 5. Interest Rate _____ %
3. Down Payment $_____ 6. Est. Mtg. Paym't $_____

I. ASSETS: *(ALL FAMILY MEMBERS)*

1. Cash – – – – – – – – – – – – – – – – – – –$_____
2. Checking or Savings Accounts – – – – – – – – –$_____
3. Bonds and Stocks *(include U. S. Saving Bonds)*– – – –$_____
4. Real Estate Holdings –
   (a) Original Sale Price – – –$_____
   (b) Less Unpaid Balance – – –$_____
   (c) Equity *(4(a) minus 4(b))*– – – – – – – – – – –$_____
5. Total Assets – – – – – – – – – – – – – – – ▲ $_____

G. ASSISTANCE CALCULATIONS:

1. Area Income Limit for this Family – – – – – – – – – ▲ $_____

2. Based on ▲☐ 135% of Public Housing
   ☐ 90% of 221 (d)(3)

		FHA REVIEW
3. Monthly Mortgage Payment *(H-6)* – – – –▲	$	$
4. 20% of Adj. Monthly Income *(F-16)* – – – –	$	$
5. Formula (1) for Mo. Subsidy *(G-3 minus G-4)*	$	$
6. Monthly Payment *(Principal + Int.+ MIP)*– –	$	$
7. Monthly Payment *(Principal + Int.+ @1%)*– –	$	$
8. Formula (2) for Mo. Subsidy *(G-6 minus G-7)*	$	$
9. Assist. Paymt. Auth. *(lesser of G-5 or G-8)*–▲	$	$
10. Mortgagor's Monthly Paymt.*(G-3 minus G-9)*▲	$	$

J. ASSETS ALLOWANCE:

1. Dependents *(F-12)* _____ x $ 500) – – – – – – – – –$_____
2. Annual Share of Mortgage Payment *(Mortgagor's Monthly Payment (G-10 x 12))*– – – – – – – – –$_____
3. If Mortgagor is 62 or Older, enter $5000 or if Mortgagor is less than 62, enter $2000– –$_____
4. Total Assets Allowance – – – – – – – – – – – – –$_____
   (Total Assets (I-5) may not exceed total Assets Allowance (J-4)

K. PROPERTY ELIGIBILITY: ▲

(a) Approved Prior to Beginning of -

☐ (11) New Construction.

☐ (12) Substantial Rehabilitation.

(b) Unit in Condominium or Cooperative not Previously Occupied in -

☐ (21) New Construction Completed within 2 years.

☐ (22) Substantial Rehabilitation within 2 years.

(c) Unit in Existing Dwelling - *(30 Series)* OR (d) Unit in Condominium or Cooperative Over 2 Years Old - *(40 Series)*
▲ When Occupants Qualify as one of the Following:

☐ (31) ☐ (41) Displaced Family.

☐ (32) ☐ (42) A Family with 5 or more Minors.

☐ (33) ☐ (43) Family Occupying Public Housing.

☐ (34) ☐ (44) Previous Owner or Cooperative Member Received Assistance Payments.

(e) Unit in Existing Project - (f) ☐ (60) Other Existing Dwelling.

☐ (50) Insured under Section 236.

☐ (52) Receiving Rent Supplement Payments.

L. CERTIFICATION:

I/we hereby certify that the foregoing information is true and complete to the best of my knowledge and belief. If the application results in approval of Assistance Payments, I/we agree to furnish the Mortgagee, on FHA Form 3101, the required recertification of family income and composition and occupancy of the property. Inquiries may be made to verify the statement herein. I/we fully understand that if we rent or sell this property, or cease to occupy it, I/we must immediately notify the lender in writing.

Date_____ Signatures_____

(Husband or Head) *(Spouse)*

WARNING Section 1001 of Title 18 of the United States Code makes it a Criminal Offense to make a willfully false statement or misrepresentation to any Department or Agency of the United States as to any matter within its jurisdiction.

M. REVIEW AND ELIGIBILITY: ▲ ▲ IF NOT ELIGIBLE CHECK REASON:

The above information has been reviewed and the applicant

☐ is ☐ is not eligible for Assistance Payments in an amount of $_____ per month.

1. ☐ Income Too High *(F-15 exceeds G-1)* 3. ☐ Property Ineligible
2. ☐ Assets *(I-5)* exceeds limits *(J-4)* 4. ☐ Other_____

Date_____ Signature_____

(FHA Official)

Figure 8–8

established. A low-income family, otherwise eligible for the regular FHA housing programs but unable to meet the credit requirements of those Sections, may apply under Section 237. The special form used is the same Form 3100 used for the Section 235 application. The limitations on maximum amount that can be insured are the same as under 235.

A special requirement under 237 is that the applicant must agree to accept budget advice, debt management, and related counseling with an acceptable nonprofit organization equipped for such service. The FHA makes its determination of eligibility for mortgage insurance based on a finding that the mortgagor should be able to make his monthly payments if he does receive proper counseling.

There is another restriction for the 237 applicant: the total of his monthly payment consisting of principal, interest, mortgage insurance premium, hazard insurance, and taxes cannot exceed 25% of the mortgagor's average annual income. This is mandatory and not a guideline as is a similar requirement in other programs, although sometimes the percentage limitation is raised to 30% or even higher if stabilizing factors warrant it.

VETERANS ADMINISTRATION

The popularly called G.I. Bill of Rights passed Congress in 1944. It was designed to give returning World War II veterans a better chance upon resuming civilian life than their fathers had after World War I. While the initial bill and subsequent additions provided numerous other benefits such as hospitalization, education, employment training, and unemployment benefits, our interest here will be confined to the home loan section.

Section 501 of the Act provides for a first mortgage real estate loan that is *partially* guaranteed by the Veterans Administration and is subject to the strict rules covering all phases of the loan: the borrower, the lender, the property, the interest, and the term and loan amount, plus collections and foreclosures. The primary interest of the VA is to aid the veteran, and to this end the rules are directed.

Unlike the FHA that *insures* up to 97% of some loans, the Veterans Administration *guarantees* a portion of the loan, which in effect covers a reasonable down payment for the lender. Since the VA does not require a veteran to pay any portion of the closing costs, forbids him to pay any discount, and eliminates the need for a down payment, many veterans can move into their houses with no cash requirements. In the beginning Congress set the maximum guarantee at $2000, which proved to be much too small. Over the years these limits have been increased periodically to improve the assistance program and to recognize inflationary pressures. In 1968 the present limits were set at 60% of the loan or a maximum of $12,500, whichever is least, less any guarantee already used.

Eligibility of Veteran

In handling a loan for a veteran, some of the principal problems come in properly qualifying him. Basically, he must be able to prove that he served in the armed forces for certain minimum periods at various intervals of hot and cold wars. Because of a rather continual change in these rules, the best way is to make application through the Veterans Administration for a Certificate of Eligibility. This Certificate will also show the amount of guarantee actually available to the veteran and is one of the instruments needed at closing the loan.

In regard to the amount of eligibility, if a veteran has never used his privilege, it would be $12,500 today. But, suppose a veteran had bought a $10,000 house in the early 1950s; his guarantee then would have been 60% of the $10,000 loan or $7500, whichever is least. So he would have "used" $6000 of the guarantee. He still has $1500 remaining to use; and in 1968 the increase to a $12,500 maximum gave him an additional $5000 of guarantee. Now he would actually have $6500 of guarantee remaining with which he might secure another house loan of perhaps $22,000.

There is considerable misconception about how a veteran may obtain a restoration of his eligibility to use the veteran's assistance program. A *release of liability* upon the sale of his house does *not* restore his entitlement to another guarantee.

There are two ways to achieve this restoration of eligibility: (1) a full payoff of the original loan, thus relieving the VA from further exposure, or (2) a compelling reason for the sale. On the latter point, the VA distinguishes between necessity and desire. Only necessity is accepted for a release, which would be such reasons as a change of jobs or medical requirements for a different climate. An increase in the size of the family is classified by the VA as "desire," not "necessity"!

The release of liability needs a special application, but the law does require the VA to grant the release if the veteran meets the following three requirements: (1) the loan must be current, (2) the purchaser must qualify as an acceptable credit risk, and (3) the purchaser must agree to assume the veteran's obligations on the property. It is good advice for a veteran to make the sale of his house contingent upon the VA acceptance of the purchaser and a release of liability for himself if the sale involves assumption of the GI loan. While the law specifies no time limit for obtaining the release of liability, once a sale is closed the veteran will find little interest from the new purchaser in helping him secure his release.

The reason that a release of liability alone does not restore the veteran's entitlement to a full guarantee again is that the VA remains liable under the original contract of commitment to the mortgagee. Only a payoff of the loan removes this exposure for the VA. But if the veteran is forced to sell for compelling personal reasons, and is so accepted by the VA, the veteran can recover his full entitlement and not be further penalized.

Form 26–1802a–Application for Home Loan Guaranty. Figure 8–9 shows Form 26–1802a, which is prepared by the loan originator for submission to the VA. The form incorporates the usual essential information on the amount and terms of the loan, the security being offered, the personal and financial status of the veteran, and the certifications by the veteran and the lender to make sure the veteran has been advised of the reasonable value of the property he wants to buy.

FORM APPROVED
BUDGET BUREAU NO. 76-R0515

VETERANS ADMINISTRATION **APPLICATION FOR HOME LOAN GUARANTY**	1A. VA LOAN NUMBER	1B. LENDER'S LOAN NO.

2A. NAME AND PRESENT ADDRESS OF VETERAN *(Include ZIP Code)*	2B. RACE OR ETHNIC ORIGIN OF VETERAN
	☐ WHITE *(Non-Minority)* ☐ NEGRO/BLACK ☐ SPANISH AMERICAN ☐ AMERICAN INDIAN ☐ ORIENTAL ☐ OTHER

3. NAME AND ADDRESS OF LENDER *(Include number, street or rural route, city or P.O., State and ZIP Code)*	2C. SOCIAL SECURITY NUMBER
	4. PROPERTY ADDRESS INCLUDING NAME OF SUBDIVISION LOT AND BLOCK NO. AND ZIP CODE

	5. AMOUNT OF LOAN	6A. INTEREST RATE	6B. PROPOSED MATURITY
		%	YRS. MOS.

The undersigned veteran and lender hereby apply to the Administrator of Veterans' Affairs for Guaranty of the loan described herein under Section 1810, Chapter 37, Title 38, United States Code to the full extent permitted by the veteran's available entitlement and severally agree that the Regulations promulgated pursuant to Chapter 37 and in effect on the date of the loan shall govern the rights, duties, and liabilities of the parties.

SECTION I — PURPOSE, AMOUNT, TERMS OF AND SECURITY FOR PROPOSED LOAN

7. PURPOSE OF LOAN — TO:		7a. PURCHASE CONDOMINIUM UNIT
☐ PURCHASE EXISTING HOME — PREVIOUSLY OCCUPIED ☐ CONSTRUCT A HOME-PROCEEDS TO BE PAID OUT DURING CONSTRUCTION ☐ PURCHASE EXISTING HOME — NOT PREVIOUSLY OCCUPIED		☐ NEW ☐ EXISTING

8. TITLE WILL BE VESTED IN	9. LIEN	10. ESTATE WILL BE:
☐ VETERAN ☐ VETERAN AND SPOUSE ☐ OTHER *(Specify)*	☐ 1st MORTGAGE	☐ FEE SIMPLE ☐ LEASEHOLD *(Show expiration date)*

11. ESTIMATED TAXES, INSURANCE AND ASSESSMENTS		12. ESTIMATED MONTHLY PAYMENT	
A. ANNUAL TAXES	$	A. PRINCIPAL AND INTEREST	$
B. AMOUNT OF HAZARD INSURANCE ON SECURITY		B. TAXES AND INSURANCE DEPOSITS	
C. ANNUAL HAZARD INSURANCE PREMIUMS		C. OTHER	
D. ANNUAL SPECIAL ASSESSMENT PAYMENT			
E. UNPAID SPECIAL ASSESSMENT BALANCE			
F. ANNUAL MAINTENANCE ASSESSMENT		D. TOTAL	$

SECTION II — PERSONAL AND FINANCIAL STATUS OF VETERAN

13. MARITAL STATUS	14. AGE OF SPOUSE	15. AGE(S) OF DEPENDENT(S)
☐ MARRIED ☐ WIDOWED ☐ DIVORCED ☐ SEPARATED ☐ NEVER MARRIED		

16. ASSETS		17. LIABILITIES *(Itemize all debts)*		
A. CASH *(Including deposit on purchase)*	$	NAME OF CREDITOR	MO. PAYMENT	BALANCE
B. SAVINGS BONDS, OTHER SECURITIES			$	$
C. REAL ESTATE OWNED				
D. AUTO				
E. FURNITURE AND HOUSEHOLD GOODS				
F. OTHER *(Use separate sheet, if necessary)*				
G. TOTAL	$			

18. Monthly Payment on Rented Premises Vet. Now Occupies					
A. RENT	B. UTILITIES INCLUDED ☐ YES ☐ NO		TOTAL	$	$

19. INCOME AND OCCUPATIONAL STATUS			20. ESTIMATED TOTAL COST	
ITEM	VETERAN	SPOUSE	ITEM	AMOUNT
A. OCCUPATION			A. PURCHASE EXISTING HOME	$
			B. ALTERATIONS, IMPRV., REPAIRS	
B. NAME OF EMPLOYER			C. CONSTRUCTION	
			D. LAND *(If acquired separately)*	
			E. PURCHASE OF CONDOMINIUM UNIT	
C. NUMBER OF YRS. EMPLOYED			F. PREPAID ITEMS	
			G. ESTIMATED CLOSING COST	
D. GROSS PAY	MONTHLY $	HOURLY $	MONTHLY $	HOURLY $	H. TOTAL COST *(Add items 20A through 20G)*	$
			I. LESS CASH FROM VETERAN	
E. OTHER INCOME	$	$	J. LESS OTHER CREDITS	
			K. AMOUNT OF LOAN	$

NOTE—IF LAND ACQUIRED BY SEPARATE TRANSACTION, COMPLETE ITEMS 21A AND 21B.	21A. DATE ACQUIRED	21B. UNPAID BALANCE $

SECTION III — CERTIFICATION *(Must be signed by veteran and lender)*

THE UNDERSIGNED VETERAN CERTIFIES THAT: (Complete Item 22A and Check Items 22B and 22F in all cases.) (Check Items 22C, 22D and 22E whenever the contract price or cost exceeds the VA reasonable value determination.)

22A. ☐ I have been informed that $ _____ is the reasonable value of the property as determined by the VA.

22B. ☐ I now actually occupy the property identified herein as my home or intend to move into and occupy it as my home within a reasonable period of time after completion of the loan.

22C. ☐ I was ☐ was not ☐ aware of the VA reasonable value determination when I signed my contract.

22D. ☐ Having been informed of the VA reasonable value determination, I do hereby represent that I desire to complete the transaction at the contract price or cost.

22E. ☐ I have paid or will pay in cash from my own resources at or prior to loan closing the difference between the contract price or cost and the VA reasonable value, and I do not now have and will not have outstanding after loan closing any unpaid contractual obligation on account of such cash payment.

22F. ☐ The foregoing information contained in these certifications and in Section II of this application are true and complete to the best of my knowledge and belief.

READ CERTIFICATION CAREFULLY — DO NOT SIGN APPLICATION UNLESS IT IS FULLY COMPLETED

23. DATE	24. SIGNATURE OF VETERAN *(Read certification carefully before signing)*

THE UNDERSIGNED LENDER CERTIFIES THAT: ALL INFORMATION REFLECTED IN THIS APPLICATION IS TRUE TO THE BEST OF MY KNOWLEDGE AND BELIEF.

25. DATE	26. NAME OF LENDER	27. TELEPHONE NO.	28. SIGNATURE AND TITLE OF OFFICER OF LENDER

FEDERAL STATUTES PROVIDE SEVERE PENALTIES FOR ANY FRAUD, INTENTIONAL MISREPRESENTATION, OR CRIMINAL CONNIVANCE OR CONSPIRACY PURPOSED TO INFLUENCE THE ISSUANCE OF ANY GUARANTY OR INSURANCE BY THE ADMINISTRATOR.

VA FORM 26-1802a
FEB. 1971

SUPERSEDES VA FORM 26-1802a, MAR. 1969
WHICH WILL NOT BE USED.

VA 2

Figure 8–9

Form Approved
Budget Bureau No. 63-RO267

VETERANS ADMINISTRATION
AND
U. S. DEPARTMENT OF HOUSING AND URBAN DEVELOPMENT
FEDERAL HOUSING ADMINISTRATION

REQUEST FOR VERIFICATION OF EMPLOYMENT

INSTRUCTIONS: LENDER - Complete Items 1 thru 7. Have applicant complete Item 8. Forward directly to employer named in Item 1.
EMPLOYER - Please complete Items 9 thru 16 and return directly to lender named in Item 2.

PART I - REQUEST

1. TO *(Name and address of employer)*	2. FROM *(Name and address of lender)*

3. SIGNATURE OF LENDER	4. TITLE	5. DATE	6. FHA OR VA NUMBER

I have applied for a mortgage loan and stated that I am or was employed by you. My signature below authorizes verification of this information.

7. NAME AND ADDRESS OF APPLICANT	8. SIGNATURE OF APPLICANT

PART II - VERIFICATION

EMPLOYMENT DATA	PAY DATA		

9A. IS APPLICANT NOW EMPLOYED BY YOU? *(If "Yes," complete Items 9B,10 and 11.)* ☐ YES ☐ NO *(If "No," complete Items 9B,9C,9D and 10.)*

12A. BASE PAY *(Enter amount and check period)* ☐ ANNUAL ☐ HOURLY ☐ MONTHLY ☐ OTHER ☐ WEEKLY *(Specify)* $

12C. TO BE COMPLETED FOR MILITARY PERSONNEL ONLY

9B. LENGTH OF APPLICANT'S EMPLOYMENT *(If Military, enter total service)*

PAY GRADE

12B. EARNINGS LAST 12 MONTHS		TYPE	MONTHLY AMOUNT
TYPE	AMOUNT	BASE PAY	$
BASE PAY	$	RATIONS	$
		FLIGHT OR HAZARD	$
OVERTIME	$	CLOTHING	$
COMMISSIONS	$	QUARTERS	$
		PRO PAY	$
BONUS	$	OVER SEAS OR COMBAT	$

9C DATE APPLICANT LEFT

9D. REASON FOR LEAVING

10. POSITION OR JOB TITLE

11. PROBABILITY OF CONTINUED EMPLOYMENT

13. REMARKS

The above information is provided in strict confidence in response to your request.

14. SIGNATURE OF EMPLOYER	15. TITLE	16. DATE

THE INFORMATION ON THIS FORM IS CONFIDENTIAL. IT IS TO BE TRANSMITTED DIRECTLY, WITHOUT PASSING THROUGH THE HANDS OF THE APPLICANT OR ANY OTHER PARTY.

☆ U.S. GOVERNMENT PRINTING OFFICE: 1972—779—070/2017

Figure 8–10

The application must be accompanied by a number of substantiating documents as follows:

1. A credit report on the veteran from an approved source.

2. Verification of employment as shown on page 186, which is a standard form used by both FHA and VA. Verifications are needed for both veteran and spouse, if employed, and must show the amount of regular income separately for overtime, commissions, and bonuses. The report should show probability of continued employment.

3. Verification of deposit on the form reproduced on page 188. This form is used to verify any cash assets claimed by the veteran.

4. A copy of the executed sales or construction contract.

5. The Certificate of Reasonable Value (CRV), Form 26-1813a, which is the appraised value as determined by the VA.

6. The veteran's Certificate of Eligibility, Form 26-1870. This is the statement that shows the veteran's eligibility for assistance and the amount of his entitlement, i.e., the amount of the guaranty available to him.

7. Any other data or documents as may be required by the VA office. Often clarifications are needed regarding the veteran, and statements giving acceptance of unusual conditions must be submitted.

Essential Qualifications for VA Loans

The concern of the Veterans Administration is to make sure that the veteran is assuming an obligation within his financial capability, that the property is fairly represented, and that the appraised value (CRV) is fully disclosed to him. As mentioned earlier, the VA is offering a program of assistance to the veteran as a part of the nation's expression of gratitude for his service. It would miss the mark if the veteran were burdened with an impossible debt load or with a grossly misrepresented house to live in. It is with these guidelines in mind that the VA underwriter analyzes the information submitted to him for approval of a home loan guaranty.

The lender on a VA loan can be classed as supervised or

Form Approved
OMB No. 63-R0266

VETERANS ADMINISTRATION
AND
U.S. DEPARTMENT OF HOUSING AND URBAN DEVELOPMENT
FEDERAL HOUSING ADMINISTRATION

REQUEST FOR VERIFICATION OF DEPOSIT

INSTRUCTIONS: LENDER – Complete Items 1 thru 7. Have applicant complete Items 8 and 9. Forward directly to bank or other depository named in Item 1.
ADDRESSEE – Please complete Items 10 thru 14. Return directly to Lender named in Item 2.

PART I – REQUEST

1. TO: (Name and Address of Bank or other Depository)	2. FROM: (Name and address of lender)

3. SIGNATURE OF LENDER	4. TITLE	5. DATE	6. FHA OR VA NUMBER

7. STATEMENT OF APPLICANT

A. NAME AND ADDRESS OF APPLICANT	B. TYPE OF ACCOUNT	BALANCE	ACCOUNT NUMBER
	CHECKING	$	
	SAVINGS	$	

I have applied for a mortgage loan and stated that my balances with the bank or other depository named in Item 1 are as shown in Item 7B.
My signature below authorizes verification of this information. Your response is solely a matter of courtesy for which no responsibility is
attached to your institution or any of your officers.

8. SIGNATURE OF APPLICANT	9. DATE

PART II – VERIFICATION

10A. DOES APPLICANT HAVE ANY OUTSTANDING LOANS?	11A. IS APPLICANT'S STATEMENT IN ITEM 7B CORRECT?
☐ YES ☐ NO (If "Yes," enter total in Item 10B)	☐ YES ☐ NO (If "No," complete Item 11B)

10B. TYPE OF LOAN	MONTHLY PAYMENT	PRESENT BALANCE	11B. CURRENT BALANCES	
			CHECKING ACCOUNT	SAVINGS ACCOUNT
SECURED	$	$	$	$
UNSECURED	$	$	12A. IS THE ACCOUNT LESS THAN TWO MONTHS OLD?	
			☐ YES ☐ NO (If "Yes," complete Item 12B)	
10C. PAYMENT EXPERIENCE			12B. DATE ACCOUNT WAS OPENED	
☐ FAVORABLE ☐ UNFAVORABLE (If unfavorable, explain in Remarks)				

13. REMARKS

The above information is provided in strict confidence in response to your request.

14A. SIGNATURE OF OFFICIAL OF BANK OR OTHER DEPOSITORY	14B. TITLE	14C. DATE

*THE INFORMATION ON THIS FORM IS CONFIDENTIAL. IT IS TO BE TRANSMITTED DIRECTLY, WITHOUT PASSING THROUGH THE
HANDS OF THE APPLICANT OR ANY OTHER PARTY.*

Figure 8–11

nonsupervised. A supervised lender is subject to periodic examination and supervision by a federal or state agency, such as savings and loan associations or insurance companies, and needs no further VA clearance. A nonsupervised lender is anyone else and must have prior VA approval in order to make the loan.

The property can be one to four units and must be used by the veteran borrower as his residence. The VA is normally very lenient in accepting less desirable properties if the veteran certifies to his knowledge of any shortcomings and still expresses a desire to buy the property. The VA until recently has always required its own appraisals of any property before issuing a guaranty commitment. But in some sections of the country experimental work has been going on to accept the same appraisals as used by the FHA.

Interest rates are set by Congress, which has empowered the Secretary of HUD to adjust the rates for the FHA, and the same rate is used by the director of the VA. But the VA has no mortgage insurance fee, and so any losses through foreclosures are collected from the veteran obligor and/or anyone else who assumes the indebtedness. Any discount on a VA guaranteed loan, and it is identical to the FHA scale as the interest rates are the same, must be paid by the seller as the veteran buyer is expressly forbidden to pay any premium for his loan.

The amount of the loan is not limited by the VA, only the amount of the guarantee. The *term* of the loan can be up to 30 years.

The servicing, or loan administration, of a GI loan is not prescribed, but mortgagees are expected to follow the normal standards and practices of prudent lenders. The VA encourages reasonable forbearance on the part of the mortgagee as the underlying aim is to assist the veteran. While there is no time limit on when a foreclosure action can be instituted after default, or a claim filed, the VA is very specific on the timely filing of a "notice of default" with them. Failure to file within the limits can cause a reduction in the guaranty for the mortgagee. The time limits for filing a notice of default are: (1) 60 days after nonpayment of an installment, (2) 90 days after demand for curative action under the mortgage terms other than nonpayment, and (3) 180 days for nonpayment of taxes. If foreclosure becomes necessary, the VA must first appraise the property and set a "specified value," which becomes the minimum amount for which the property can be sold, as a protection to all parties concerned.

Present Practices and New Programs

Now we come to a major point that has made the VA guarantee highly acceptable to lenders. The terms of the guaranty would permit the VA to pay the amount of the guaranty in cash to the mortgagee in case of foreclosure action, and force the lender to dispose of the property as best he could. However, in practice, the VA steps in when foreclosure becomes necessary, pays off the balance of the loan with interest and costs to the mortgagee, and takes title to the property itself, when necessary. Periodic listings of VA foreclosed houses available for resale are advertised in metropolitan daily papers. These must be handled through a VA-approved real estate broker, who is entitled to a 5% commission for handling the sale and closing the loan agreement for the VA.

One of the more recent additions to the veterans' loan program has been the handling of mobile homes. On this type of loan (and it must still meet the requirement of being the veteran's principal residence) the maximum amount is $10,000 for a term of 12 years. Interest is set at 10.75% simple interest, which is permitted in most states as it is considered consumer-type credit. There is also a package deal that permits the acquisition and preparation costs of a mobile home lot up to $7500 additional with a 7% interest rate. The guaranty for this program has been a maximum of 30%. It has not been well accepted as yet, primarily because of the lower guaranty allowed. Lenders feel there is a more rapid depreciation rate on a mobile home, and after deducting rig-up costs, the 30% guaranty provides too slim a margin of security.

Four major changes or additions were included in the Veterans Housing Act of 1970, passed in October of that year, indicating some new trends.

1. A program was instituted to put the VA into the mobile home business as described above.

2. A GI loan can now be secured to refinance an existing loan—this was not previously possible. It was designed to help the veteran whose eligibility had expired under previous laws, and who may have been forced into taking a higher cost conventional loan. In this particular loan, the veteran is permitted to pay any discount points necessary. However, the program has not found wide acceptance as refinancing is not often economical because of new closing costs, even at a lower interest rate.

3. All expiration dates for veterans' qualifications have been dropped.

4. A GI loan can be used to buy a condominium, provided one or more units in the same project have been sold under a government-underwritten program.

GOVERNMENT NATIONAL MORTGAGE ASSOCIATION

In the partitioning of the Federal National Mortgage Association in 1968, the Government National Mortgage Association was established as a part of the Department of Housing and Urban Development. GNMA presently operates from a single office in Washington, D.C. and, under a service agreement, uses all of the FNMA regional offices to handle its field requirements. For these services a fee is paid to FNMA. GNMA is authorized to develop programs as may be directed in the following two areas; (1) special assistance projects, and (2) management and liquidation.

Special Assistance Projects

The broad commission granted by the charter act of the GNMA for special assistance projects gives the President of the United States authority to direct the Association to make purchase commitments on certain types and categories of home mortgages as he may determine. The Association is authorized to buy such mortgages as are insured under other government programs and as may be committed by the

Secretary for Housing and Urban Development. Further, GNMA carries special authority to make mortgage purchases in housing programs for the armed services, in emergency areas, for below market-interest rate mortgages, and for construction advances; and most recently, under the "Tandem Plan" it is empowered to subsidize discounts on government-insured mortgages.

Tandem Plan

One of the important methods that GNMA has used to render special assistance to the housing market in times of tight money and high discounts on federally underwritten fixed-interest loans, is to provide a subsidy for payment of a portion of the discount. This is handled under the "tandem plan," which means the Association works in conjunction with the private lenders as a support mechanism rather than as a competitive purchaser of mortgages. Under the tandem plan, the Association early in 1971 established a purchase price of 97 for all Section 235 mortgages and par (100) for all Section 236 mortgages. As of August 6, 1971, the program was extended to new house loans at 96 and existing house loans at 95, with a limitation of $22,000 on such a loan, or $24,500 if the house is a four-bedroom unit and the family is five or more. The initial program has undergone several revisions.

In operation, the tandem plan is intended as a back-up measure and not as a means of outbidding the private investor. To accomplish this purpose, the plan offers two incentives for the mortgage banker to place his mortgage loan with private sources rather than dump the full load on GNMA.

First Incentive. When the mortgage banker buys, say a $100,000 commitment at 95 through FNMA for existing housing, he normally pays a half-point commitment fee. If, at the time of commitment, he asks for a "buy back" privilege from GNMA, the fee drops to 1/100th point (which goes to FNMA). Based on the market price of mortgage loans on the same commitment day, an "immediate selling price"

(ISP) is established. Let us say, for our example, that the ISP at this time is 93.50. Now, GNMA steps in and guarantees to pay 1.50 from its subsidy money to the mortgage banker (or any other authorized seller) for this loan package. The mortgage banker, in agreeing to the "buy back" privilege, has 45 days to decide what to do with his mortgages. If the market moves upward, say to 94 (the guarantee was at 93.50), the mortgagee can pick up some extra money by selling at the higher price to the private investor, and still collect his full 1.50 guarantee from GNMA.

Second Incentive. If GNMA does end up buying the mortgage commitment itself at the 95 price, there is no servicing contract granted. Normally, the mortgage banker earns .3% to .5% on the unpaid balance of a loan as a servicing fee for handling the collections and escrow accounts. It is a major source of income for the mortgage banker and is a strong reason to place a tandem plan loan into private channels where the servicing fee can be retained.

The tandem plan had barely been placed into operation in 1971 when interest rates on mortgage loans began to decline and very little subsidy money from the $2 billion then authorized was actually needed. The tandem plan alone had very little direct effect on interest rates at the time, as a slowing economy was the principal cause of the lower interest rates. But, the plan did provide a psychological indication of the government's intent to help reduce money costs for low-income house buyers.

Again, in 1973, the tandem plan was activated to give an assist to a declining housing industry suffering from high money costs.

Management and Liquidation of Loan Portfolio

Under the management and liquidating portion of GNMA operations, the Association carries the burden of orderly liquidation of the FNMA portfolio as of October 31, 1954. It is in the interest of the government to transfer these older mortgages into private financing channels as rapidly as possible and return the funds to the Treasury. Another major function under this section is the authority granted to GNMA to guarantee securities issued by the Association itself, or by any other issuer approved for this purpose, in the form of a full government guarantee.

Mortgage-Backed Securities

In an effort to provide greater liquidity to its own pool of mortgages and to tap the growing source of funds in the hands of pension and trust funds, GNMA devised a method to issue a separate certificate of guarantee covering a specific block of FHA, VA, or Farmers Home Administration mortgages, or combinations of these federally underwritten mortgages. The block of mortgages for this purpose can be assembled by a mortgage banker, or a group of them, or by any other approved lending institution in a minimum amount of $2 million. After examination of the block of mortgages by GNMA, if all are found to be in order, a certificate of guarantee is issued for the entire block. For a purchaser of the guarantee certificate, the purpose is to provide a security of a quality similar to a government bond and paying a slightly higher yield for a long term.

After the first four years of operations in this type of certificate, GNMA had guaranteed and sold over $7.5 billion of such securities. In the beginning of the program, most of the purchases had been made by thrift institutions. But, by fiscal year 1974, over 80% of these securities were being purchased by pension funds and other nonmortgage-oriented institutions at a rate of over $3 billion per year. The general public also participated in the purchase of certificates which are issued in smaller denominations.

Source of Money

The source of funds for GNMA purchases of mortgages is primarily the United States Treasury. The Chartering Act authorizes the Association to issue its obligations and the Secretary of the Treasury to purchase these obligations, redeemable within five years and at interest rates determined by the Secretary of the Treasury. Actual operating expenses of the Association must be paid for by fees collected on its transactions, and it is required to be self-supporting.

Continuing Role of GNMA

As an agent of the federal government, GNMA will continue to exercise considerable influence over real estate financing through its various moves in the residential mortgage market. The government effort is in the direction of (1) minimizing the fluctuations in mortgage money that directly affect the ability of the housing industry to operate on a stable basis, and (2) providing the housing the country needs. It can be generally stated that with each successive recession since the depression years of the 1930s, the swings have been a little less violent. While complete stability may neither be obtainable nor desirable, the role of GNMA will continue to be directed toward reducing the cycles and to provide various forms of assistance when money rates climb and the market falls off.

In striving to reduce the extent of housing cycles, GNMA provides the government with one more tool to utilize.

RESIDENTIAL LOAN ANALYSIS

GENERAL ANALYSIS OF LOANS

The process of analyzing and approving a loan is called *underwriting*. The individual who assembles and analyzes the necessary data, and usually gives his company's consent to a specific loan, is referred to as the *underwriter*. Properly underwriting any loan requires a complete analysis of all pertinent factors, including: (1) the borrower, his ability and willingness to pay; (2) the property, its condition, location, and usage; (3) all relevant economic influences; (4) laws controlling foreclosure procedures and assignments of rent; and (5) any unusual conditions that may exist.

An underwriter must try to foresee the future and estimate the continued stability of the borrower, and must also try to judge the future values in a specific property. The underwriter must look beyond a normal appraisal, which provides an estimate of past or present value, and weigh the forces that affect the future based on the experience of the underwriter in this field.

A loan analysis covers a wide assortment of information; and from these diverse elements, an underwriter must determine the degree of risk involved. There is no such thing as a risk-

free mortgage loan. It is the underwriter's prime responsibility to determine the magnitude of the risk, and to compensate for it in the terms and conditions of the loan. The degree
of risk determines the ratio of loan to value, the length of
time for repayment, and the interest rate required by the
lender.

In this and the two succeeding chapters, various classes
of properties, the economics involved, and the principal
sources of income to repay each type of loan will be discussed.

CONVENTIONAL RESIDENTIAL LOANS

In Chapter 8 on government programs the requirements for
and methods used by the FHA and VA in handling residential loans have been outlined. In conventional lending, the
procedures employed are basically not very different because
the goal is the same, namely, to make a sound loan, and this
requires adequate information. The variations in conventional lending lie chiefly in the multitude of interpretations
and special viewpoints that derive from the vast variety of
conventional lenders exercising their individual ideas regarding requirements.

Gradually, however, the individuality associated with conventional loans is giving way to an increasing effort to
conform with the outlines for loans prescribed by the secondary market operators. FNMA has its particular forms,
FHLMC requires certain procedures, and the private mortgage insurance companies have their own requirements. All
of these agencies have established minimum standards of
acceptability and maximum limits, which are subject to
change as conditions may require.

The expression "conventional loan" is simply a loan that
is not government-insured or government-guaranteed. Without such a government commitment, the conventional loan
stands more on its own; the credit-worthiness of the borrower
and the value of the property held as security become more
important to the ultimate lender. Until recently there was no
one else a lender could turn to in case of default on a conventional loan except the borrower and to foreclose the prop-

erty. Lenders in distant places were reluctant to accept loans that might require the management and disposal of a repossessed house in a remote place. It is in this area of relieving a lender of the post-foreclosure problems that the FHA and the VA gained strength and acceptability.

Beginning in 1971, during a period in which private mortgage insurance became a requirement for home loans in excess of 90%, conventional loans grew more acceptable to the large lending institutions in the secondary market. For the borrower, private mortgage insurance made higher loan-to-value ratios more readily available, which permitted lower down payments and broadened the potential market for homes.

Conventional residential loans may be categorized in many ways, including loan-to-value ratio, size of loan, type of property, location of property, and also the present or proposed usage of the property. Following is a discussion of the more important categories and elements affecting residential loans.

Loan-to-Value Ratio (LTVR)

The loan-to-value ratio denotes the amount of the loan as a percentage of the value of the property. The ratio applies to all types of loans. In line with this formula, the value of the property is the single variable. The most common definition of value favored by lenders is the appraised value of the property, or the selling price, whichever is the least. If a loan is being made where a sale is not involved, then the appraised value is the controlling factor.

Banking regulations have long permitted savings associations to make loans up to 90% of the property value, but many in the past have used a more conservative 80% limit. With the advent of low-cost private mortgage insurance and permission to make 95% loans, these ratios are changing and most banks and mortgage companies will negotiate 95% loans that are covered by mortgage insurance.

Size of Loan

Federally chartered savings associations from 1971 on have been permitted to loan up to $36,000 on a 95% loan-to-value ratio and up to $45,000 on a 90% loan. The Federal Home Loan Mortgage Corporation set a limit of $35,000 for single-family residences, permitting 95% loans, as a requirement for purchase. Mortgage bankers are not eligible to sell to FHLMC and savings associations are not obligated to sell, however, this $35,000 limit of Freddie Mac has prevailed as it is a substantial purchaser of mortgages, and most associations prefer to make loans that can be readily sold if needed.

The separate states set their own limits for state-chartered associations, banks, and insurance companies. Many states elect to follow the pattern set by the national regulatory body, the Federal Home Loan Bank Board. As the controlling authority for member savings associations which are the largest single source of residential mortgage money, the FHLBB holds a dominant position.

There is no real minimum for a loan except pure economics. When a mortgage loan goes under about $10,000, it becomes more expensive to service, and the fee received does not justify the time and expense involved. Of course, the efficiency of organizations varies, and the minimums they can handle fluctuate accordingly. Some mortgage companies consider $20,000 as the minimum conventional loan that can profitably be accepted. To undertake loans of lesser amounts might mean the company would be forced to sell at greater discounts, which would prove unprofitable.

Loans exceeding a lender's limits can be handled by several banks or associations joining together, with one institution responsible for administering the loan. For home loans exceeding approximately $50,000 to $60,000, the prudent lender would expect the borrower to show a sustaining annual income of approximately 75% of the loan amount, plus some depth in other personal assets.

There are no rules requiring any lender to make loans up to the maximum amounts permitted. Each lender maintains his own guidelines as to strength of borrower, type of property, neighborhood, etc., that would qualify for a maximum loan. Some states, such as Texas, no longer set maximums on residential loan amounts, and depend upon the lender's good judgment to establish the correct limit for any one loan. However, as interest increases in secondary market sales, lenders are reluctant to negotiate a loan that exceeds the dollar limits established in the secondary market.

Economic Stability

In considering geographical areas for purposes of making residential loans, lenders examine the future growth pattern of the entire region as well as the immediate neighborhood involved. Thus, loans in areas of high unemployment, or where there are mostly seasonal business patterns, or where the population depends heavily on a single industry—in all of these locations, loans are considered less desirable by many lenders. Home buyers in such locations can look only to local sources for lendable funds, without much access to the lower cost national market.

The Physical Property

Classifications of the physical property cover a multitude of factors. Most conventional residential loans are concerned with single-family units, but also include duplexes, triplexes, and fourplexes. Houses can be identified, too, by the number of bedrooms, or more commonly by the size of the property expressed in square footage of living area.

Townhouses are classified as single-family residences if the land is divided and can be pledged with the building. The use of common walls between the townhouses is acceptable if proper delineation is made in the deed description.

Houses located on unpaved streets are not acceptable to many lenders. One problem that occurs is the decreasing desirability of such a house, in case of a foreclosure sale, due to dust and wet weather inaccessibility. There is also the question of future paving assessments against the land.

For lenders, the classification of materials used in construction is generally confined solely to the exterior or facade of the house. Among the most commonly used materials are aluminum, asbestos, and wood sidings, or brick and stone. Brick and stone are more acceptable to lenders even though some types of wood may have longer lasting qualities.

The utilities available to the house are a consideration.

Top preference is shown to an organized, municipally operated water and sewage system. With situations in which a small privately owned water system or private well is the source of water, a lender is concerned about the quality and continuity of the supply. Sewage systems are subject to increasingly rigid requirements as to the quality of effluent that may be released into a river or other waterway. The smaller systems may have difficulty financing an expanded plant. The use of septic tanks does not automatically result in a rejection, though many lenders refuse to make loans on such types of property.

The placement of electrical wires and telephone lines underground serves as an added attraction to the appearance of a neighborhood. However, this feature has little effect on the loan decision. Other niceties (amenities) such as a neighborhood club or a swimming pool or recreation area actually do increase values to some degree and are duly noted in the property appraisals.

Minimum square footage or ground area restrictions are not generally set out as such in a conventional loan. This is in contrast to the FHA, which has a number of such rules detailing minimum room size, number of people per room, maximum amount (one-third) of the lot that may be covered by housing, and other rules, which are not generally disqualifying factors in conventional loans. The overall area of living space is the main concern in conventional loans and many lenders use a thousand square feet as the acceptable minimum. Some lenders may refuse to loan on a single-bedroom detached house. The essential question here is, "Does the property have a sufficiently broad market to facilitate resale if this becomes necessary?"

Location of Property

Lines are drawn by most conventional lenders between urban, suburban, and rural housing. The differences are not always clearly delineated, but they do provide a broad classification that is useful in describing packages of loans.

Due to the sprawl of our great metropolitan areas, the term *suburban* now means almost any location in a recorded subdivision of land in the general area surrounding cities—the region of greatest growth in our country. *Urban* means the downtown and near downtown areas of our cities. *Rural* identifies farm housing and, to many lenders, houses existing in the smaller towns. Rural is also occasionally used to identify housing without access to a central water and sewage system.

Lenders are accustomed to specifying areas or neighborhoods within a city that are acceptable or unacceptable areas within which they will or will not make house loans. Their reasons are linked to possible future changes in value; obviously, a neighborhood that is deteriorating and losing value would not be a good place to make loans expecting re-payment over a long period of time.

Age of Property

The age of a house is a simple, frequently used criterion for determining acceptable and unacceptable loans. The range varies from an insistence on exclusively new houses, which is very rare, to no fixed limit. Many lenders couple the age of the property with the neighborhood or location of the house. Some neighborhoods maintain their desirability over the years and 30- to 40-year-old houses may qualify for prime loans. However, the big secondary market purchasers of loans usually hold to a maximum age limit of 15 to 25 years to qualify for the best, or prime, rates.

Older houses that are not in the more acceptable neighborhoods may still qualify for mortgage loans but at higher interest rates and for shorter terms. The originator of a loan must always keep in mind what the specific requirements of his various sources of money are in regard to age.

Appraisers on conventional loans are expected to specify the actual age of a house in their report. Normally this can be determined from the owner or the builder or from building records. A knowledgeable appraiser can adjust this age to an "apparent age," which could vary in either direction. A neat, well kept house and yard that has been carefully maintained would have a lower apparent age than a run-down, unkept property.

Another possibility for mortgage loans on the older houses is through the Federal Housing Administration programs. Contrary to the procedure used in conventional loans, the FHA appraiser is asked to state his opinion of the remaining economic life of the house. The FHA limits its insured commitment to 75% of the remaining economic life; i.e., a remaining life of 40 years would permit an insured commitment for 30 years.

Usage of Property

Residential properties can be said to fall into four categories of usage insofar as mortgage loans are concerned. These include:

1. *Owner-occupied.* This property is considered to show prime security usage and accounts for most residential loans. Only owner-occupied units can command the highest ratio loans.

2. *Tenant-occupied.* Such property falls more into the commercial category of loan analysis, though it is still considered a residential loan for tax purposes and so far as banking regulations are concerned. Since a rental house would not command first call on the owner's income, a lender could downgrade the collateral and make a smaller loan of, perhaps, 75% or 80% of the value.

3. *Resort Housing.* Until recently resort houses could be described as cottages, sometimes poorly built of nonpermanent materials, and generally not acceptable as security for loans. The locations often lacked proper fire and police protection, were subject to vandalism and excessive storm damage, and were often not connected to municipal utility systems. In recent years the growth of new, higher class subdivisions in lake front or mountainous areas has greatly improved the quality and, thus, the acceptability of these homes as collateral. Lenders do, in fact, make many resort home loans, but they adjust the amount downward from, perhaps, 65% to as high as 90% loan-to-value ratio.

In resort-type developments, it is not unusual for a developer to buy a loan commitment himself, paying the discount fee necessary to provide his potential customers with a dependable, economical source of mortgage money.

4. *Second Homes.* Second homes are a close corollary to the resort home, though they differ in several ways since the more affluent society of the 1960s and 1970s has produced a growing number of families financially able to live in two different houses. On occasion, the house in the city might be less lived in and less occupied, on the whole, than the so-called second home in the country. With regard to financing, a lender usually makes a careful determination as to which house might be considered the primary housing entitled to preferential treatment, and which one should be downgraded as a second home, receiving an 80% or lower loan. A decision such as this would be required where the borrower was interested in making a purchase that is primarily based on a substantial annual income and not enough other assets. The lender must then consider the loan from the viewpoint of a sudden decrease in income due to job loss or working disablement. Which house, then, would most likely have to be forfeited under adverse circumstances?

UNDERWRITING GUIDES

The foregoing classifications of housing help to determine if a particular property will fall within the guidelines acceptable to a particular lender. For example, a lender might advise his correspondent that he is accepting applications for single-family residential loans in certain specified areas, or particular subdivisions of a city, for houses that are not over ten years old, and for loans not less than $20,000. This gives a broad range to work with, but then the evaluation must be focused on the individual property.

The most important piece of information is the appraisal, which provides a professional study of the physical property and the neighborhood. The photographs usually will show one or two views of the house, plus a shot of the street to give some clue to other houses in the neighborhood. The appraised value is compared with the selling price of the property, and a maximum loan limit is determined. The actual amount of the final loan offered is tempered by the borrower's own qualifications. The loan limit, as well as the interest rate and term of the loan, are determined by the amount of risk involved.

An experienced underwriter further checks the property for such factors as:

Location. Assuming the neighborhood has been approved, the actual location within a subdivision can be important. If the property under consideration backs up to an undesirable neighbor, such as an all-night drive-in food shop, a lower loan limit might be prudent.

Conformity. A house substantially out of step with others on the block gives cause for refusing or reducing the amount of the loan. The question is one of future resale. A larger, higher priced house in a neighborhood of smaller homes loses some of its value. A house of an unusual or different design, although very attractive in its proper setting, can present something of a freakish appearance in a conventional type neighborhood.

Topography and Soil Conditions. The contours of the land are important as some houses in an otherwise acceptable subdivision might be prone to flooding. As the federal programs for flood insurance grow, this particular problem will become of less importance to the lender. Soil conditions over the country show considerable variation from very solid to highly unstable bases and include geological fault lines. The problems caused by these factors have the same results—the house can become structurally defective and, therefore, unsalable long before the loan is paid off.

Local Regulation. A loan underwriter is always cognizant of the housing codes and should watch for any unusual deed restrictions that can affect future resale. In addition, there are sometimes legal situations that can create problems such as privately owned water districts with their own rules or requirements, flood control districts exercising certain controls, or neighborhood maintenance associations with nearly unlimited authority to raise assessments. As long as the property is occupied and the payments are made, the problems, if any, belong to the home owner, but the lender must always keep in mind the unfortunate possibility of having to take over the house in a foreclosure.

CONDOMINIUMS

The outright purchase of a vertical or horizontal apartment unit effectively detached from a piece of land has required state-enabling legislation declaring such a unit to be in the category of "real property." By means of these legal provisions, controlled lending institutions are permitted to accept such property as collateral. Legislation allowing condominium sales was initiated in the eastern states and has spread across the country over a period of years. It has only been in the past few years, however, that a nearly explosive growth has overtaken condominium sales, accompanied by the necessary mortgage loan programs.

By 1970, condominiums accounted for 11% of the total volume of new home sales and continue to grow more popular each year. The groups most interested in this type of property purchase are the young marrieds and senior citizens, together comprising over half the adult population.

The increasing popularity of the condominium concept of home purchase stems from the desire for home ownership, with the tax advantages of deducting interest and property taxes against an individual's income. In addition, there is a measure of inflation protection gained in property ownership plus tax deferment (within code limits), or capital gains treatment of a profitable sale. And, finally, the right to rent the unit as a landlord is possible, if desirable.

The mortgage loan for a condominium is handled similarly to the loan negotiated for a detached single-family residence, using the proper legal description of the condominium, et al. In this case the condominium with no actual physical attachment to a piece of land is pledged as security for the loan.

Since the lender must always foresee the possibility of foreclosure and subsequent resale of the property, it is necessary to examine some additional problem areas peculiar to a condominium. One of the more important items directly involved in condominium-style living that concerns the lender is that of maintenance costs. In order to sell the unit, a developer may be able to hold costs down or may even defer some necessary maintenance in order to show a low monthly charge. Subsequent to the project being sold, however, with the builder no longer responsible for its maintenance, the true problems may show up along with added costs for the unwary purchaser. Therefore the maintenance agreement on the property must be acceptable to the lender.

The voting control of the management board for the project can be held by the developer without a time limitation. It is the general practice for developers to assure proper operation and maintenance during the sell-out period of a project, and provided that the individuals involved have high ethical standards, this is a legitimate selling attraction. The problems of management most often arise under circumstances where not all the units are sold, and the developer must reduce his prices, or even rent unsold units, leaving the initial unit owners at a disadvantage. It is good practice to place a time limitation on the developer's absolute voting control; a limitation of perhaps two years would minimize potential problems of this nature.

Utilities should be controlled by the unit owners if at all possible. Unfortunate results may occur when a developer continues to exercise control over all utilities such as gas, electricity, sewer, water, and television channels. Such unwarranted control may expose unit owners to excessive rates and poor performance.

An intention to increase the size of a condominium project should be publicly declared in advance and made known to prospective buyers and lenders. If a developer withholds adjacent land for possible additional units, the later construction of them might overload existing recreational facilities and reduce the value of existing units by the sheer size and numbers of the completed project.

The management contract may affect future values and should be examined by the lender. These contracts are normally written prior to the sale of the units, and it is possible to tie down the rights to sell or lease all units for a lengthy period of time. Any restriction on resale rights would be detrimental to the lender's position.

SUMMARY FORM OF INFORMATION

Because of the importance of the Federal Home Loan Mortgage Corporation as a secondary market for savings association loans, its specific requirements will provide a good example of the instruments and information needed to properly submit a loan to it for purchase. Figure 9–1 (a and b) is a reproduction of Form 356 (Program Summary of Home Mortgages), which spells out eligibility requirements.

CONCLUSIONS

The purchase and financing of a home, for many buyers, are not just a routine business transaction but involve emotions as well. In today's economy, the availability of mortgage money to a home buyer often means the difference between decent and marginal housing. Thus, a loan rejection on a home can involve more personal feelings than a loan on commercial property.

A lending officer carries a responsibility to structure any loan so as to minimize the risk for the lending institution's depositors or policyholders. While a home loan looks most strongly to the borrower's present and potential income for repayment, the property represents the ultimate collateral for the loan. It is essential that the lender is reasonably certain that the property will continue to be of adequate value and offer protection to the lender for the life of the loan.

Unfortunately, one of the leading reasons for a loan refusal

Federal Home Loan Mortgage Corp.

PROGRAM SUMMARY—HOME MORTGAGES
ELIGIBLE MORTGAGES FOR SALE TO FHLMC
CONVENTIONAL WHOLE LOAN & PARTICIPATION PROGRAMS

A. MORTGAGE REQUIREMENTS
(Sec. refers to Convention Sellers Guide Jan. 1, 1973)

I. LOAN TO VALUE RATIO (Sec. 3.01 a)
a. Maximum Original Loan 95%
b. Calculate ratio on *lower of purchase price or appraised value.*
c. Whole Loan Program—P.M.I. required on amount over 75%.
   Participation Program—P.M.I. required on amount over 80%.
d. Maximum Loan 80% on 2-4 Family Dwellings.
e. Maximum Loan 80% on any loan made for the purpose of refinance (Sec. 301 k).
f. Private Mortgage Insurer must be approved by FHLMC.

II. MAXIMUM ORIGINAL AMOUNT OF MORTGAGE (Sec. 3.01 b)
a. One Family $35,000
b. Two Family $37,000
c. Three Family $39,000
d. Four Family $43,000
(Alaska, Guam & Hawaii may increase by 50%)

III. AMORTIZATION & TERM (Sec. 3.01 c & d)
a. Each loan must provide for amortization in accordance with regulations established by the FHLBB.
b. Mortgage term:
   (1) Original term, not more than 30 years.
   (2) Remaining term, not less than 10 years from Purchase Contract Date of Acceptance.

IV. ORIGINATION (Sec. 3.01 e)
Each loan must be closed in the Seller's name. (See Sec. 3.01 e regarding packaging loans.)

V. AGE OF LOAN (Sec. 3.01 f)
a. Must be closed at least one day before delivery of mortgage to FHLMC if a Whole Loan or before Purchase Contract Date of Acceptance if a Participation.
b. Cannot have been closed *more than 1 year* prior to Purchase Contract Date of Acceptance.
c. Date of closing is date of final disbursement of the mortgage proceeds.

VI. JUNIOR FINANCING (Sec. 3.01 j)
Total financing cannot exceed 95% of appraised value or purchase price, whichever is less. Junior Mortgage must comply with minimum established in Sec. 3.01 j. (Minimum of 5% cash down required.)

VII. DEBT SERVICE (Sec. 5.03)
a. Use borrower(s) stable monthly income (Read Sec. 5.03).
b. P.I.T.I. (principal, interest, tax and insurance), of all mortgages, *normally* should not exceed 25% of stable income.
c. Total monthly obligations including P.I.T.I.—*normally* should not exceed 33⅓% of stable income.
   Note: Justifiable exceptions to these generalizations will be considered. Present sufficient information to substantiate exceptions.
d. A mortgage which is or has been 30 days delinquent is not eligible for purchase.

VIII. OCCUPANCY (Sec. 3.01 l)
a. Single Family must be owner occupied at time of delivery.
b. 2-3-4 Family—owner must occupy 1 unit at time of delivery.
c. Property must be owner's principal residence.
d. Vacation, seasonal or mobile homes NOT eligible.
e. Mortgages of corporations or partnerships are not eligible.
f. 70% of the units in each condominium development must be sold or under contract for sale prior to submission of first unit to FHLMC.

IX. MORTGAGE DOCUMENTS (Sec. 3.01 n)
a. Whole Loan Program—Each mortgage must be closed on FHLMC Uniform Mortgage Instruments without modification.
b. Participation Program—FHLMC Uniform Mortgage Instruments optional, but if FHLMC uniform documents are not used then Sellers document must be acceptable to FHLMC.

X. HAZARD INSURANCE (Sec. 3.04)
a. Policy is with a company having a Bests' Financial rating of at least BBB+ or better.

b. Amount of coverage must be at least:
   (1) the full amount of damage or loss, or
   (2) the full amount of the unpaid balance of the mortgage, or
   (3) an amount not less than that necessary to comply with any co-insurance percentage stipulated in the policy.
c. Scope of insurance—at least fire and extended coverage.
d. Policy must contain a standard mortgagee clause showing note holders interest.

XI. TITLE INSURANCE (Sec. 2.1 g Agreement)
a. Seller must possess a title insurance policy written by a title company acceptable to FHLMC; or, certificate of title, or such evidence of title as is commonly required by institutional lenders in the jurisdiction of the mortgaged premises.
b. The title policy or other evidence of title must protect mortgagee up to the principal balance of the loan.
c. The protection and benefits must run to the noteholder.
d. The policy must be written on the current standard form of the American Land Title Association, or, if such form is not available in a jurisdiction, the form approved by such jurisdiction.
e. Title insurance is required on Condominiums, Leasehold Mortgages and P.U.D.s.

XII. LEASEHOLD PROPERTIES (Sec. 3.07 a)
a. Must be readily marketable type of ownership in area.
b. The lease must be recorded.
c. The leasehold must be in full force and effect and be subject to no prior lien or encumbrance by which it can be terminated or subjected to any charge or penalty.
d. Lease term must exceed mortgage maturity by 10 years.
e. FHLMC may require that Lease documents be reviewed by outside counsel (at Seller's expense).

XIII. CONDOMINIUMS (Sec. 3.03)
a. Either horizontal or vertical units are acceptable.
b. Read carefully Sec. 3.03 warranties.
c. Submit written designation of those warranties which Seller is unable to make.

B. DELIVERY OF LOAN PACKAGE TO FHLMC FOR UNDERWRITING & PURCHASE

I. IDENTIFY THE PURCHASE CONTRACT AS CORRECT AND CHECK THE REQUIRED DELIVERY DATE ON THE PURCHASE CONTRACT.

II. SEND THESE DOCUMENTS ON EACH LOAN: (Sec. 6.01)
(See reverse side for assembly instructions)
a. FHLMC Form 13SF—Mortgage Submission Voucher.
b. Mortgage Note (Copy if Participation Loan, Original if Whole Loan).
c. Loan Application
d. Credit Report
e. Profit & Loss Statement (or Federal Tax Return.) *
f. Appraisal Report
g. Photographs (2) (original—copy not acceptable).
   (1) Front view of subject property.
   (2) Street scene showing subject and adjoining properties.
h. Opinion of Counsel for Non-Domiciliary Property *
i. FHLMC Form 12—Mortgage Schedule

III. DO NOT SEND ORIGINAL OR COPY OF THESE DOCUMENTS TO FHLMC. (Retain in Seller's file.) (Sec. 6.02)
a. Mortgage or Deed of Trust.
b. Recorded Assignment (assignment required only on Whole Loan Purchase).
c. Title Insurance Policy (unless there is a Title problem not covered by waivers in Sec. 3.02).
d. Survey.
e. Hazard Insurance Policy or Certificate of Insurance.
f. Closing Statement or Verification of Down Payment.
g. Private Mortgage Insurance Policy or Certificate of Insurance.
h. Condominium, Leasehold or P.U.D. documents *unless Seller is unable to comply with warranties set forth in Conventional Sellers Guide, Sec. 3.03.*
*Submit when applicable (See Assembly Instructions).

FHLMC 356 3/73

Figure 9–1a

ASSEMBLY INSTRUCTIONS

I. **The following documents are to be assembled for each mortgage submitted. Arrange them in the order listed below, with first item listed (Form 13SF) on top. Secure documents with an Acco-type fastener at the top of the right side of a legal size manila folder.**

  A. FHLMC FORM 13SF—MORTGAGE SUBMISSION VOUCHER (Sec. 6.01).
    1. This form is used by FHLMC to:
      a. Expedite processing.
      b. Establish our loan file, servicing record, and accounting records.
    2. Form 13SF must agree with:
      a. Purchase Contract. (FHLMC Form 1 or 57) as to Contract number.
      b. Note & Mortgage (or Deed of Trust), as to:
        (1) Name of borrower.
        (2) Original loan amount.
        (3) Original note term.
        (4) Mortgage interest rate.
        (5) Monthly installment (Prin & Int).

  B. MORTGAGE NOTE (Sec. 6.01 b)
    1. Whole loan program—send original note properly endorsed. (No modification permitted)
    2. Participation program—send photostat of signed note. (Both sides if 2 sided form is used.) Any modification to note prior to delivery must be included.
    3. Endorsement must be complete from original lender to FHLMC.

  C. RESIDENTIAL LOAN APPLICATION (Sec. 5.02)
    1. Submit Residential Loan Application (FHLMC Form 65) or, submit Seller's application form. Seller's application form must be acceptable to FHLMC.
    2. Signed loan application must contain following information:
      a. Identical name(s) conforming to Form 13SF and mortgage note.
      b. Number of dependents.
      c. Listing of Assets & Liabilities. (Must indicate source of down payment.)
      d. Installment debts showing outstanding balance, monthly payment, and name of creditor.
      e. Borrower's job title and length of employment. (Show employment for at least 2 years.)
      f. Borrower's monthly income.
      g. Employer's name and address.

  D. CREDIT REPORT (Sec. 5.03)
    1. Name and address must be same as on application or explain difference.
    2. When slow payments, collection problems, liens, judgments or bankruptcies are shown, Seller must explain to justify credit worthiness.
    3. Verify debts shown that were listed on application and confirm employment and salary.
    4. Credit Report must be prepared by a FHLMC qualified credit reporting agency and dated within 90 days of note date.

  E. PROFIT AND LOSS STATEMENTS (Sec. 6.01 e)
    If applicant is self-employed, submit latest annual Profit and Loss Statement or Federal Tax Return to substantiate income shown on application.

  F. APPRAISAL (Sec. 6.01 f)
    1. Submit appraisal on Residential Appraisal Report (FHLMC Form 70), or submit Seller's appraisal. Seller's appraisal form must be acceptable to FHLMC.
    2. Appraisal must report:
      a. Property address conforming to Form 13SF.
      b. The legal description (the property appraised must agree with the legal description as shown on Mortgage or Deed of Trust).
      c. Description of improvements.
      d. Complete cost computations.
        (1) Total livable area. (Show in square feet.)
        (2) Basement area.
        (3) Other improvements.
          (Indicate cost factors for each of above.)
        (4) Depreciation.
        (5) Land value.

      e. Comparable sales data (properly adjusted) on at least three similar properties.
      f. Purpose of appraisal.
      g. Certification of value.
      h. Date of appraisal.
        If appraised prior to construction, value must be certified after completion.
      i. Appraiser's signature.
    3. Discuss any substantial difference between purchase price and appraised value.

  G. PHOTOGRAPHS (Sec. 6.01 g)
    1. Submit two clear photographs of the mortgaged property.
      a. Front view of subject property.
      b. Street scene showing subject and adjoining properties.
    2. The photographs are to be attached to an $8^{1/2}$ by 11 sheet of paper.

  H. OPINION OF COUNSEL FOR NON-DOMICILIARY PROPERTY (Sec. 6.01 i)
    1. In the event the mortgaged property securing the note is outside the state of the Seller's principal office, the first mortgage for such non-domiciliary state delivered by the Seller must be accompanied by an opinion of counsel.
    2. See Sec. 6.01 i for required content of counsel's opinion.

  I. CONDOMINIUM WARRANTIES WHICH SELLER IS UNABLE TO MAKE (Sec. 6.01 h).
    If the mortgage covers a condominium unit, designate any warranties set forth in Section 3.03, which Seller is unable to make. (If no designation is set forth, Seller shall be deemed to have made the warranties set forth in Section 3.03.)

II. **Upon completion of the preparation of each individual mortgage for submission to FHLMC, the following should be accomplished.**

  A. COMPLETE MORTGAGE SCHEDULE (FHLMC FORM 12) IN DETAIL AS FOLLOWS:
    1. List each individual loan that is being submitted for purchase.
    2. Prepare separate page for each mortgage interest rate.
    3. Sub-total each page.
    4. Grand total final pages.
    5. Double space all entries.

  B. COMPLETE CONTRACT DELIVERY SUMMARY (FHLMC FORM 381) IN DETAIL AS FOLLOWS:
    1. Original loan balances entered in Purchase Control Reconciliation section must be the total of original loan amount from all Form 13's (SF or Multi) submitted for purchase under this contract.
    2. Enter name of bank (must be member of Federal Reserve System or FHLB) that you desire FHLMC to use in transferring purchase proceeds.

  C. SUBMIT PACKAGE TO FHLMC SET UP IN THE FOLLOWING ORDER:
    1. Original of FHLMC Form 12 with contract delivery summary (FHLMC Form 381) attached.
    2. Individual mortgage files, in same order as listed on Form 12.

III. **After completion of Underwriting & Documentation Review, the appropriate FHLMC Regional Office will contact Seller regarding inspections of the properties, underwriting results and documentation problems.**

  A. Loans acceptable to FHLMC will be identified and replacement loans may be requested for those loans determined not eligible for purchase or FHLMC will purchase the lower amount.

  B. If Seller submits replacement loans, the same procedure should be followed as for an original submission; however, the total amount of unpaid principal on these loans cannot exceed total amount of unpaid principal on the loans being replaced.

  C. After determination as to which loans are to be purchased, FHLMC will update the principal balances from the Seller and also set a closing date for the purchase.

Figure 9–1b

has nothing to do with the analysis of borrower and property, but lies in the availability of funds within the lending institution itself. In order to maintain a balance within its own portfolio of loans between geographic areas, residential and commercial loans, and the various classes of houses, any one lending source may not be able to handle a particular loan application. This is one of the areas where a mortgage banker or a broker can perform a service of matching a borrower with a lender.

In summing up, a lender must look at a property offered as collateral in much the same way as a buyer; the property may some day belong to the lender to dispose of.

LOAN ANALYSIS OF INCOME PROPERTIES

GENERAL INFORMATION

Loans against all types of income properties require the same type of background information as would be needed for analyzing a residential loan. This information package would include a study of the location, the construction and other physical characteristics of the building, the local zoning laws and deed restrictions that may be involved, and the economic potential of the region and local area. In addition, and of greater importance to most investors, is an analysis of the income and expense factors. The lender wants to know how much of the total income is, or will be, available to pay the debt service—those periodic payments of principal and interest on the mortgage loan.

The most accurate method of obtaining the information needed is an *audited statement* by an independent accounting firm showing the actual income and expenses over a period of several years. For new developments such figures, of course, would not be available.

A second method used by many developer-builders is to use actual operating figures but incorporate *adjustments in both income and expenses* to more accurately portray a full year of operation. In this manner expenses might be leveled to show average annual figures. For example, if the exterior of the building was repainted and paid for upon completion, the total expense could be spread over the three-to-five year life of the paint job to give a more accurate annual expense factor. Annual payments, such as taxes, may have been delayed into the following year and should properly be returned to the current year to give a true picture. Similar adjustments may be made for unusual fluctuations in income. These calculations are often referred to as "stabilized" figures, which are expected to indicate a more accurate operational picture. Stabilized figures should not be confused with adjustments that are intended to mislead the analyst by overstating profit potential.

A third method of preparing an analysis of income property is a *projection of income and expenses*. Obviously, this is the only method that can be used on a new development. It is sometimes called a "pro forma" statement, which is really a knowledgeable estimate of the future cash flow. Since it is a projection, a pro forma statement should be prepared by a professional accountant who is aware of all the facts. It is difficult to accept a property owner's projection as an objective statement.

FEASIBILITY REPORT

The analysis of a new project investment often includes an additional study termed a *feasibility report*. By definition the word feasible means "capable of being used successfully." Therefore, the purpose of such a study is to ascertain the probable success or failure of the project under consideration.

There is a similarity in the background information needed for both a property appraisal and a feasibility report. The difference lies in the focus of conclusions regarding the timing and the usage of the property. A feasibility report seeks conclusions on the profitability of future operations, whereas the appraisal relates future profitability to present property value. A feasibility report is a preliminary study conducted before plans are drawn or financing is obtained. The information is used to guide the builder-developer and also serves as additional material for a potential lender to analyze.

A feasibility study draws certain conclusions concerning cost estimates and then analyzes the market available for the particular project under consideration, such as an apartment, office building, or other project. The detailed market analysis is the real meat of the study because it attempts to determine the probability of future income. Almost any income property can be projected into an appearance of profitability by using an arbitrarily high figure that may or may not be substantiated by the actual market available. It is the purpose of the market study portion of the feasibility report to show by actual canvass or survey, by charts of population and business growth, by analysis of present and future traffic and transportation patterns, and by actual comparisons of occupancy and income of comparable existing income properties whether or not a need exists for the proposed project.

Feasibility reports are not guided by any professional group pressing for accuracy and integrity and are therefore subject to a wide variety of interpretations. The best reports are prepared by experts in marketing analysis who have no personal interest in the subject property and are therefore able to make objective judgments. It is not unusual for a report to contain a presentation of information and facts regarding the project and its potential market, leaving the conclusions to be drawn by the reader.

More in the nature of an illustration, rather than as a standard pattern that does not really exist, the following outline could represent the material covered in a comprehensive feasibility study:

1. *Conclusions*—Presented first as these are the answers to the practical questions that the rest of the study has developed.

2. *Property*—A description of the property, location, type of building or buildings, and an estimate of costs showing some detail as to how costs are determined.

3. *Market Evaluation*—A study in depth of all factors that affect the marketing of the property, such as traffic patterns, population growth, type of income, other services available in the immediate area, direct and indirect competition, and any

laws, regulations, or other restrictions that will affect the project.

4. *Environmental Effect*—As local environmental rules expand, the impact of larger projects on the area are becoming the subject of intensive and lengthy coverage. The cost of the research and its effect on the cost of the project must be considered in the overall investment.

5. *Expense and Income*—An experienced analyst can develop reasonably accurate projections of operating costs. These are best approached as (1) *fixed*, which covers such items as insurance and taxes that do not vary with occupancy, and (2) *operating* expenses such as water, electricity, and maintenance that do fluctuate with occupancy. From these figures, a break-even ratio can be determined. The income projection must be based on some factual data of comparable rents and occupancy figures, but does remain essentially an estimate drawn from knowledge and experience.

A feasibility report does not attempt to recommend financing methods or detail the expenses involved with interest costs. The conclusions stop with an estimate of total cash that would be available for debt service. The timing of the financing, how it is arranged, and under what type of commitments —these are problems for the developer to resolve.

USE OF A LOAN CONSTANT

In discussing a loan, the prospective borrower will find it difficult to mentally convert an interest rate and the term of a loan into a dollar cost for his project. In order to facilitate negotiations, it is customary to use a multiplier, referred to as a *constant*, which means the constant percentage of the original loan that is paid annually for principal and interest. This constant payment is also referred to as *debt service*.

For example, an 8% loan with a 25-year term has an annual constant of 9.26. Thus, on a $1 million loan, the debt service amounts to $92,600 annually. Now, if the interest rate is increased to 9%, this would change the constant to 10.07 for the same term. If a change occurs in the term from, say 25 years to 15 years, then the original 8% rate calculates out at an 11.47 constant.

Tables compiled by statistical experts are available at technical bookstores showing the progression of constants. A variety of other tables are also available for reference on exact mortgage yields, equity build-ups, and amortization statistics.

APARTMENTS

Apartments, or multifamily housing, as the FHA broadly classifies them, can range from a four-family building to upward of 2500 units or more. Since apartments are residential housing, qualifications similar to single-family housing are necessary. This would include location, type and stability of the neighborhood and the region, laws governing foreclosure procedures, and the architectural style of the building itself.

Because an apartment is an investment property as well as a residence, there are many variables involved in determining the risks. Experienced apartment operators judge three factors to be of almost equal importance in a successful operation. These are: (1) location, (2) physical facilities, and (3) management. Obviously, a careful underwriting analysis must consider all three factors in determining the risk involved.

Location is usually the first limiting requirement of an apartment seeker, along with size of the unit and its price. A major consideration of location is easy access to jobs; freeways affect and broaden accessibility. Also important in judging location is the nearness to schools and churches. The availability of recreational facilities, such as parks and golf courses, along with restaurants and other entertainment, are all to be considered. Apartment dwellers, as a group, are not as burdened with housework and yard maintenance as a single-family resident would be.

Since location is a major determinant of the available

market, it is necessary to evaluate the market in that area. For instance, does the proposed rental structure fit the requirements and will it be competitive? And do the size and type of units meet these demands?

The physical plant must meet the market requirements, not only in size of units, but also in architectural style and amenities available. Amenities would include such factors as playground areas, tennis courts, swimming pool, club room, and entertainment facilities. If the market is primarily a family type, the two- or three-bedroom units would be the most popular choice; if intended for younger singles, the one-bedroom and studio design would be in greatest demand. The elderly, on the other hand, might prefer one or two bedrooms with a minimum of stairs to climb. Sometimes an assortment of units is used with the hope of covering all phases of the market. This "shotgun" approach is a poor substitute for a careful analysis of the market as it may result in one type or style of unit easily rented and maintaining good occupancy while others go begging for tenants. Before building begins on an apartment complex, knowledgeable operators (developers) study the market for particular requirements and then use their merchandising power to attract suitable occupants.

Management is a major factor known well to experienced operators and too often underestimated by newcomers to the field. Together with the location and the physical plant, management, too, can be a "make or break" factor. Larger cities throughout the country have companies that specialize in apartment management, offering a complete management service for a fee of 3% to 5% of the gross revenues. Maintaining routine cleanliness of the public areas, prompt repairs of equipment or damaged sections of the building, and fair enforcement of tenant rules for the mutual well-being of the tenants are all necessary to achieve and maintain a high occupancy rate. Experienced operators learn how to cope with the special requirements of rental properties such as initial screening of tenants, the most effective methods of collecting rents and keeping them current, the special problems created by domestic pets, the handling of skip-outs and of tenants who create disturbances for other occupants. Consequently, an underwriter will look much more favorably, riskwise, on a property under the management of competent individuals or companies.

As apartment-style living proliferates in the cities, an underwriter must recognize that the better planned, better maintained facilities are those that will maintain the occupancy in soft or competitive markets. And a continuous high occupancy rate is the key to survival in this business.

Analysis of Income and Expenses

On proposed apartment construction, a projected statement can be prepared to show anticipated gross revenues from each unit and all miscellaneous revenues such as that from laundry rooms, less a vacancy factor and credit losses. This will produce an effective income from which deductions can be made for all expenses. Fixed expenses include such items as taxes and insurance, and operating expenses such as utilities, maintenance, supplies, labor, and management. A special expense that is frequently overlooked or underestimated is the replacement costs—items such as drapes and carpeting, equipment such as stoves or dishwashers, all in continuous use, have a tendency to wear out, and allowances must be set aside for replacements. The cash remaining after these deductions then becomes available for debt service. Any remaining cash, after all expenses and debt service have been covered, serves as a cushion against a loss or a slow period.

It is apparent then that there are many variables among these figures that are subject to interpretation. For example, what occupancy rate may be reliably projected? FHA uses a percentage figure of 93. Conventional lenders generally tend to select an occupancy rate substantiated by actual rates prevailing in a particular area. Most lenders require proof of an occupancy rate near 90% before they will entertain a loan application. Rental rates also must be in line with the going market. Expenses can be projected with reasonable accuracy. In general, they range from 36% of the gross effective income to 45%, depending on the size of the operation and the efficiency of the management.

As previously defined, debt service is the monthly or annual cost of interest and principal payment and should be tailored to insure the timely retirement of the full loan. By careful analysis of the cash available for debt service, the underwriter can determine the most effective loan for the proposed apartment. Adjustable and negotiable factors are the *term*, which under conventional loans ranges from 15 upward to 30 years, and the *loan-to-value* ratio, which determines the equity cash required. The interest rate is generally pegged at current market rates and is less subject to negotiation.

Depreciation as an expense item is expected to be covered under items allocated to maintenance and replacement. However, the principal use of the rules governing depreciation on apartments at the present time is how it can be used as an offset against taxable income. The 1969 Tax Reform Act recognized the need for housing in this country by allowing continuance of accelerated depreciation on residential type property investments, while reducing this type of tax shelter on other investment properties. An investment in a new apartment can qualify for the accelerated double declining balance depreciation. From a loan analysis standpoint, the depreciation allowance against taxes is important in that it reduces the overall tax liabilities but cannot be counted on for the life of the loan. While the amount of depreciation available to an apartment investor depends on his income bracket and is complicated by formulas limiting his overall tax preference deductions, it is a fair statement that for the first four or five years of a new apartment operation, the interest cost and depreciation deductions will more than offset the available income for tax purposes.

Cooperative Apartments

Cooperative apartments are a variety of apartment in which the ownership of a given unit is vested in the tenant-owner, and the ownership of the land and public facilities is vested jointly with all the other tenant-owners of the complex. The most practical method of operating this type of facility is to set up a corporation with shares of stock representing the jointly-owned interests. Another method would be to place the joint interests in trust with a trust company, which then issues certificates of beneficial interest. Construction of this type of apartment has waxed and waned in the past, primarily stimulated by rising land costs, and the desire for ownership equities, and for obtaining certain tax advantages, as well as a means of exercising some control in the selection of neighbors and enabling more individually styled apartments. The problem of financing a co-op is finding a means of carrying the costs while the units are in the process of being sold. One reasonable solution to the problem is to require a certain percentage of presold units prior to the release of any loan money.

Rule-of-Thumb Analysis

In order to properly analyze an apartment income property, a detailed study of all information regarding operating costs, fixed expenses, and gross income, with allowances for credit loss and vacancies, must be considered in relation to the total investment required. However, from long and hard-won experience, investors have developed certain guidelines that are useful in providing a quick evaluation on an apartment loan application to determine if it is worthy of further analysis. The use of these methods varies among investors and according to practices of the area of the country in which they do business, but some of the more commonly employed ratios and evaluations can be listed as follows:

Mortgage Multiplier. The factor that converts effective gross rent to an estimated mortgage amount ranges from four to six. For example, if a project grosses $2400 per unit annually, it could attract a mortgage loan of $12,000 per unit if a multiplier of five is used.

Loan per Room. The required size of a "room" in an apartment is not standardized. One company might consider a minimum living-room size for a two-bedroom apartment to be 160 square feet with the smallest dimension being 11 feet, or a living-dining alcove combination for a two-bedroom apartment with 200 square feet would be counted as one and one-half rooms. The average loan per room will vary from $2000 to $4500.

Gross Rent Multiplier. This is a rule-of-thumb method for converting gross project rental income into an estimate of value or sales price. The measure varies from 5½ (or 66 months income) to 7 times annual income.

Site Value Ratio. The site value ratio is the ratio of the value of the site to the total value of land and improvements. The percentage varies from 6% to 20%.

SHOPPING CENTERS

Shopping in urban areas has relocated substantially from the downtown section to outlying districts and suburbs. The movement dates from approximately World War II and was brought about largely by the automobile, which along with freeway systems produced a major change in our living patterns and altered our population centers.

Merchants in the downtown areas recognized these changing patterns and, for the most part, were in the vanguard of the development of regional shopping centers. Specialized development companies grew up in this period whose purpose was to organize the merchants, locate proper land sites, arrange for financing, and then handle construction and even management of the completed center.

Size, Services, and Development

The size, shape, and structure of shopping centers, as well as the methods used in their development, show such extreme variation as almost to defy classification. Common observation shows a range from small, localized strips of stores along a frontage road, to a supermarket with perhaps a half-dozen satellite stores served from the same parking lot called "convenience centers," and on up to the huge complexes.

In terms of financing, the smaller strip-type shopping centers referred to are often built as speculative ventures and remain merely bare-wall shells until suitable tenants are found. Larger centers, however, almost always commence with a major store as a focal point and a traffic generator, and are preleased before construction begins. A developer seldom builds a large facility without leases in hand, for it is the lease that determines the financing. And the type and the amount of the lease supply the key to the money.

Summing up the major varieties of shopping centers from the simplest to the most complex would include: (1) the *neighborhood center*, which provides daily essentials such as food, drugs, hardware, and everyday services; (2) the *community center*, adding to the neighborhood category with apparel, furniture, professional services, and some recreational facilities; and finally (3) the *regional shopping center*, utilizing major stores and scores of lesser shops including a variety of restaurants and substantial recreational facilities, the whole arranged in an attractive manner and esthetically appealing to today's shopper.

Classification for Financing

Shopping center facilities fall into three major categories when considered for financing: (1) owner-occupied, (2) preleased space built by a developer, and (3) space-built for speculative leasing. These categories are not always clearly differentiated in that many centers carry a combination of all three types, but they are used here to distinguish differences important to an underwriter's analysis.

Owner-Occupied. While this type of store building is not as common as it once was, there are still many of this type being built. The largest of all retail merchants, Sears, Roebuck and Co., generally leases its smaller stores but buys the land and builds its own facility for the larger centers. A free standing discount store is usually owner-occupied as are many of the newer warehouse-type furniture stores. Some of the largest local merchants undertake development of their own outlying stores. In all cases of owner-occupied facilities, the financial strength and credit record of the owner are the key to good financing. The type of merchandiser capable of building a substantial new facility for sales expansion generally has the experience to know the extent of the market. Regardless of the merchandiser's experience or reputation, however, comprehensive independent market studies are undertaken and made available to the underwriter.

The largest merchants may resort to the sale of bonds for financing expansion rather than a mortgage loan, depending on the cost of the money. In either case, it is the credit reputation of the borrower, rather than the real estate pledged, that determines the interest rate as well as the term set and the amount of the loan.

Preleased. Many merchants prefer to utilize their cash and borrowing capacity for growth in inventory and accounts receivable, rather than for real estate investments. Consequently, they work with investors or builder-developers who are knowledgeable in construction and property management. In order to obtain the physical facility desired, the merchant is often willing to sign a long-term lease ranging from 15 to 25 years, thus assuring the builder-investor of a continuing income. The lease payments must be calculated to cover such maintenance as the owner is held responsible for, plus the debt service. Taxes and insurance increases can be passed on to the tenant with an escalation clause in the lease.

The actual lease, the strength of the leasee, and the terms of the lease itself are the keys to financing the building. For a strong lease, a lender will fund a major percentage of the total amount of the lease payments without substantial reference to the building itself. The percentage may run as high as 75% of the total amount of the lease payments and can provide for an assignment of the lease payments directly to the lender.

If the leasees are less credit-worthy or of smaller size, the lender will still take an assignment of rentals but also looks more to the strength of the lessor. In this case, too, the size of the loan may be reduced to a percentage, say 70%, of the actual investment in land and buildings. The rental from smaller shops such as barber shops, boutiques, and fashion stores, with little established credit would not be considered as a measure for the loan except that such leases in hand would provide an addition to the overall occupancy of a multistore center.

One of the problems that becomes particularly important regarding preleased space is the ability of the developer to complete the building within the projected cost figures. Leases do not provide for rental increases to cover a builder's mistakes. Consequently, the prudent lender must not only determine the accuracy of projected costs of building with the income and expenses that will be generated, but must also be reasonably certain that the builder is sufficiently experienced and capable of completing the project within the specified budget.

Speculative. The substantial growth of all business, and particularly the service-oriented businesses requiring limited store type space, has provided a lucrative field for the speculative builder. This is space built in bare-wall form, from the small corner shopping strip to portions of the large regional centers, without a lease or even a prospective tenant. When a tenant is found, the store space is completed to the particular tenant's requirements, either at the tenant's initial expense or added into his lease payments.

From the lender's standpoint, speculative store space rates rather low in desirability and is one of the first types of mortgage loans to dry up in periods of tight money. An empty store, after all, is only an expense. The reason a lender will entertain such a loan is due to his reliance on the ability and financial strength of the builder-owner. If the builder is strong, or if he has an excellent record of finding qualified tenants for previous projects, a lender will look with some favor on the project if money is available.

The building of space for speculative leasing is accepted by lenders when it is a relatively small portion of a large regional center, most of which is already preleased. It has been well proved that major stores generate traffic that benefits and thus attracts many smaller merchants and service-type facilities.

Specific Shopping Center Areas for Underwriting Analysis

There are some problems common to the development and continued successful operation of all types of shopping facilities, from the very largest down to the single-store operation. Problems that must be examined include: (1) location, (2) the physical facilities to be constructed, (3) the management and general plan of operation, (4) tenants and sales volumes, (5) types of leases, and (6) lease terms. Discussion of these problems with possible answers to questions that arise follows.

Location. As in other types of real estate, location of a shopping center dictates the market. The population of the surrounding area should be studied for density, potential growth, family purchasing income, and the number of retail stores per family to determine if there is a real need for the proposed store or shopping center. From this study it should be possible to project the total retail volume in the general area and to reduce this to an estimate of sales per store. With regard to a large-scale center, it would be advisable to employ a market analyst for such a study, as it becomes intricately involved with such facets of the problems as the nature of the center and accessibility and shopping habits of the prospective customers in or near this location.

The location should also be selected for ease of entry and exit. Since surveys indicate that the principal shoppers are women, planning should take into consideration that women drivers dislike difficult traffic patterns, which may in turn lessen their enthusiasm for shopping at that particular center. Long-range plans should also recognize the fact that the flow of traffic at any given center might be substantially altered by future developments.

Physical Plan. There are many ways to build a shopping center, and no single plan insures success. The huge regional centers show great imagination in design, layout, decor, and various attractions offered to the shopper. Many have become recreational centers as well as shopping centers. Entertainment is often provided in the public malls in the form of musicians, demonstrations, art shows, and other types of exhibits. Modern centers exude something of a carnival atmosphere at times in their all-out efforts to attract shoppers and overshadow the competition from smaller centers. Inevitably, middle-level centers are finding it more difficult to compete with the many extra attractions offered by the largest centers. However, the smaller convenience centers in good locations hold onto a local trade and are generally sound investments.

Since parking is one of the big advantages of a shopping center, these facilities should be adequate. As a general rule, three square feet of parking area should be provided for every one square foot of rentable shop space. An alternative rule would be to allow five or six parking spaces for each 1000 square feet of shop. Employee parking is best designated and kept apart from the prime locations. Supermarkets require the most parking space of any type of store.

The physical plan should be carefully examined to make certain that floor plans are of proper size with access readily available, that there is adequate heating and air conditioning, and that sufficient space has been provided for the handling of incoming merchandise and outgoing waste materials. These are mainly architectural and engineering concerns, but if costly mistakes can be prevented, the lender's money will be better secured. Considering the complexities involved, it is always a safer investment to employ experienced builders.

Management and Operations. Management plays a very important role in all types of income properties, and shopping centers are no exception. The larger centers rely heavily on competent management, not only to clean and maintain the facility, but to provide attractive decorations, timely promotional advertising, control of traffic, policing of crowds, and even some entertainment. The management usually works with an organized merchant's association in providing some of these services. Good promotional organization provides assurance to the lender that there will be a continuity of the entire project as all shopping center store units have a degree of interdependence.

In the area of operations, management can either place much of the responsibility for interior maintenance and daily upkeep on the tenant, or provide the service as a separate charge that can be adjusted as costs change. In the smaller operations and in the single-building facility, the owner usually takes responsibility only for exterior maintenance and the parking areas.

The experience of the operators is very soon evidenced by the manner in which they detail the responsibility for costs: both in how the costs for finishing out a store for a particular lessee are allocated between the owner and the tenant, and in how the operating costs are detailed. Such seemingly minor items as an electric eye-controlled doorway can cause continual maintenance problems. Is this an interior or exterior feature? The knowledgeable operator does not leave such items to later negotiation but spells them out in the written agreement. The lender should have an interest in any potential problem that he might inherit.

In the analysis of a proposed shopping center, the underwriter should definitely determine that adequate allowance has been made for initial planning and start-up costs. The new emphasis on environmental impact adds another cost for the investor who must now prepare studies and submit the necessary reports to authorized officials. Lease-up costs and initial advertising must all be provided for in the financing proposal as well as allowances for probable tax increases on any undeveloped land that is held for future growth.

Tenants. Another area of management responsibility to be examined by the underwriter is the policy used in selecting tenants and locating them within the center. The granting of exclusive franchises is not beneficial to the owner but may be necessary for a large store such as a supermarket. Any franchise granted in broad or general terminology, such as allowing a restaurant an exclusive franchise for "food handling," can be very restrictive to future growth of the center. Tenants should have the financial strength to under-take the lease obligations plus the ability to serve the public in a successful manner. Customer problems involving any single store can cast a poor reflection on the entire shopping center. Also a good diversity of stores is helpful in luring shoppers back again.

As previously indicated in this section, the quality of the tenants in a preleased center is a major factor in securing a mortgage loan. Sometimes there is an overemphasis on the desirability of the national chain-type stores as lucrative tenants. Recent statistical data indicate that localized chains and independent stores are very effective sales producers and that more often than not they turn over a larger volume of sales per square foot of floor space than do national opera-tions. Sales volume is the key to larger rental income on percentage leases. The continued security of the mortgage payments rests to a considerable extent on the ability of the merchants to achieve profitable sales volumes.

Types of Leases. The type of lease used and the detail it contains are vital to the loan analysis. Three main types are:

1. *Term Leases*—Term leases are used by most of the smaller shops and by some of the larger stores. This means paying flat monthly rentals figured on a basis of store size or square foot-age. These leases can allow for automatic increases every year or two and can provide renewal options.

2. *Percentage Lease*—The larger merchants (such as drug stores, supermarkets, and department stores) operate on mini-mum or base rentals plus a percentage of the gross sales. Percentages can vary from 1 to 6% of gross sales depending on type of store and sales volume. A no-minimum lease sets up a risky situation for a lender as the store may be able to operate profitably at a sales volume that does not pay the cost of the space occupied.

3. *Net Leases*—Another form of lease arrangement consists of operating the bare property strictly as an investment for the owner with the tenant paying all maintenance, taxes, and in-surance. This type of operation is known as a net lease to the owner, covering only a reasonable return on his property in-vestment. Management and operational problems would all be

minimized by passing the entire burden on to the tenant. The net lease procedure is frequently used by individuals or by development companies who have decided to build a facility in a distant location for a major tenant, a supermarket for instance, but simply do not have the personnel available and are not interested in accepting management responsibilities.

Lease Terms. The investment required to furnish a large store requires a long-term lease, which has advantages and disadvantages for the owner. The long term gives the lender good assurance of repayment and makes for better loan terms. The disadvantage lies in the fixed return on an investment over a number of years when costs of all kinds continue to increase over a period of time. Insurance costs also tend to increase and are related to risks that tenants may introduce. Consequently, long-term leases will normally carry escalation clauses that provide for any increase in taxes and insurance to be passed on to the tenant.

The smaller stores or shops, such as beauty parlors, florists, and boutiques, generally contract a three-to-five year lease, which is subject to rental increases periodically in anticipation of rising costs. The smaller shops seldom agree to percentage leases as they lack the necessary sales volume and the more complicated bookkeeping procedures required.

There are some lease provisions of special concern to a lender, particularly those that could bring about a premature cancellation of the lease. For example, leases that tie the occupancy of one store to the continued occupancy of another store present an obvious problem. Any type of exclusive clause restricting other shops from carrying competing lines or type of service can be detrimental. Stores can and do change their sales patterns over the years.

Occasionally special leases are permitted a major tenant based on a below-cost figure as a means of capitalizing on the inherent attraction of well-known merchants. The traffic generated by one big store is expected to provide sales for the lesser merchants. For a lender's standpoint, however, this type of subsidized rent structure suggests an undesirable pattern since it places a heavier burden on the remaining tenants to compensate for the loss sustained on the single below-cost lease.

Costs that continually escalate without realistic controls can be set out in a lease agreement as separate expenses, or in clauses allowing an equitable rental adjustment. Such services as heating and air conditioning, participating advertising, waste disposal, janitorial services, and security services may be covered under a separate service contract that can be adjusted for escalation, as may be necessary. Such a contract should contain protective clauses for the tenant to prevent the unscrupulous use of terms as a device for increasing costs unfairly, which might bring about default on the lease itself.

Example of a Shopping Center Lease

An example of a *percentage lease* for a supermarket of 20,000 square feet would be as follows:

> Assume the rental is set at a minimum of $1.50 per square foot, per year, based on a 1½% of the gross sales. The $1.50 for 20,000 square feet would amount to a rent of $30,000 per year. So, calculating a gross sales volume of $2,000,000 or less per year, the supermarket would pay the $30,000 per year minimum. If the total volume goes over $2,000,000, the 1½% of the gross would apply above that amount.

A *typical* shopping center deal would vary considerably across the country, depending upon land values and construction costs in a particular area. However, the proportions are similar, and the figures confirm this similarity. Assuming land cost at $1 per square foot and using the three-to-one ratio on parking space, the rentable shop space would then cost $4 per foot in land contributed. For a reasonably simple structure, the building costs would come to about $15 per square foot, which includes paving and lighting the parking lot. The total investment, using these figures, would add up to $19 per square foot. At this investment level, operating costs run approximately $1.00 per square foot, per year. Rentals for space such as this would average $3.00 per square foot per year. The following table (Table 10–1) shows how the investment works out using a highly simplified procedure for greater clarity:

TABLE 10–1

Projection for Shopping Center Investment
(Figures are hypothetical using a 50,000 square foot building
located on 200,000 square feet of land. Total cost—$950,000.)

Capital Investment		
Equity investment (20%)	190,000	
80% mortgage loan	760,000	
Total investment		950,000
Income—Annual Basis		
Gross income (3.00 per ft.)	150,000	
Less 5% vacancy and credit loss	7,500	
Operating income		142,500
Expenses—Annual Basis		
Operating costs, taxes and insurance	50,000	
Debt Service—9% loan for term of 25 yrs.		
Constant — 10.07 × 760,000 =	76,532	
Total cash outflow		126,532
Cash return		15,968

Based on the above figures, the investment would show slightly more than 8% cash return on the equity investment. However, many unforeseen contingencies could upset this return, such as lower occupancy than expected, failure to collect all rentals due, and run-away operating costs. In the example cited above, the cash return cannot be considered as the only profit since the principal payments on the loan are also a part of the profit, and it does not constitute taxable income since the depreciation allowed offers an off-setting deduction. The lender must look to the margin of cash over-and-above the operating costs, plus the debt service, in order to estimate the margin of financial safety that can be counted on in any given investment.

OFFICE BUILDINGS

The owners of all types and sizes of office buildings, ranging from the largest to the smallest, acquire or construct them for one of two purposes: (1) their own occupancy, or (2) for lease to others.

Owner-occupied Buildings

Many owner-occupied office buildings are held by companies or persons with a financial history that makes the decisions on underwriting such a property somewhat easier for the lender. This is due to the fact that the credit reputation of the owner is the major qualifying factor under consideration, whereas the real estate that is to be pledged is of secondary importance. Ultimately, the source of loan repayment is closely tied to the owner-occupant's record of profitability and the manner in which previous financial obligations have been met.

Unlike a shopping center or store, the office building occupied by an owner produces no additional income. But rent and other operating costs can be substantially reduced through more efficient office layouts.

In financing owner-occupied buildings of larger size, an alternative choice to straight mortgage financing would be the sale of first mortgage bonds through an investment banker or a mortgage banker. Acquisition of large office buildings by investing institutions, such as banks or insurance companies, is a common practice. In this way, the owners simply finance large buildings from their own investment funds.

Various local, state, and federal governments and their agencies build office buildings for their own use with legislative appropriations. But some government buildings, such as post offices, are built by private investors under long-term lease contracts and are financed through private sources.

Office Buildings for Lease to Others

The underwriting of buildings intended for lease to others calls for some specialized techniques of real estate mortgage financing and requires extensive analysis of the property involved. In this category there are three main groups: (1) a builder-investor with preleased office space to build, (2) the speculative builder hoping to attract tenants before the building is completed or soon thereafter, and (3) the owner-occupied building with extra space for lease.

Preleased Office Space. *The preleased building* is the more conservative method and provides the underwriter with a lease to analyze, a tenant to examine for credit-worthiness, and a building and location to study. If the building is specialized to meet a tenant's unusual requirements (such as heavy electrical gear, raised or lowered floors, or special wall patterns), the term of the lease should be sufficient to recover the extra investment. Most underwriters will limit a loan to a percentage of the total lease payments as this is the main source of the loan recovery. Similar to a shopping center, a preleased office building faces an inflexible situation in regard to an overrun on construction costs. The building must be designed and located in such manner that it meets the projected costs, and the contractor must have the ability to complete the project within the contract terms. Bonding of the contractor is a normal requirement. Escalation clauses should be provided in any long-term lease agreement to cover rising taxes and insurance costs. Preleased office buildings for single tenants are usually "bare-wall" leases; i.e., the tenant finishes and furnishes the interior and provides his own maintenance.

Speculative Office Buildings. *The speculative builder* presents a greater risk to an underwriter and only the more experienced and credit-worthy builders can command this type of loan. In addition to the usual analysis of the building and its location, consideration must be given to the market and the regional economic pattern. What are the chances of the speculative building becoming fully leased? The underwriter, however, is not in the business of chance by choice, so a protective restriction can be established that would require the building to have a 75%, 80%, or, perhaps, 85% occupancy with bona fide tenants before the permanent loan will be released. Of course this throws a real burden on the construction financing and usually means that the builder of a speculative building must have the credit strength or cash reserves to build and lease the building without an assured permanent commitment. It is not unusual for a knowledgeable builder-contractor to build and lease an office building with his own funds, then mortgage-out for more than his costs. In such a case the loan security rests as much on an assignment of the lease income as on the mortgage pledge. With regard to speculative office buildings, lenders often set rental minimums to protect their repayments. Buildings with multi-tenant occupancy usually provide for janitorial service, which can be a separate agreement subject to escalation if costs increase.

Owner-occupied Building with Space to Lease.   The third type of building loan in this office building category is the owner-occupied with space to lease. In this situation there is a mixture of several types of income including the owner's normal rental payment, plus rent from space for speculative lease, as well as rent from space already preleased; but there is no one source providing sufficient revenue to assure recovery of a normal ratio loan. The underwriter must analyze the property as a whole and make certain that the full loan has a reasonable chance of recovery before any portion of that loan is permitted to be released.

General Guidelines

In today's business world, office buildings are under construction in many locations with one major aspect in common—business growth. Even though downtown areas are somewhat congested and offer only limited parking, they are still highly desirable locations for businesses requiring convenient access to banks, accounting firms, attorneys, or other service-oriented facilities, plus easy contact and association with customers, suppliers, other allied businesses, hotel accommodations, and transportation.

As freeway patterns have developed in urban areas, many businesses have opted for outlying locations that provide ease of parking and close proximity to potential office workers. The decline of mass transportation systems, hastened by the increasing use of cars, has made freeway locations in some cases nearly as accessible as downtown. It should be noted in passing, however, that the next generation may very possibly witness a reversal of this trend, especially in view of the energy shortage.

Even though it is a generally accepted idea that the true value of an income property is what it will earn, the physical aspects of the office building should be fully covered in an underwriting analysis. Factors such as the flexibility of interior partitions will affect future ability to rent space. It has been demonstrated that excessive public space may become a heavy burden as the building grows older. Also mechanical equipment can cause problems, and in the case of older buildings may need replacement.

The ability to maintain high occupancy in office buildings is less dependent on economic inducements than on such intangible qualities as prestige and status. For example, ground-floor space rented to a dignified, prestigious merchant can enhance the value of upper-floor space. The class of tenants can add to a particular building's value; i.e., a building known for top-rate law firms or a medical office building of high caliber tenancy will attract other professional people. Companies and business concerns seeking a high-class clientele are often willing to pay a few dollars more each month in rentals for the advertising value of a prestige address.

The expenses of operating an office building must be considered in the total loan picture. Unlike other types of real estate properties, office buildings usually furnish a janitorial service for the tenant as well as for the public areas. There are many companies specializing in contract cleaning services that will allow some control to be exercised over these costs, but these costs are subject to escalation over the years. If a building is new, projected operating costs must be utilized, but actual operating costs should be available in the records kept on existing buildings. Care must be taken in analyzing any cost figures to minimize distortions that might lead to misleading conclusions. For example, expense items may be omitted, maintenance work can be neglected, incidental repairs may sometimes be capitalized to reduce expense figures, and tenant services can be held to a dangerously low level in order to distort earnings figures in an upward direction.

All of these factors should become apparent to the experienced underwriter and properly weighed in the final loan analysis.

Like other properties, the operating management is a key ingredient in continuing success. Poor management can discourage occupancy and drive good tenants away.

Example of an Office Building Loan

Several years ago in a period of tight mortgage money, a mortgage loan was negotiated for a high-rise office building to be built with 150,000 square feet of space. The borrower showed a total investment of $4 million including land and building, and requested a 90% loan, or $3.6 million. The financial projections were outlined as shown in Table 10–2.

In this particular example, the lender felt that the high

TABLE 10–2

Projected Statement for Office Building

Land Area and Costs		
150,000 sq. ft. @ $26.67 per sq. ft.		$4,000,000
(127,500 sq. ft. net rentable		
costing $31.50 per sq. ft.)		
Investment		
Equity capital	400,000	
90% mortgage loan	3,600,000	
Total investment		4,000,000
Income		
Gross @ 100% occupancy calculated		
@ $6 per sq. ft. per year	765,000	
Less vacancy and credit loss at 5%	38,250	
Effective income		726,750
Expenses		
Operating costs including janitorial		
services and taxes @ 34.5% of income	250,730	
Debt service at 9.75% interest for a term of		
25 years—Constant 10.69 × $3,600,000	384,840	635,570
Cash return		$ 91,180

ratio loan request justified a participation of a greater amount than the 9¾% interest would yield. The time was a period of very tight money, and lenders were in good position to demand greater yields. Hence, the following features were added to the loan agreement:

1. The land amounting to 100,000 square feet was purchased by the lender for $3 per square foot and then leased back to the owner of the building for a ground rental of $50,000 per year.

2. As additional ground rental, the lender took 3% of the gross annual income, which amounted to approximately $21,000 more.

3. With the repayment of the loan calculated on a $6 per square foot rental, the lender demanded 15% of any rentals earned in excess of $6 per foot as a hedge against inflation.

With the substantial participation protection available to the lender in this loan agreement, there was no requirement for personal endorsement on the part of the borrower.

WAREHOUSE BUILDINGS

Another type of income property that is preferred by many investors because of its relatively low maintenance and management requirements is the warehouse building. The demand for warehouse space has grown substantially in this past decade for several reasons. Many types of companies use general warehouse space to store merchandise in peak seasons or to keep a product closer to its ultimate market, or perhaps there is a need to house an unusually large stock of some raw material.

Somewhat like office buildings, this type of facility can be built for use by an owner, such as a grocery chain operator; or it can be built for use in part by an owner, such as a light manufacturer with portions available for lease to others; or it can be built for speculative leasing as commercial warehouse space. It is the speculative warehouse that requires the most careful loan evaluation of the property. Owner-occupied or partially occupied buildings provide an established business with a source of income to substantiate and undergird the loan analysis. Warehouses are built fully preleased and partially preleased in much the same way as office buildings and shopping centers, so that the analysis of the two different types would be similar.

There are several basic requirements for effective warehouse space that would make it more easily rentable during the life of a loan. Like all other income properties, location is of paramount importance. The location of a warehouse should include accessibility by roads running in several directions and capable of handling large trucks. The warehouse should also be accessible to rail spurs, if possible. The land need not be in high-density traffic zones as required by shopping centers and some office buildings, but neither should it be locked into small street patterns that limit the size of the truck that can be accommodated. Availability of a rail siding is not essential to every user, but lack of this facility may limit future marketability. Another requirement that must be checked out is the availability of adequate water lines and pressures to support proper fire extinguisher installations. Without adequate fire protection, insurance rates skyrocket and greatly increase storage costs for the prospective tenant.

In the construction design of the building itself, provision should be made for loading docks capable of handling truck and freight-car loadings at the proper heights. The ceilings must be high, generally over 15 feet for more efficient stack storage of merchandise.

The costs of construction of a warehouse building are similar to those for a shopping center building inasmuch as both are fairly high ceiling buildings with little or no interior finishing provided by the builder. Warehouses require heavier floors to support more weight, but use much less parking space than a shopping center building. However, the cost of land suitable for a warehouse is much lower than that required for freeway-accessible shopping sites.

Warehouse leases often provide for a net return to the owner, which means the *tenant* pays all maintenance and operating costs, plus paying for all insurance and taxes on the building. In such a lease, management expenses would be held to a bare minimum. The cash available for debt service is thus very easy to calculate. On general warehouses with multi-tenant occupancy, the owner may provide some services and, most likely, will be responsible for taxes and insurance costs.

LOAN ANALYSIS OF INDUSTRIAL, RURAL, AND DEVELOPMENT PROPERTIES

SPECIAL-PURPOSE BUILDINGS

Buildings erected for specific purposes have more limited marketability or access to income than those categorized in the preceding chapter as income properties. Under this limited usage category falls industrial plants with specially designed floors to support heavy machinery or technical equipment, and/or with overhead structures carrying large cranes and conveyor systems. Also, processing plants such as refineries and chemical and mineral handling facilities all have singular usage. Other specialized type buildings, with a somewhat broader usage because of the large retail markets they serve, are such buildings as service stations, food franchise outlets, and automobile dealerships.

Large companies, who are the principal builders and owners of specialized properties, have the capability of generating investment money through the sale of bonds or through an increase in their issues/shares of stock. The discussion here focuses only on those circumstances in which an individual or company is seeking a mortgage loan to finance the construction or purchase of a special-purpose plant or building.

In evaluating a building of limited usage for a mortgage loan, the lender will obviously look to something in addition to the real estate value represented in the property itself. There are three methods that can be used to justify such a loan, which are as follows:

Money Good. To establish the amount of a loan that might be made, the "money good" approach would determine at what price the property could be liquidated under a forced sale. This is the amount of money that could be realized through foreclosure.

A loan made for such an amount would be reasonably well secured by the property. But the loan amount would probably be too small, relative to the total investment required, to be of practical value to the borrower. This method is not very common in today's financial markets, but it has been used.

Earnings Record of Borrower. Since the recovery of the loan in an orderly manner depends on the borrower's ability to produce income, the past record of profitable production is of paramount importance in the underwriting of a special-purpose property loan. A large company with established credit presents little problem. A smaller company, seeking to expand with a major investment, would require closer scrutiny. This would not only involve the credit record but also a review of the management personnel with their experience and capabilities.

Any *new venture* into a specialized area of business or production is generally not suitable for the mortgage lender's portfolio. Such enterprises can find suitable capital in the equity funding provided by the sale of stock. The security required by a mortgage lender limits the loans to reasonably well-proven and experienced people and companies.

Endorsement. The endorsement of a loan either by a customer or by a supplier is a fairly common practice when it proves advantageous to both parties.

An example of a customer giving loan support to a supplier might be a major grocery chain furnishing credit support to a truck gardener or a cattle feeder. Or a large equipment distributor could be giving financial assistance to one of its smaller manufacturing sources. The purpose, of course, is to assure the customer of a continued or enlarged source of product to sell. The method can be in the form of an outright endorsement of the mortgage note for a new facility. Or it can be given in the form of a letter-agreement guaranteeing certain amounts of purchases and providing for an assignment of the payments to a lender if required.

There are many instances in business today of a manufacturer or other supplier of materials assisting its customers by endorsement of their mortgage loans. The reason is to provide the supplier with better facilities through which he hopes to sell more products via the customer. Examples of this type of assistance abound in the manufacturer-automobile dealer relationship, and also in the pairing of major oil companies and their dealer-owned service stations. Some fast-food franchise operations, motel chains, and some equipment rental and distributorships commonly use the endorsement power of the licensing company to facilitate expansion. The endorsement need not be in the full amount of the loan to be helpful, but may entail underwriting a certain portion or specific amount.

By spreading the risk of the mortgage loan over several borrowers or endorsers, the lender may offer a lower interest rate and a longer term for repayment, if that is desirable.

FARM AND RANCH LOANS

At the turn of this century, 90% of our country's population lived on farms. Today, farmers make up less than 4% of the total population. And the farm loan business has changed, also. Two general categories of farm loans are: (1) the family-resident loan, and (2) the agri-corporate loan.

Family-Resident Farm Loans

The family-resident farm loan has not changed a great deal in the past 30 years. It is still based on the three legs of any good mortgage loan: (1) a credit-worthy borrower, (2) a piece of real estate of sufficient value to provide good collateral, and (3) the ability of the property and the borrower to produce an income assuring repayment of the loan. Judgments on farm land value require good knowledge and experience in a given geographical area. A single-crop farm is the most vulnerable to failure and subsequent loan default. A diversified crop operation, plus some livestock, gives the best security. So the ability of the farm to produce a continued income, regardless of an occasional crop failure or a fluctuating market, is a prime consideration in making a sound farm loan. The land value itself may be distorted by outside pressures such as a city growing nearby, or a large neighboring farm desiring to expand, or possibly a new freeway providing much frontage acreage. But the farm underwriter should confine his analysis to the producing factors: soil conditions, weather, available irrigation, type of crops, nearness to markets, and condition of the markets, for it is these factors that will produce the income from which the loan can be recovered. To give any substantial weight to the rising land values takes the loan into the category of land development.

Agri-corporate Farm Loans

Our agri-corporate loans show some similarity to special-purpose property loans. Large commercial farm companies control most of the nation's agriculture today and usually provide good business records to assist an underwriter in making an evaluation. Studies of land productivity with various crops and fertilizers, of the most effective methods of breeding and feeding livestock, and of the management techniques of cost control are all helpful in evaluating the operating procedures of commercial farms. These large farms have proved economical in their operations, and they are willing to test new technologies. Equipment can be more fully utilized and better maintained than on smaller holdings. But, along with the advantages, a word of caution: the dependency on hired labor and the management costs of a large commercial farm make them less flexible and more difficult to retrench in periods of lowering prices. The lender should hold his loan-to-value ratio at a conservative level in this type of operation.

The term of a farm loan varies as to need and may run from 10 to 40 years with 33 years a popular term, partly because the Federal Land Bank uses 33 years. More leniency is given in the repayment of farm loans than other real estate loans. A farmer's income is subject to greater variation, and a rigid payment schedule can be self-defeating. But any long-term farm loan should have full amortization as a goal.

Ranch Loans

A *ranch* presents only slight variations to a farm loan in that it produces livestock as the principal source of revenue. Because ranches are predominately in the water-short south-western regions, an underwriter must take care to analyze the water situation. Often water rights can be of greater value than the land since without water the land may be worthless. A common practice in ranching is to lease public lands for grazing. The acreage so leased becomes of value to the ranch only in the productivity the land can add to the ranch, and this can be limited by the term of the lease. But leased land or grazing rights do add value and should be included in the appraisal for loan purposes. Sometimes ranches produce additional revenues from the sale of timber rights, from mineral leasing, and even from hunting leases and dude ranching. All income has its value but must be considered according to its tenure and stability.

LAND PURCHASE LOANS

With the increasing interest in urban and suburban growth, the purchase of land for the purpose of speculative resale has grown substantially in the past ten years. A limited number of lending institutions do make loans for raw land purchases, notably some commercial banks and a very few savings associations. The loan-to-value limits are generally lower, perhaps 50% to 60% of the value, and the term is seldom over three years.

Lenders do not like to look at the actual sale of the collateral as the normal means of recovering on a mortgage loan (exceptions: house construction and land development loans). And lenders are particularly wary of a tract of raw land that may or may not have a market. Hence, such loans are made primarily to persons or companies that represent substantial other assets, and secondarily loans are made where there is a future intended use or sale that can be confirmed.

To expand on the second type of loan mentioned above, the one with a future intended use or sale, the land may be purchased for a housing development, or perhaps a shopping center, and so more time is needed to complete plans and permanent financing. The lender assisting in the immediate purchase of the land is thus in a prime position to make the construction and permanent loans if the conditions meet his requirements.

Sometimes a land broker or a developer will locate a tract of land highly suitable for a particular purchaser. It could be a small tract for a service station, or a larger parcel on which to erect a retail store outlet. But at the time the property becomes available, the ultimate user may not be in a position to consummate the land purchase. In such a circumstance, a binding letter of intent issued to a real estate broker or developer of some substance would greatly facilitate a raw land loan to acquire the chosen site. The land broker would be presenting the lender a reasonably sure sale for the land within a specified time period, with the land itself as collateral.

A loan for the purchase of raw land, regardless of its intended use, classifies as a commercial loan for a savings association and therefore falls into the limited, nonresidential end of the loan portfolio.

LAND DEVELOPMENT

The next step after the purchase of raw land is its development. "Land development" for loan purposes means the building of streets and utilities to prepare lots for resale as homesites. The development work associated with the construction of an apartment or office building project is in the category of "site development" or land preparation and is an integral part of the project construction costs.

Since the work called for in the land development plans can easily identify the project for residential purposes, such a loan is much more acceptable to a savings association than the land purchase itself.

A development loan can be made for as much as 75% or 80% of the appraised value of the finished lots, but is seldom permitted to exceed the costs incurred in the land acquisition and construction costs. This is one of several similar types of loans that generate what might be called a certain distortion in values, due to the fact that the very development being financed greatly enhances the value of the raw land. Federal regulations for savings associations permit a loan at 75% of the appraised value for residential land development. Conceivably, the appraised value of the completed lots based on an existing market would be substantially greater than the development costs. A 75% loan would permit the developer to borrow an amount in excess of his actual investment. In lending terminology, the amount of a loan that exceeds a borrower's actual costs is called "walking money"—money the borrower can walk away with upon completion. The prudent lender is reluctant to permit a borrower to obtain a cash "profit" from a development or construction loan since this has a tendency to lessen the incentive to sell the property as intended.

An integral part of a land development loan agreement is the release mechanism. This is the clause that spells out when, how, and at what price any lot or lots may be released. The release terms may call for an order of priorities by which the land can be developed and will state in what manner the lot will be released, and most important, they will specify the amount of money from each lot sale that must be paid to the lender for the release.

The release itself is a specific release of the mortgage lien on the lot or lots being sold, and is intended to permit the delivery of a clear title to the lot purchaser by the developer. The amount of money required to release a lot may be a percentage of the sales price of the lot, stating a minimum sales price. In this procedure any increase in sales price over the minimum would increase the payment to the lender and amortize the loan more rapidly. Another method is to set a flat sum on each lot for release and let the developer sell at whatever price he can. The flat sum per lot is usually calculated so as to repay the development loan with interest in full when somewhere between 50% and 75% of the lots have been sold.

Since 1968, the Department of Housing and Urban Development (HUD) has had an Office of Interstate Land Sales charged by Congress with the responsibility of establishing guidelines and procedures for land developers in an effort to minimize deceptive practices and outright frauds. Sale of lots, developed and undeveloped, has grown to $6 billion per year in this country and has brought out some unscrupulous operators. Basically, the rules require nothing more than a full disclosure of the essential facts for the land buyer and can serve as a protection for both buyer and seller. As one explanation goes, a developer can still sell a lot that is completely under water, but he must state in writing that it is under water! The rules apply to any development with over 50 lots for sale, of less than five acres each, and on which no construction is required. Failure to comply with the HUD regulations can involve a fine and imprisonment for the *lender* as well as the developer and his agents.

CONSTRUCTION LOANS

The construction industry employs approximately 5 million people in this country and is a considerable factor with its need for money. Construction lending is a highly specialized field and one that relatively few lenders become involved in. The loans pertinent to this text are those secured by first mortgages on the property under construction and are for short terms ranging from six months to three years, depending upon the type of project being funded. Due to the relatively high risk involved, interest rates are at the top of the spectrum, depending greatly on the financial strength and experience represented by the borrower.

One of the largest areas of construction is under government contracts (streets, highways, utilities, dams, public buildings, etc.) and under contracts for major corporations. In both of these, the owner can pay for the construction out of its own revenues, or from the sale of bonds. Contractors are paid on a monthly basis for work completed. No mortgages can be allowed on the land involved. If a contractor needs cash to carry through from month to month, it could be accomplished by pledging the contract payments with a commercial bank. This text will be confined to construction lending that involves the pledge of real estate for collateral.

Definition

The definition of a construction loan focuses on the special requirements for this type of financing. A construction loan is initially a loan commitment; the money is disbursed to the builder during construction in such a manner as to insure payment of all construction costs and financing charges and to require completion of the building in accordance with the plans and specifications so as to deliver a valid first mortgage at completion.

In dissecting this definition, we find first of all that a construction loan is normally paid out as the building progresses, not issued in a lump sum payment at the beginning. The disbursements are made only for work completed, either based on regular calendar periods, monthly or bimonthly perhaps, or on a progress point, such as the completion of all underground work or the pouring of foundations. To insure that payment goes to the proper parties, checks can be disbursed directly to subcontractors and suppliers with the consent of the general contractor, or by including both the general contractor and the subcontractor as payees on the check. If any laborer or supplier is not paid, he can file a lien on the property, which must be cleared before a valid first mortgage can be passed on to the permanent lender. The amount of a progress payment is a matter of determination by the lender. It is a common failure of the inexperienced lender to overpay on progress and thus jeopardize the final completion. An inspecting architect often serves as a final arbiter between the contractor and the lender to determine the proper progress payment.

The building must be completed in order to release the permanent loan funds, and it must be in accordance with the plans and specs or the permanent loan can be withheld. Consequently, the construction loan must be handled at all times so as to require adherence to the plans and to make sure sufficient money is on hand to complete the building. A cost overrun should be covered by demanding a cash deposit from the builder or sponsor. It is customary to withhold 10% of each construction payment until final completion as a protection against unexpected liens and as a hedge to insure completion.

The principal sources for construction money are commercial banks with specialized construction loan departments, savings associations, and recently the Real Estate Investment Trusts. The commercial banks' interest is in the higher yields and short terms represented in construction lending; savings associations and the REITS prefer the higher yields, but also are usually in a position to pick up the permanent loans at a minimum of expense to themselves.

There are many variations in the handling of construction loans. Some procedures used in major categories of buildings are outlined below:

Construction Loans for Residential Properties

Single-family detached houses and some townhouse projects are financed by builders on both a contract basis and a speculative basis.

Contract Basis. A house built for an owner under contract represents a reduced risk to the construction lender. The normal sales contract is a firm commitment by the purchaser and includes a permanent loan commitment for closing. Often the permanent commitment is made by the same lender handling the construction financing as a sort of packaged deal, which minimizes paper work. On such a loan the risk to the construction lender is primarily in the builder's ability to complete the house within the contract terms. The builder's record must be known to the lender.

In smaller communities and rural areas, houses are often constructed under contract by a local builder, who also operates his own lumber yard, with the builder providing the construction financing from his own resources. A nearby savings association will have already agreed to make the permanent loan when the house is completed.

Speculative Basis. Many builders, mostly in the growing suburban areas, build houses with the expectation of selling them by the time they are completed. To the risk of being able to complete the house within the projected cost figure is added the risk of selling the house at a profitable price upon completion. A lender must look at the strength and capability of a speculative builder before accepting such a loan. As a builder proves himself to the lender, his construction line of credit can be expanded.

When the housing market fluctuates downward, the speculative builder is the first to be hurt. He can be caught with many unsold houses on which the high interest of the construction loan continues to eat at any profits. More and more, construction lenders are seeking to protect themselves against a soft market by demanding a "take-out commitment" before they will agree to the construction loan. As described in Chapter 6, a take-out commitment for a house loan would be an agreement to make the permanent house loan directly to the builder if the house is not sold within one year from the commitment date. The cost of the commitment is usually one point payable at issuance. The loan so committed to the builder would be at the same ratio as the construction loan, usually 80% of the sales value of the house, but the rate of interest would be one to three percentage points over the going rate and the term much shorter, probably ten years, than if the loan had been made to the intended occupant-buyer. The builder still has the problem of selling the house, but has a little breather in facing a monthly amortization payment rather than full repayment of the construction loan, while the construction lender is clear with all his money back.

Construction Loans for Income Properties

Apartments, office buildings, shopping centers, and ware-houses all use construction financing, sometimes termed *interim financing*, to accomplish the building of the project. As pointed out earlier, only the very strongest builder-developers are capable of commanding construction financing of any income property without a permanent loan commit-ment to pay off the construction loan at completion. The terms of the permanent loan influence the manner in which the construction money can be handled. Special requirements for funding the permanent loan, such as an 80% lease-up before release of the loan proceeds, place the construction lender in a far more risky position. If a permanent lender is currently unavailable, the developer may resort to a standby commitment in the same genre, or identical to, a take-out commitment that calls for much higher payments. The con-struction lender must have a closing date for the take-out within a reasonable period (one to three years) for proper recovery of the construction loan.

Construction lending calls for highly experienced person-nel who can work with builders and who understand con-struction progress and procedures so as to make timely releases of the loan proceeds. Most lenders will not release a progress draw without physically inspecting the project or having an independent architect inspector submit his esti-mate of work accomplished. The trick is to be able to com-plete the project within the money available and still have 10% of the loan amount retained at completion to protect the lender against any unforseen contingencies. When the lender is satisfied that all bills are paid and that no valid liens can be filed, he can then release this 10% retainage.

MOBILE HOME PARKS

A fairly recent addition to the national scene as a property investment is the mobile home park. This type of project has long been developed in such resort areas as California,

Arizona, and Florida, but only since the late sixties has the mobile home park concept spread to most of the country as a way of life.

Mobile home parks considered in this text are those projects that are built for the leasing of land space to the owners of mobile homes. Some mobile home parks are handled much like ordinary subdivisions in that the land is sold to the mobile home owner. As a subdivision development for the sale of lots, the financing would be much the same as discussed earlier in this chapter under the heading of Land Development. The use of the completed park facility for the *rental* of lots presents the problem of permanent financing for the entire development. This can be done either with a conventional loan similar to an apartment loan, or with an FHA-insured commitment.

The original impetus for mobile home parks, outside of resort areas, was to provide a lower cost type of housing. The mobile home, no longer just a trailer that could be pulled behind the family car, became a completely furnished living unit 40 to 60 feet in length. The smaller units can be purchased, including furniture, for $4000 or $5000, can be parked in a space that provides little more than a parking lot, and can provide adequate living accommodations at considerably less cost than a normal house. The larger units with "double width" sections can exceed normal housing costs, running upward of $25,000 to $30,000.

So again there is considerable variation in the size of investment involved in a mobile home park. The more spartan projects provide ten or twenty spaces, often built personally by the owner of the land, and can be very lucrative if kept occupied. One of the major attractions to this form of land use is the low maintenance costs.

The middle-size mobile home park has shown the greatest growth and was spurred by a broadening of the Federal Housing Administration insuring requirements in 1969. In an effort to provide more housing for middle and lower income families, the FHA increased their insurable limits to 90% of the finished park's value and to terms of 30 years. The insurance provided by the FHA brought in many private investors who would otherwise not have been able to finance such an undertaking. And the FHA set some sound standards of quality for their parks to avoid the "parking lot syndrome." Paved streets were required, minimal landscaping was specified, and some storage space for each housing unit was included. The density of units per acre was limited to a maximum of eight, and recreational facilities such as a clubhouse, swimming pool, or tennis courts were encouraged.

Because the FHA procedures called for a final closing of the permanent loan that would include the entire project, it was necessary to complete all spaces, or pads, in one stage. Lease-up of the large parks thus developed was often slow and caused financial drains to the investors.

Conventional lenders for mobile home parks permit the development in stages to allow for lease-up and growth of income before proceeding.

In 1970, the Veterans Administration added a new benefit for veterans to permit a mobile home to be financed and a lot to be purchased under its guarantee programs. The interest rate and term allowed have not been sufficient to provide much enthusiasm among lenders, but this new development has helped promote some growth in mobile homes as a living accommodation.

Analysis of a Park

Like other forms of income property, a mobile home park must be well located and serve a market demand. The "building" consists of site preparation, underground utilities connecting streets, and concrete or all-weather pads for placement of the housing units. The only structures involved are usually a clubhouse-office building, a laundry building, and such recreational facilities as the developer elects to provide.

Maintenance requirements are minimal as the tenant is primarily leasing a piece of land. Mobile home parks operate on a cost as low as 20% to 25% of their gross rental income.

Mobile home living has been most popular where at least one of the following five situations exist: (1) a military base, (2) a construction project, (3) a college or university, (4) a resort area, (5) a retirement-oriented community.

One of the problems in the profitable development has been the longer lease-up period. Unlike apartments, which can be leased to good occupancy over fairly short periods in a strong market, the mobile home park tends to lease-up at a slower rate. Sources within the industry have reported an average rate of rent-up at ten-to-twelve spaces per month for a new park. However, it has also been observed that once a mobile home is moved into location, it seldom moves out of the park. One reason, of course, is that mobile homes are not built for travel, but are actually semipermanent dwellings. Also, where moving is contemplated, the cost of moving at 50¢ to $1 per mile serves as a deterrant since the moving costs could easily exceed the value of the equity in the mobile home. Hence, it is far more common for an owner who may be transferred to a new location to simply offer his mobile home for sale on its present location and purchase another at his future destination. The result for the owner of a mobile home park is that he can actually count on a more stable income than he could look to in an apartment investment. Once the pad is leased, there is a security provided by the mobile home itself that provides good assurance of continuous rental payments.

The lending industry does not respond quickly to anything new, preferring instead the comfortable security of a proven good thing. So, in many areas of the country, conventional loans have been slow to surface for the development of mobile home parks. As more experience has demonstrated the values of this type of investment, financing is more easily obtained. A park loan can now be insured against default by private mortgage insurance companies, thus facilitating the trading of these loans in the secondary market.

FINANCING MOBILE HOMES

Mobile homes do not fall in the category of true real estate, but are regarded as personal property in the same way as an automobile. Financing of these homes will be considered briefly here, since they represent some 20 to 25% of the housing units built for sale or rental in this country each year.

Partly because they are an outgrowth of the much smaller house trailer, the mobile home is financed in a similar manner to an automobile. Most states will license and tax them as a highway vehicle, causing some dissension and controversy within communities where mobile homes locate and utilize local schools and police and fire protection facilities.

Underwriting programs by both the FHA and VA have provided some impetus to the growth of mobile home sales. And conventional procedures have kept pace. All these loans follow the pattern of a consumer loan, not a mortgage loan, and are secured by an assignment or a lien on the title registered with the state agency for vehicles.

The term for mobile home loans is longer than for a car, generally running for ten to twelve years. But the interest is the same "add on" type used in car loans. According to this method, for example, a 7.5% add-on interest produces a 12.41% annual rate for a ten-year loan and a 12.10% annual rate for a twelve-year loan.

The majority of conventional lenders handling mobile home loans employ the services of one of several companies specializing in the insuring and processing of vehicle loans. For a small fee, a percentage of the monthly payment, the service company sells a default insurance policy to the lender. The service company uses this fee to handle delinquencies and if repossession becomes necessary, will pay off on the default insurance and assume responsibility for recovering and reselling the repossessed unit. Some service companies act as the regular monthly collection agency for the loan with the lending source, such as a savings association, simply providing the cash for acceptable loans. This service is similar to that of a mortgage banker handling real estate loans for a lender.

ALTERNATIVE FINANCING METHODS

SALE OF MORTGAGE BONDS

At several points in the text, reference has been made to the sale of bonds as a method of financing a real estate project. Years ago, the sale of bonds was the principal means of raising real estate investment money because the repayment had been a consistently good one. An additional advantage for the issuer and seller, prior to the establishment of the SEC (Securities and Exchange Commission), was the lack of regulation. Security sales during the Depression of the 1930s came to a near cessation. The rebirth of mortgage companies after the Depression utilized existing pools of investment funds rather than sales to the general public as a primary source of lendable money.

The creation of the SEC in 1934 introduced some measure of control to the securities industry, and the enforcement of these regulations was helpful in preventing fraud, deception, and abusive practices in connection with the sale of stocks and bonds. In today's market, only a few of the very largest companies, such as American Telephone, attempt to sell large issues of bonds direct to the general public. The majority of companies work in tandem with investment bankers who are knowledgeable in securities regulations, and whose organizations are staffed with sales personnel capable of handling the distribution.

Because the sale of any kind of security, whether stocks or bonds, requires some established record and credibility, developers taking this step are usually limited to better known companies and individuals of strong financial worth. Considerable initial time and expenses are required for the proper registration of a bond issue, involving extensive legal work and accounting data to be submitted to the SEC, which must then approve the issue, clearing it for sale to the public. The cost of registration alone, for instance, can run as high as several hundred thousand dollars.

A bond issue secured by a pledge of real property would be termed a mortgage bond. There are also equipment bonds secured by such things as freight cars or airplanes. A bond that is not secured is called a "debenture" bond and is similar to a promissory note. What the SEC requires is that the issuer fully disclose all information relative to the company and its key personnel, the security behind the bond issue, and how the proceeds of the sale will be used. Failure to comply with SEC requirements is a felony offense, subject to fine and imprisonment.

Once a bond issue has been registered and approved, the investment banker can handle the sale in two different ways. First, he can make an outright purchase of the entire issue at a discount off the full value. He then resells the issue to his investor clients at a higher price, usually with the help of a network of associated investment banking firms across the country. With very large issues, several of the major investment houses may join together to underwrite the issue. It takes an intimate knowledge of the market conditions to handle a block purchase with the expectation of making a profit from the mark-up of its discount price.

The second method can be termed the "best efforts" plan. This actually means just what the name implies—the investment banker will sell the issue at whatever the market will bring, retaining a fixed commission for his services.

PRIVATE PLACEMENT OF SECURITIES

The growth of major investors, such as the insurance companies, the mutual funds, and pension funds, has up to now dominated the activity on the national security exchanges. However, there is a growing trend to bypass these public markets and place both stock and bond issues directly with an investor. From the point of view of the issuer, the procedure has some advantages, including: (1) no SEC registration required, (2) no publicity—no public pronouncements, on proprietary information regarding company products or processes, (3) financial conditions of closely held companies remain confidential information, (4) more flexibility in terms with a negotiated private placement, thereby benefiting both the borrower and the lender, and (5) lower sales costs for the issue.

It is within this field of the private placement of securities that mortgage bankers have become increasingly active and directly competitive with the investment banker. Mortgage companies have good contacts with many sources of money and are familiar with the special needs of each for investments. The sale of a block of securities to their regular investors is a natural expansion of their business relationship.

SEC REGULATIONS FOR REAL ESTATE-TYPE SALES

The growth in sales of various types of "certificates" to finance real estate developments has brought increased scrutiny by the SEC as to any violations of the securities laws. In general, the SEC considers the sale of any form of a partial interest in land to the general public as a type of security and subject to its regulations. The many forms in which real estate developers present their various "deals" has brought a number of new rulings, all with the purpose to protect the general public against fraud and misrepresentation. In various new rulings, the SEC has considered a predevelopment sale of certificates for lots as a form of securities; the sale of condominium units that may be available for rental purposes has come under registration guidelines; and if the sale of partnership interests is solicited publicly, as opposed to a contact *from* an interested purchaser, then a clearance is needed from the SEC.

In any real estate project involving ownership by a group of persons or companies, the prudent lender will obtain a legal opinion to determine if proper compliance is being made with both federal and state security regulations.

PURCHASE AND LEASE-BACK

One method of financing a real property acquisition is to find a willing investor who will buy or build the property and lease it back to the intended user. Tax laws have made this procedure very practical for charitable institutions or tax-exempt organizations such as churches in order to purchase land and build as may be required to lease, without being subject to property taxes. In addition, the income from the lease payments is exempt from income tax and can be set on a somewhat lower scale to benefit the lessee. This mutually advantageous plan can be used for many types of buildings, stores, service stations, industrial plants, or office buildings, to name a few.

The purchase and lease-back procedure is not confined to a tax-exempt user only; it is also used by major companies, such as oil companies seeking to expand their marketing operations, who will build and lease a property for a particular tenant. Another variation of this procedure is the municipally owned industrial park. A city that wants to increase business and the number of jobs for the community will acquire a suitable tract of land, develop it, and build buildings for lease to acceptable tenants, all for the purpose of attracting more industry. The money for such land purchase and construction is generated by the sale of municipal bonds, not always guaranteed by the issuing community, but always in the tax-exempt municipal category.

LAND LEASES

Businessmen have always felt a strong need for owning something tangible, and with some individuals there has been an almost fanatical pursuit of, and obsessive attraction to, land ownership and the consequent feeling of security such ownership provides. The all-powerful urge to own land simply as land, however, is gradually giving way in this era to a more realistic approach that values land for the uses that can be made of it, instead of just for its ownership alone. Most of the material things we consider essential to sustain and maintain our life style can now be rented, such as houses, cars, appliances, and furniture. Business enterprises have long been accustomed to renting buildings as well as owning them, but they have usually insisted on owning their own equipment. Now, through specialized leasing companies, even the most intricate machinery and equipment can be leased. The advantage to the lessee is that his capital is not tied up, the lease payments are all tax-deductible expenses, and the equipment may be more easily exchanged for newer models, thereby reducing the problem of obsolescence.

As land becomes less available there has been a tendency for land owners to lease rather than sell property. Many land areas in Hawaii cannot be purchased at any price, but these areas can be leased for very long terms, thus allowing home building to continue. Some of the more densely populated areas of California, as well as much midtown urban land in all major cities, are subject to acquisition by long-term lease only. Mortgage lenders are able to finance buildings on leased land through agreements that recognize the land lease and provide for certain assignments of rights in case of default. This would not be a first mortgage loan in most states, but is acceptable to some lenders who are permitted to make such a loan. From a practical standpoint, for the lender's protection, the land rental payments can be handled much the same as property taxes.

USE OF OTHER COLLATERAL

Mortgage loans can be made on the basis of the real property plus some other form of collateral that may be pledged. If the borrower needs more money than the property alone will permit, the lender can ask for more security: additional property, stocks or bonds, an assignment of equipment, or such other assets mutually agreed to by the lender and borrower. With additional collateral, the lender has recourse to other assets for recovery of his loan if it becomes necessary.

Personal Endorsement. The personal endorsement of the borrower for the benefit of his company, relative, or associate is a form of additional collateral to the lender. Large corporate borrowers do not use personal endorsements, but with smaller companies and those under majority control by one stockholder, it is not uncommon to request the personal endorsement of the principals—one or all of them. A personal guarantee on a mortgage loan can be limited. For example, if five men are endorsing a $100,000 loan, each might ask to limit his liability to $20,000. Approval would be a matter of decision by the lender. Without a specific limitation, each endorser of a note is exposed, or is said to carry a contingent liability, to the full amount of the debt.

Compensating Balances. Cash balances carried in an account with the lending institution, when it is a commercial bank or savings association, can be deemed additional collateral when a minimum balance is required as a condition of the loan agreement. This procedure is also called a *compensating balance*. The requirement to maintain a certain minimum cash balance is not unusual since it gives the lender some assurance that cash is on hand, and this does add some strength to the borrower's financial statement. Compensating balances have also been used to entice or pressure a bank to grant a line of credit to the borrower.

Assignment of Life Insurance. Life insurance companies are probably more interested than other lenders in adding the assignment of life insurance policies on the principal borrowers' lives to the list of additional collateral. This practice is a reasonable requirement for any lender when the successful payout of a loan is heavily based on the ability of one or two principals to operate a business. Some home owners also carry mortgage pay-out life insurance, a declining balance form that covers the amortized balance due on a loan in case of the premature death of the borrower. However, no lender yet requires this particular type of insurance in conjunction with the granting of a home loan.

SALE OF EQUITY INTERESTS

Two types of equity investment have become popular as methods for financing real estate—syndications and realty funds.

Syndication

In real estate ventures, a syndicate is a form of limited partnership organized to carry out a specific project, and upon completion of that project, is dissolved. Syndicates operate in a number of other businesses, motion pictures for example, and are composed of groups of people or companies formed to carry out a particular enterprise. The purpose is to generate a large amount of capital by increasing the number of investors, or simply to spread the risk of a project and jointly share in the rewards.

The sale of participating interests in the large real estate developments, or in the purchase of a large tract of land to hold for speculative growth in value, has increased substantially over the past decade. Escalating land values have attracted the interest of many smaller investors, and by joining a group the risk is spread and the benefits are a bit more secure.

Most states have set limits on the number of persons that can comprise one syndicate, or in the total amount that can be sold, or in the manner of sale. Any effort to sell a syndicate interest across state lines or through the mails involves the federal rules spelled out by the Securities and Exchange Commission. Competent legal counsel is needed for guidance in any sales effort involving joint ownership interests.

Realty Funds

Whenever a larger group is formed to participate in a real estate venture, and registration with federal and state regulatory agencies is necessary, the participation can be in the form of "units" purchased in a realty fund.

Realty funds are organized by persons or companies wishing to raise equity money for real estate projects, such as the purchase of raw land, a construction development, or the purchase of existing income properties. The interests are sold in the form of participating certificates at a fixed price per unit. A unit generally costs anywhere from $100 to $5000, depending on the plan of organization, and represents a certain percent of interest in the total fund. Federal and most state laws classify the sale of such participating interests as a sale of securities that must be registered and approved before any sale can be made.

The participant is actually a limited partner and may share in the tax losses and depreciation as well as the profits generated through the fund's investments. The organizer of the fund is usually the general partner, or a company he controls is so designated, and he also serves as the managing agent for the partnership properties.

SPECIAL TYPES OF FINANCING

While most mortgage financing follows a fairly standard pattern of a first mortgage as security based on a reasonable loan-to-value ratio and fully amortized over the term of the loan, there are some interesting variations that can be used in special circumstances. When the situation calls for a more flexible approach to a loan, the following basic methods might be considered, either separately or in combination, as need or imagination may demand.

Although some proposals become more imaginative than

realistic, proper use of specialized financing techniques can rescue a faltering real estate sale or breathe new life into an otherwise stalled project. In the hands of a skilled promoter, some of these procedures reflect the so-called wheeler-dealer concept of development financing. But there is a telling story in an old cartoon depicting a rather seedy looking tramp relaxed on a park bench and picking his teeth with a piece of straw. The caption reads, "I never quite got the hang of it. I was always dealing when I should have been wheeling, and wheeling when I should have been dealing."

Wrap-around Mortgage

The wrap-around mortgage is a method used to facilitate the sale of a property by encouraging the seller to accept a second mortgage note as partial payment in lieu of cash for his equity. It is most commonly used when the equity has built up substantially over the years and the first mortgage carries an earlier, lower interest rate. The purpose is to hold the advantage of the lower first mortgage interest for the benefit of the seller and, in so doing, to substantially decrease the initial cash requirement for the benefit of the buyer.

To illustrate with a hypothetical example, let us say a building is offered for sale at a price of $100,000, which is acceptable to the buyer. The first mortgage loan, now 10 years old with an interest rate of 5¼%, is paid down to a balance due of $55,000. On a straight assumption basis, the buyer would need $45,000 cash. Or with a new first mortgage loan on the older building, the maximum loan-to-value ratio being offered would be 75%, which would require $25,000 cash. But the buyer does not want to use even that much initial cash in the purchase. Under such conditions a "wrap-around" mortgage might well resolve the problem and make the sale possible. The proposal is for the buyer to pay just $10,000 cash and grant to the seller a wrap-around mortgage on the property for $90,000 at 7¼% interest, which would acknowledge the existing first mortgage. Under this arrangement the seller is actually undertaking a second mortgage loan in the amount of $35,000, at a fair interest rate, plus earning an additional 2% of interest on the first mortgage.

Normally, the seller would continue to make the regular payments on the first mortgage obligation, using the proceeds from the second mortgage payments to do so. The buyer, paying on his $90,000 obligation each month, would of course require some protective clause granting him the right to make the first mortgage payments direct to the first mortgagee if a potential default should arise.

Balloon Note

The purpose of a "balloon" payment is to permit smaller monthly installments for the first few years and to retain the loan in a short-term classification for the lending institution. The smaller monthly payments (less than the amount to fully amortize the loan) are made for, say, three years, at which time the full unpaid balance becomes due.

If, for example, the borrower needed $25,000 and offered adequate collateral, the lender under this type of loan would accept principal payments of $200 per month, plus accrued interest, for up to three years. At the end of the third year, the final payment due in full would be $18,000, plus interest. (Payments of $200 each for 35 months amount to a principal reduction of $7000.)

It is often assumed that if the payments are promptly made, the lender will renew and extend the final balloon payment for another limited term of small principal payments. But the lender is by no means legally obligated to do so, and circumstances can force him to require a full pay-off on the note when due.

"Interest Only"

The expression "interest only" covers a variation of the balloon note procedure in that for the first year or so nothing is paid on the principal, and only the interest is due. This method is most commonly used today in the sale of raw land, but is applicable to any kind of loan.

If a seller is commanding a good market price for his land and does not need immediate cash, he has a better chance of selling the property by handling his own financing and making it attractive to the speculative buyer, such as a syndicated group. In such a case, the purchaser buying the land for resale rather than development wants as small a cash investment as possible, hoping to resell within several years at a profit.

To use an example: if a person owns 40 acres of land and sells it for $5000 per acre, or $200,000 total, he may carry the sales amount as a loan to the buyer and collect 8% interest for the first two years. Thus, the buyer takes title to the property, subject to the seller's mortgage in the amount of $200,000, and each year pays $16,000 to the seller as tax-deductible interest. Before the two years have elapsed, the buyer finds another company who will pay $8000 an acre for the land in cash. Now, the second sale at a later date for $320,000 clears the $200,000 first mortgage and any accrued interest, leaving a substantial profit on a relatively small cash investment.

The trick is being able to make that second sale.

Extended Terms

Most companies selling a service or product need their accounts receivable paid promptly and often offer cash discounts for such payments. A few companies utilize credit terms as an incentive to do business with them and, in so doing, provide additional financing for the customer.

In building an apartment, an office building, or even a house, a major supplier such as a lumber dealer, a cement company, or an electrical or plumbing contractor may agree to extend his payment terms for 60 or 90 days, or in some cases, until the project is finished and sold. This method does conserve cash for the builder-developer, but usually comes at a higher price—an increase in the product or service price plus interest. And the supplier exposes himself to a payment delay that usually means a forfeiture of his lien rights if it exceeds 120 days.

This "extended terms" method of auxiliary finance is not to be confused with slow payment or nonpayment of material-men's bills; both are very poor procedures. Building supply companies are fully aware of the 90- to 120-day time limits within which to file liens for nonpayment and normally make sure that their interests are protected.

Supplier Loans

In recent years some of the major appliance companies and, in a few cases, utility companies have given larger builder-developers financial assistance with outright loans secured by second mortgages. The ulterior motive in such cases is always to insure the use of the lender's products. This could be heating and air conditioning equipment or a full range of kitchen equipment, or it could be a utility company seeking a competitive advantage.

Subordination

Subordination is a procedure used to grant priority to a specific lien so as to permit better financing of a project. In this method, a landowner or a mortgage holder, for a consideration, might subordinate his position in favor of a specific lending institution in order to meet a loan requirement.

A possible situation wherein this procedure could be used would be a landowner, not wishing to sell his land, but desiring development and income, agrees to a long-term land lease to, say, a motel chain. In order to help finance the construction of the motel building, the landowner would agree to subordinate (to make inferior) his ownership rights to the mortgage lien, as arranged by the motel chain. Normally, the motel chain would have to be sufficiently strong financially to give the landowner reasonable assurance of performance under the lease terms. And the landowner would expect to retain the right to step in and assume the mortgage payments, with rights to the motel's income, in case of an act in default by the motel chain.

Leverage

The word *leverage* is defined as the mechanical advantage of a lever. In real estate jargon, the term has several variations, but in essence it means the use of a relatively small amount of cash to induce a large mortgage loan for the purchase of a property. The term belongs more properly in the vocabulary of the promoter-developer who feels the escalation in land value will provide a lucrative return on the equity investment. As long as values inflate, the theory holds up well.

From a lender's viewpoint, the high-ratio loans, i.e., those of low cash equity, are not highly desirable. The rapid rise in land values generally, since the mid-sixties, has provided a safety margin of its own for existing properties, as the values appreciate instead of depreciate in some areas. But the underwriter cannot always count on a speculative increase in value to prove the soundness of the loan.

ANALYZING
BORROWERS

Most of the attention of previous chapters has been focused on the physical property and its evaluation as collateral for a mortgage loan, with only occasional references to the borrower. In this chapter, discussion will be focused primarily on the borrower together with the information required for evaluating an individual borrower's ability to repay a loan.

Since borrowers applying for loans through FHA and VA procedures have been discussed in Chapter 8, this chapter will consider the problems of the borrower seeking a conventional real estate loan, the information supplied in a loan application, and analysis of the application, plus the necessary credit report and the information it must disclose.

The last part of the chapter will turn from individual home borrowers to corporate analysis.

SOURCES FOR INDIVIDUAL HOME LOANS

Most people borrow money to purchase a home only once or twice in a lifetime. Often, it is a brand-new experience for the average borrower. How should this uninitiated person proceed?

271

Fortunately, there are many specialists in the field to turn to for advice and guidance.

The Real Estate Broker

Since the house is normally selected before a loan is considered, one of the first knowledgeable experts to look to is the broker handling the house sale. Most states have licensing and bonding statutes to assure the public of the broker's qualifications. The more competent brokers maintain current information on the various local sources of mortgage money, the type of loans each are negotiating, the interest rate, and the current fees charged for service. In the past, some brokers made arrangements with a cooperative lender to send customers to that lender for a split of the fee. The FHA banned this practice as it could be used to the disadvantage of the home buyer. And, in conventional loans, it is not considered to be a good procedure because it limits competition.

In some areas of the country, particularly in the smaller communities, a knowledgeable real estate broker can and does perform a valuable service for the lender by taking a loan application and handling some of the preliminary steps of asking for verifications. For this work the broker earns a portion of the finance fee. When actual work is performed on the loan application by the broker, the FHA permits payment in relation to the services rendered. Payments of this kind are not considered as "fee splitting."

Loan Broker

Independent loan brokers in some areas of the country are very active, maintaining contacts with real estate sales personnel, local savings associations, architects, attorneys, bankers, and any others who would have need for assistance in securing loans for their customers or clients. The independent broker could be called by the real estate broker, for example, at the consummation of a sales contract to assist the buyer in the proper placement of his loan.

The independent broker carries current knowledge of where the best loans can be secured and performs a valuable service for both borrower and lender. He earns his brokerage fee, usually ½ to 1% of the loan, by taking the loan application from the borrower to make certain it is complete and accurate. He assists in the verification of data and assembles the essential information needed in the application package by the lender. The independent broker generally works with smaller lenders who cannot afford the fixed cost of a salaried representative making calls on potential customers.

Mortgage Companies

Leading the way in the field of merchandizing mortgage loans is the mortgage banking industry. In the larger communities, mortgage companies compete heavily with each other through their loan representatives. In periods of easy money, some real estate brokerage firms are besieged with calls from mortgage companies seeking loan business. Those firms that can continue funding loans in periods of tight money gain considerable support from the real estate industry in easier times.

The mortgage company field representative is a trained specialist in the intricacies of loan applications, and sensitive to the points that need clarification or verification for proper underwriting evaluation. The mortgage company representative can take an application at the place and time most convenient to the applicant. It has been this type of assistance to the borrower that has enabled the mortgage companies to handle well over half of all home loans in the country.

Savings Associations

As pointed out in Chapter 4, the leading source for mortgage money—the savings and loan associations—handle loans both through intermediaries, such as mortgage companies or brokers, and also directly to their customers. Some of the more aggressive savings associations have followed the mortgage companies practice of sending loan representatives into the field to call on potential loan applicants. But most savings associations rely on their own depositors and the business contacts made by their officers to attract loan applicants into their own building locations to make applications for loans. Qualified lending officers take the loan applications, obtain the necessary substantiating information, and in most cases, personally present the application to the loan committee for approval. In this manner, the committee can interrogate the lending officer for any details they consider pertinent to their judgment of the loan.

Builders

When the purchase is a new home direct from a builder, there can be an existing commitment of mortgage money available to the home buyer. Or the builder may suggest that the purchaser obtain his own financing. Some of the variations are discussed below.

Competitive Method. The small-to-medium-sized builders may have their construction money secured without any commitment for the permanent loans. For example, a commercial bank carrying the construction financing would have little interest in making a permanent loan. If there is no commitment, the purchaser is free to seek whatever source of mortgage money he may select.

Commitment Method, Construction. When a builder, and this would cover all sizes of builders, obtains construction money, he may be requested to give the lender a first refusal right to all permanent loans on the project. The construction lender thus ties up a good source of loans for the future, which is one of his incentives to make the construction loan in the first place. To enforce this right, the lender can add a penalty provision in the construction loan agreement that provides for an extra ½ or 1% of the construction loan to be paid for a release of the construction mortgage if the loan is not handled through the same lender. A purchaser cannot be required to borrow money from a particular lender, but it can be a bit more costly to go elsewhere.

Commitment Method, Purchase. Some of the larger builders who can qualify for the lowest rates on their construction money, or use their own funds for this purpose, may purchase a future commitment for money direct from a savings association or other major source to protect future customers needing loans. The builder will pay at least 1% of the total commitment amount to hold the money. Or he may pay additional fees to assure his future home buyers a lower, more competitive interest rate. This expense, which in effect is a prepayment of interest by the builder for the benefit of the buyer, is charged back into the cost of the house. It is in this manner that some builders can advertise lower than market interest rates and obtain a competitive advantage in the home market.

Associated Companies. A few of the larger builders who are almost national in scope are organized with their own affiliated mortgage companies or money sources to provide permanent loans. The tie-in is generally competitive with the market rates for money and is intended as a convenience for the buyer. These companies seldom use any pressure to press their full range of services upon a customer if not desired, but they carry a competitive edge by being available at the proper time.

Other Sources

Each community has a variety of other potential sources that a borrower may find helpful. These include insurance company loan offices, employer credit unions, or fraternal, religious, or labor union organizations that the potential borrower may be affiliated with, plus other more localized lending organizations. In utilizing these sources the borrower must take aggressive action to seek the loan, as the helpful assistance provided by the mortgage companies and savings associations is not always available. However, the cost for the money borrowed could be a bit lower, offsetting the disadvantages.

FINANCIAL EVALUATION OF THE BORROWER

The high loan-to-value ratio (LTVR) of the loan negotiated for house purchases today places a premium on the borrower's repayment ability. The conventional lender, or the private mortgage insurance company selected, cannot expect a recovery of money from the collateral in the first few years of the loan. Proper analysis of the borrower to determine his total available income, any claims against that income, as well as his credit record, is important for a home loan. A borrower's other assets are helpful as additional security for a loan and can result in a lower rate of interest, but other assets cannot always be counted on for use in repayment. The lender knows that in many cases of actual default in payments the borrower has met with financial problems that were beyond his control, such as accidents, job lay-offs, or serious illness in the family; and that such problems can deplete most of the family's financial assets, leaving the lender with few means of recourse beyond the house that has been pledged.

Inevitably then a loan is "good" to the extent that the borrower is good. To initiate the collection of information necessary to analyze a borrower, a loan application is taken. On the following two pages is one example of this loan application. There are many variations of these forms, but the essentials are always there, including (1) identification of the borrower, (2) description of the property, (3) the amount of the loan requested, (4) the borrower's employment and income record, (5) the borrower's assets and liabilities, and (6) the borrower's credit references and his certification as to the validity of the information being submitted.

No two borrowers ever present the same credit picture. Analysis of a borrower still defies any attempt to impersonalize the procedure to the point of computerization. But

APPLICATION FOR RESIDENTIAL LOAN

Application is hereby made for a loan described below as to amount and terms, to be amortized by the payment of equal ☐ monthly; ☐ quarterly; ☐ semi-annual installments for principal and interest.

Total Amount of Loan	Rate of Interest	Number of Years	Payment for Principal and Interest	Estimated Payment for Taxes and Hazard Insurance Premiums	Total Payment
$	%		$	$	$

Prepayment Privilege: _____

_____

The mortgage (will) (will not) provide for escrow payments for taxes and insurance

Source of Equity _____

Details of secondary financing: _____

Purpose of loan: _____

The loan will be secured by a first mortgage or deed of trust upon real property located at:

_____

(Street Address)　　　(City)　　　(P. O. Zone)　　(County)　　　(State)

Legal Description: _____

_____

Property Description: _____

Lot Size: _____

	Cost	Date	Mtge.	Present Balance	Name of Holder	Interest	Payments
Land	$		1st	$		%	$
Building	$		2nd	$		%	$
Total	$			Estimated Annual Taxes:	Applicant (will) (will not) occupy property.		

Improvements made since Purchase: _____

Special Judgments or Assessments: _____

Applicant _____ Age ____ Spouse _____ Age ____

Ages of dependents _____

Applicant's Address _____

Applicant's Phone Numbers: Home _____ Business _____

SOURCE OF ANNUAL INCOME		PERSONAL INFORMATION
Base salary	$	Occupation or Type of Business
Overtime wages	$	
Bonus and commissions	$	Employer
Dividends and interest income	$	Address
Real Estate Income (Net)	$	Position held　　　No. of years
Wife's income	$	Partner or officer in any other venture or other employment
Other income—itemize	$	
		Previous Employer
		Address
TOTAL	$	Position held　　　No. of years
CONTINGENT LIABILITIES		WIFE'S EMPLOYMENT
As Endorser or Co-maker on Notes	$	Employer
Alimony payments (Annual)	$	Address
Are you defendant in any legal action?		
Have you ever taken bankruptcy?		Position held　　　No. of years

I (We) agree to pay all expenses incident to appraisal, credit investigation, photographs, title work, closing fees, attorney fees, survey, and any other necessary closing expense.

In the event I (We) do not close this loan, I (We) will pay _____ a fee of _____.

I (We) agree to furnish through _____, agent, fire insurance with extended coverage for at least $_____.

I hereby certify that the information contained in this application is true and complete to the best of my knowledge and belief.

Signed _____

Date _____　Signed _____

Figure 13–1a

ASSETS			LIABILITIES		
Cash (Show Bank)	$		Notes payable: (Show Payee)		
			To	$	
Earnest Money Deposited			To		
Investments: Bonds and Stocks —see schedule			To		
			Installment Accounts Payable		
Investment in own Business			Automobile: Monthly ($)		
Accounts and Notes Receivable			Other: Monthly ($)		
Real Estate owned—see schedule			Other Accounts Payable		
Auto: Year Make			Mortgages payable on Real Estate—see schedule		
Personal property and Furniture			Unpaid Real Estate Taxes		
Life Insurance ($) Cash Surrender Value			Unpaid Income Taxes		
			Chattel Mortgages		
Other Assets—itemize			Loans on Life Insurance Policies (Include Premium Advances)		
			Other debts—itemize		
			Total Liabilities		
			Net Worth		
Total Assets	$		Total Liabilities and Net Worth	$	

COMPLETE THE FOLLOWING SCHEDULES IN DETAIL

SCHEDULE OF BONDS AND STOCKS

AMOUNT OR NO. SHARES	DESCRIPTION *(Extend Valuation in Proper Column)* ——⟶	MARKETABLE ACTUAL MARKET VALUE	NON-MARKETABLE (UNLISTED SECURITIES)

SCHEDULE OF REAL ESTATE

DESCRIPTION AND LOCATION	ACTUAL MARKET VALUE	MORTGAGE AMOUNT	MATURITY DATE

*Indicates sold and awaiting closing

SCHEDULE OF NOTES PAYABLE

Specify any assets pledged as collateral, indicating the liabilities which they secure:

TO WHOM PAYABLE	DATE	AMOUNT	DUE	INTEREST	ASSETS PLEDGED AS SECURITY

SCHEDULE OF INSTALLMENT ACCOUNTS

PROPERTY PURCHASED	AMOUNT OWED	MONTHLY PAYMENT

ADDITIONAL COMMENTS

Form No. 202A Mortgage Bankers Association of America, 111 West Washington Street, Chicago, Illinois 60602

Figure 13–1b

there are some guidelines and general rules, mainly based on common sense, that are helpful in determining whether or not a borrower can make good on his loan commitment. To make a sound prediction, the underwriter of the loan considers two basic questions: (1) What is the person's ability to pay? (2) What is his willingness to pay?

Ability to Pay

More than any other type of loan, the home loan looks to a family's income as the basic resource for repayment. Assets are important but are used in part to determine the spending or saving patterns practiced in the use of that income. Therefore, a careful review of the employment record, present income, and future potential is important. Below are listed some of the income elements considered by a lender, with a commentary on each topic.

Types of Income

In today's multi-job standard that includes more than one jobholder in many families, the actual total income can be difficult to arrive at, as this information suggests:

Salary. The salary is the easiest form of income to determine and generally a more secure type of income.

Bonus. A bonus should not be counted on unless a regular pattern can be established for several successive years.

Commission. A straight commission job can be very lucrative, or it can be a complete bust. Only a past record of income can be accepted as factual, culled from several years of tax returns.

Hourly Wages. The hourly wage is a solid basis for continuing income and one that can usually be confirmed from an employer.

Overtime Wages. This is an uncertain basis for making a larger loan as most employers try to avoid overtime and use it only as an emergency or temporary practice. Again, a consistent pattern of overtime payments for several years would make this an acceptable addition to the gross effective income.

Second Job. Many persons today hold more than one job on a full- or part-time basis. Teachers, policemen, skilled hourly workers, all can have other capabilities and may spend extra hours augmenting their income. If the second job has been held over a period of several years on a regular basis, it provides a substantial lift to the regular income.

Unreported Income. A few people accept extra work, or even become involved full time, in jobs that pay in cash and on which income is not reported for tax purposes. Such income, if not reported, is illegal and cannot be used under any condition as income to justify a loan. This "borrower" could reach an abrupt end to his free income via the prison route.

Wife's Income. The wife's income is an important addition to a family income, and in a growing number of families, this may be the largest and/or only source of income. In the lending industry, there is still some reluctance to place full weight on a wife's income due to time-honored obligations involving family emergencies and sickness, pregnancies, and child care. However, substantial changes, legal and otherwise, have followed in the wake of the women's liberation movement, and many lenders now give full weight to a wife's income, that is, within certain limitations. A marriage of more than five-years duration, the existence of several school-age children, the husband's job record extending over several years—all of these factors are generally favorable for full acceptance of a wife's income.

Income from Children. While many young men and women, living with their parents, earn substantial money at full- or part-time jobs, these earnings are not a recognized addition to the family income for loan purposes. The obligation on the part of the children to contribute to the family finances for support of the home is not a permanent one, since normally they will leave the homestead and set up their own household within a few years. Thus, temporary income supplied by grown children lends no real weight to the loan request.

Pensions and Trusts. Few home buyers in the past have enjoyed pensions, retirement funds, or other work benefits at a sufficiently early age to apply them toward a home purchase. However, the pattern is changing. For instance, many veterans of military and other government services have now completed 20 or 30 years of employment before the age of 50. These benefits are, of course, one of the most reliable forms of income.

Child Support and Alimony. Some states do not permit alimony but provide child support as a matter of court decree. Other states permit both alimony and child support. Such payments can be considered as regular income for a divorcee or remarried person, depending on the court ruling. However, the record of payment must show dependability over a period of time before it would constitute an acceptable addition to total income in full amount.

Self-Employed. Many persons operate their own businesses or work as individuals in professional capacities. Since there is no employer to verify actual income, the only acceptable method of validating this income is by referral to previous income tax reports. Certified copies of these returns can be obtained from the Internal Revenue Service for a small fee upon application by the taxpayer only. Some small businessmen are able to pay certain living expenses from their business (car expenses and depreciation, entertainment, travel, etc.), but weight can only be given to the actual income reported as taxable.

Interest and Dividends. These funds normally represent a stable income but must be considered from the angle of a possible sale of the asset for another purpose. Again, the past record would indicate the probable future pattern in any given case.

Stability of Income

Along with the size of an applicant's income, the assurance that it will be continued must be investigated. Two factors are involved: (1) time on the job, and (2) type of work performed.

Length of Time. Some lenders hold to a policy of rejecting all applicants with less than three years tenure at their present job. There is a basis for this restriction in that any new job may or may not work out, either due to personality factors or to lack of accomplishment. But with the more rapid changes in jobs today, the job tenure can be more fairly judged from the individual's job history. Has the applicant made a record of "job hopping" without noticeable improvement in his income? Is the present job one of greater responsibility and growth potential than the previous job? Has the applicant maintained a record of employment in his chosen field of work and qualifications, or is his present job an entirely new type of work?

The question of job tenure does not lend itself to easily defined limits due to the variables mentioned above. But most lenders hold to some minimum term of employment, generally from one to three years.

Type of Work. While a person with a long record of employment provides the soundest answer to the question of income stability, not everyone seeking loans can provide such a record. The type of work engaged in does give good clues as to future stability.

Among men, salaried jobs with the larger companies and professional men with tenure are considered the most secure. Hourly workers with the protection of union contracts are far more stable (and often higher paid) than lower level management and clerical staff workers. Government employees carry good security as do teachers, policemen, and other service workers. On the lower side of the scale, new salesmen enticed by stories of high commissions, entertainers, and seasonal workers give poor evidence of continued stable income. To some lenders, socially unacceptable types of work such as bartending carry unduly low ratings. However, most lenders find nothing wrong per se with bartending. Self-employed men should have a record of successful operations to assure stability as more small businesses fail than ever succeed.

With women, only recently has the spectrum of jobs available broadened to include almost every type of work. Rated among the highest for stability are teaching, nursing, and the growing executive group. Secretarial work as a class rates rather poorly, mainly from lack of continued interest; but the top legal, professional, and executive secretaries not only command good salaries but are virtually assured of continuous work today. A few of the less stable categories are clerical workers, models, actresses, and waitresses. A growing number of young and older women are going into commission sales work with about the same mixed success as men. But in some areas, like house selling, women have proved to be even more capable than men.

Analyzing Income Factors

Few conventional lenders have established rigid patterns or detailed forms to evaluate an applicant's income. The more common procedure is for the lenders to establish certain basic minimums to guide the loan processor and to base their lending on the record of the agent's results. Every loan underwriter builds his own record with a lender, and any difficulties or foreclosure may serve to diminish the lender's confidence in the underwriter's analysis and judgment. Broad guidelines for analyzing income stability for loan applications would include such items as:

1. An effective gross income of four or five times the monthly payment.
2. A job tenure of at least 18 months.

3. A maximum age not exceeding 50 years.

4. Determination of effective income by including base pay plus all other family income at 50% or 75%.

Variations abound in these guidelines, and the only constant is the continued effort of the lender to make sound loans that will be repaid without problems. The last item above, item (4), is an approach to income analysis called "weighting" (to adjust the income that can be counted on for five or ten years). Stable income is given full weight in determining effective income. Other sources, such as overtime pay, may be downgraded to 50% or 75% of reported income in an effort to avoid making a loan that would easily become too great a burden on a family's income.

Liabilities

All charges or obligations against an applicant's income must be considered in determining the amount available to meet the mortgage obligation. The liability connected with the *normal* costs of supporting a family and maintaining a house is taken into consideration by limiting the mortgage payment to 20% or 25% of the applicant's effective income.

It is the extraordinary charges that must be checked. If other monthly payments exceed one year in pay-off time, they should be deducted against the regular income to arrive at effective income. Such charges as car payments, boat or trailer payments, furniture payments, and loan repayments are all demands upon the monthly income. In conventional lending, these charges can also be weighed against other assets, rather than solely against income.

Assets

Most home buyers are younger couples who have not yet accumulated very many assets. The purchase of a house represents one of the largest investments they will make. But the addition of such values as stocks, bonds, real estate, savings funds, and other assets does indicate an ability to live prudently and conserve a portion of the income. Life insurance is both an asset in its cash value and protection features and a liability in its cost. Cars and boats represent some trade-in value. Furniture and personal property are often overvalued in an applicant's statement of assets because of the owner's personal attachment. Employee trust and pension funds can represent value if the interest is a vested one, i.e., if the employee can take the funds with him if he leaves his job. An interest in one's own business should be determined by an actual financial statement of that business. Accounts and notes receivable should be detailed for proper valuation.

Willingness to Pay

The element of willingness to pay, sometimes called *credit character*, or *intent*, is the most difficult to analyze and judge. Yet this factor alone can be the cause of a loan rejection, often without a reason given, or the real reason concealed by reciting some other weak spot in the applicant's record. The most tangible information concerning an individual's record of handling his obligations comes from his credit bureau report. Information may also be derived from public records regarding litigation, judgments, or criminal actions. Conversations with persons involved in the house sale transaction can sometimes bring to light information on the applicant's manner of living, his personal attitudes, and activities that might give cause for a more detailed investigation. The initial loan application often is taken at the lending company's offices, but it can be handled at the residence of the applicant. Some lenders expect a personal call to be made on the applicant by their agents, as a person's manner of living can be most helpful in judging the credit character.

Under "willingness to pay," another bit of information that can be helpful is called *motivation*. For example, is the house purchase to be used for a family? Many lenders still consider a family unit as the only acceptable borrower.

However, with the changes in life styles, the marital status has become less of a factor, and single persons, both men and women, are now considered eligible for single-family houses, with townhouses attracting the most interest. The criterion of motivation is satisfied primarily by maturity, and the age of 29 or 30 is considered to be a minimum age limit. A single person must have the income requirements to meet the monthly payments, but he or she usually does not have the demands on income created by a family.

Under this category of credit attitude, a formidable barrier must be surmounted: the problem of invasion of privacy. Attitudes are changing among lenders but still range over a broad spectrum. The older, highly personal approach to a loan is still practiced in smaller communities and by many venerable lending institutions. Some savings and loan associations will not approve a loan without personal contact with the applicant by at least one, sometimes two, lending officers.

At the other extreme we find efforts to make the analysis as impersonal as possible. The thought here is to minimize the effects of personalities, of likes and dislikes, or of prejudices that have relatively little bearing on the strength of the applicant. These efforts center around some form of a rating chart with columns such as "good, fair, and poor" for judging 10 to 20 basic factors on the applicant's credit record. Each factor carries a different value in points for "good" or "fair," and must total a certain minimum to qualify. More than one rating in the "poor" column can be an automatic rejection.

It is in this area of trying to bridge the gap for the remote lender that the mortgage banker can serve as eyes, ears, and interpreter to bring all the facts into focus. The true picture can be just as advantageous for the borrower as for the lender and is mandatory in making proper judgment on any loan. An invidual asking to borrow someone else's money should be willing to provide complete and accurate information about himself.

HELPFUL HINTS

Few individuals are experienced in making loan applications. Sometimes raw facts can be misinterpreted, and an explanation is needed to clarify the situation. Lenders vary considerably in the amount of cooperation they can or will extend to the borrower in explaining requirements or correcting omissions. Some of the problem areas and possible answers are discussed below.

Loan Amount versus Income. If the size of the amortization payments is too large for reasonable repayment within the effective income, the lender can suggest a smaller loan. This could well mean a smaller house but still an upgrading in living standards.

Large Monthly Obligations. When a debt load for other purchases, such as a car or furniture, takes too big a bite out of an applicant's income, the lender may suggest a delay in handling the loan for six or eight months to permit the repayment of nonrecurring obligations before undertaking an additional debt.

Failure to Meet All Qualifications. If the applicant fails to qualify under a minimum requirement, such as time on the job, he may add the endorsement of another person to secure the note. In a home loan, it is best that the endorser have a real and sustaining interest in the borrower, such as a parent would have.

CREDIT REPORTS

Individual Credit

In most metropolitan areas there are a number of agencies that furnish credit information on individuals and companies. Most of the agencies specialize in certain geographic sections of the city or in specific classes of business. To be of value, credit information must be accurate, current, and in depth. In selecting a source for this information, a careful examination is needed to determine the best pool of information.

The mortgage business, for the most part, has followed

the lead of the FHA and VA who make contracts with one of the major agencies for each area. The one selected is usually affiliated with Associated Credit Bureaus of America, Inc. and has ready access to exchange information from all areas of the country.

Credit bureaus are heavily dependent on the cooperation of local banks, merchants, and professional services to relay factual data to them. From the information submitted, a report is assembled, using coded data to protect the sources, and is available to member companies for a fee. There is some variation in the reporting procedures, but most furnish an identification of the source by industry only (bank, medical, real estate, department store, etc.), reporting dates and account dates, high and low credit, balance due, and the manner of payment.

It is the last item mentioned, manner of payment, that gives an immediate clue to the paying record of the loan applicant. A letter and a numeral are the code used—the letter indicates the type of account (Open, Revolving, Installment), and the number gives the paying pattern. Number 1 is "pays as agreed," which is tops, down to Number 9, which is a bad debt placed for collection.

Credit reports contain a brief history of past employment, salary or other manner of compensation, and a record of credit experience locally and from a previous place of residence if necessary. In a mortgage credit report it is customary to show a review of the county records for judgments, liens of any kind, and criminal charges that may have been filed. On the following page is a copy of a typical credit report showing how the information is presented by the Credit Bureau of Greater Houston.

One of the problems of credit reporting is the possibility of misfiling credit information. The confusion of same names, similar names, changes of married names, and just plain errors can cause an unjustified adverse report, or perhaps fail to give a true picture. Several years ago the use of social security numbers became standard procedure among the credit bureaus, but reporting companies still continue to neglect this practice and errors consequently persist.

Another problem besetting credit reporting is the recent

NAME AND ADDRESS OF CREDIT BUREAU MAKING REPORT

☐ SUMMARY REPORT	☐ SINGLE REFERENCE	☐ TRADE REPORT

CREDIT BUREAU OF GREATER HOUSTON
2309 Fannin Street
Houston, Texas 77002
Tel. 224-4744

☐ SHORT REPORT	☒ FULL REPORT	☐ PREV. RES. REPORT
DATE RECEIVED 6/4/71	DATE MAILED 6/9/71	------
DATE TRADE CLEARED 6/1/71	DATE EMPLOY VERIFIED 6/1/71	INCOME VERIFIED ☐ YES ☒ NO

CONFIDENTIAL *Factbilt*® REPORT   FOR   CREDIT BUREAU OF GREATER HOUSTON   (813)

IN FILE SINCE: 7/54

This information is furnished in response to an inquiry for evaluating credit risks. It has been obtained from reliable sources, the accuracy of which is not guaranteed. The inquirer agrees to indemnify the reporting bureau for any damage arising from misuse of this information, and this report is furnished in reliance upon that indemnity. It must be held in strict confidence, and must not be revealed to the subject reported upon. If adverse action is taken based on this report, the subject reported on must be so advised and the reporting agency identified.

REPORT ON (SURNAME):	MR., MRS., MISS:	GIVEN NAME:		SOCIAL SECURITY NUMBER:	SPOUSE'S NAME:
Doe		John	G	457-36-5077	Betty

ADDRESS:	CITY:	STATE:	ZIP CODE:	SPOUSE'S SOCIAL SECURITY NO.:
2309 Fannin	Houston, Texas		77002	436-21-5777

COMPLETE TO HERE FOR TRADE REPORT AND SKIP TO CREDIT HISTORY

PRESENT EMPLOYER AND KIND OF BUSINESS:	POSITION HELD:	SINCE:	MONTHLY INCOME:
XYZ Oil Corp	Engr.	8/12/63	$ 1,000 Month

COMPLETE TO HERE FOR SHORT REPORT AND SUMMARY REPORT AND SKIP TO CREDIT HISTORY

DATE OF BIRTH: 1909	NUMBER OF DEPENDENTS INCLUDING SPOUSE → 2	☒ OWNS OR BUYING HOME	☐ RENTS HOME

FORMER ADDRESS:	CITY:	STATE:		FROM:	TO:
1500 Strawberry Rd.	Houston, Texas	77002		10/62	10/63

FORMER EMPLOYER AND KIND OF BUSINESS:	POSITION HELD:	FROM:	TO:	MONTHLY INCOME:
Davel Constr Co.	Engr.	7/59	8/63	$ 750 Month

SPOUSE'S EMPLOYER AND KIND OF BUSINESS:	POSITION HELD:	SINCE:	MONTHLY INCOME:
First Ins. Co.	Clerk	8/62	$ 400 Month

CREDIT HISTORY (Complete this section for all reports)

KIND OF BUSINESS	DATE REPORTED	DATE ACCOUNT OPENED	DATE OF LAST SALE	HIGHEST CREDIT	AMOUNT OWING	AMOUNT PAST DUE	TERMS OF SALE AND USUAL MANNER OF PAYMENT
B 142		SATIS CKG ACCT					
C 157		1963	5/71	442	125	00	0-1
O 577		10/65	5/71	250	100	00	0-1
H 5		11/62	9/70	629	00	00	0-1
H 249		11/62	5/71	706	565	565	1-8
M 311		8/63	7/70	250	00	00	0-4
AT 25		11/65	3/70	240	00	00	I-20-1
CONROE, TEXAS	REPORTED 12/70		LST CHECKED 12/70	ON FILES 1962			
D		1965	10/70	125	00	00	0-1
C		1968	1/70	85	00	00	0-1

INDICATE IF FILE CONTAINS

☐ Items of Public Record   ☐ Any record of accounts placed for collection   ☐ Any reports received from other Credit Bureaus

IF ANY OF THE ABOVE ARE CHECKED, GIVE DETAILS

MEMBER

Associated Credit Bureaus, Inc.

FORM 100

PRINTED IN U.S.A. 4-72

Figure 13–2

successful legal attacks on credit bureaus when an erroneous report causes damage to a person or company. Information detrimental to a person's credit position can be damaging, and many retail companies follow the easiest route to avoid problems by simply not reporting information. This practice of refusing to furnish any information on credit customers in order to avoid possible damage suits diminishes the value of any cooperative report.

Corporate Credit

To analyze adequately the credit-worthiness of a company, it is necessary for the underwriter to become acquainted and fully cognizant of every phase of the business under scrutiny: management, sales, production, purchasing, research and planning, personnel policies, and the physical plant and equipment, as well as to make a careful study of the financial statements. There is wide latitude as to the quantity and quality of detail needed to answer the fundamental question of whether or not it would be advisable to make a loan at the time being considered.

The underwriter expects to have a current, preferably audited, financial statement presented along with the loan application. An audited statement is one in which all the pertinent data are verified by the independent accountants preparing the report, in which the figures are presented in a form and according to rules determined by the accountants, and in which the final conclusions are certified as correct and accurate by the accredited accountants. The principal factors a lender will look for are the record of profitable use of existing assets, the accumulation of cash and property versus outstanding obligations, and the very important working ratio of current assets to current liabilities. The latter indicates both the manner of operation and the immediate cushion of assets available to protect the company against a temporary reversal.

Personal interviews with company officers are utilized to fill in more detail of what the company's plans are and how it intends to carry them out. Where larger loans are involved, it is routine procedure to verify the company's market and its ability to sell its product. Comparative balance sheets and profit and loss statements covering the previous ten years of operations give excellent indications of how the company has handled its business and what the general trend will be. Also, a Dun and Bradstreet report (one of the largest national credit reporting services) can give something of the history on the company, which helps to project future capabilities. It is the long-range ability of the company to operate profitably that is the real key to the trouble-free recovery of a loan.

In order to evaluate the results of the loan on the company's finances, it is customary to prepare a *pro forma* statement—both the balance sheet and the profit and loss statement. These statements are a projection of what the loan will do, such as increase the investment in productivity, add a new product line, provide an additional service, or broaden a market, as well as the expected effects of that loan on the profitability of the company.

To assure the lender that the proceeds of the loan are used as projected, a loan agreement is drawn up that spells out the purpose of the loan and can provide penalties for non-conformance. In addition, certain restrictive covenants are often added to the loan agreement that will place limits on such things as loans or advances to officers or employees until the loan is paid off, control the payment of salaries and dividends, limit any other borrowing, and require approval of the lender before any major assets, patents, or leasehold interests can be sold. All terms of the loan agreement are negotiable and are designed primarily to assure the lender's interest in the company over a period of time during which the ownership and management can change drastically but the loan obligation continues on.

LOAN CLOSING

INTRODUCTION

In the preceding chapters we have tried to cover the broad areas of money sources and their motivations, the information needed to analyze a real property loan and how lenders look at various types of properties, and the more important factors of borrower examination. In completing the analysis, we will go step-by-step through the collected information needed to close a loan. The example in this chapter is a residential loan, presented just as it would be closed using a title company as the escrow and closing agent. However, the essentials could apply to any loan.

With the borrower analyzed and the property appraised, we have the information needed to accept or reject the loan application. The loan processing procedures have been placed in the hands of a loan solicitor, while the real estate agent, along with the potential buyer, awaits a decision. Up to this point, the prudent procedure is to minimize all expenses that are not essential to underwriting the loan; should the loan fail for any of many reasons, expenses incurred in anticipation of approval could be wasted.

Once the mortgage company advises a sales agent or the buyer of an applicant's approval, further steps are needed to consummate the transaction. It is the purpose of this chapter to identify the steps necessary for closing and to allocate, insofar as possible, the responsibility for performance and the costs.

INFORMATION AND FEES REQUIRED

Mortgagor's Information Letter (MIL)

The information contained in the Mortgagor's Information Letter is a part of the closing data needed, but more accurately comes under the listing requirements that a sales agent obtains from the seller when a property is offered for sale. This is the information that is requested from an existing mortgagee, at the time a property is offered for sale, showing the exact amount of loan or loans due on the property, amount of escrow balances, and any premium required for payment of the loan. The letter is normally returned to the real estate broker handling the transaction and becomes a part of the selling proposal. Title companies are normally advised of the present lien holders but seek their own information from the county records and directly from the present mortgagee so that a proper pay-off and release of any prior mortgage liens can be handled at the closing.

Preliminary Title Report

When an earnest money contract has been consummated, it is a good idea to "open title" with whatever title insurance company has been selected to handle the closing. This is usually done by the real estate broker after discussion with the seller, since the latter will be paying for the owner's title policy. The buyer may also have a voice in the selection, as the owner's title policy is for his protection. It is very good practice to clear the title company with the proposed mortgagee as the lender will not accept every title company. Sometimes the broker asks the mortgage company to select a title company. In order to simplify handling, the title company selected is normally one located in the same county as the property being sold.

The preliminary title report is furnished by the title company to both the real estate agent and the mortgage company. The information contained is a confirmation of the correct legal description, and it also includes the names of the owners of the property according to the county records, any restrictions or liens on the property, any judgments against the owners of record, and a listing of any requirements the title company may have to perfect title and issue a title insurance policy. It is an assurance that if the requirements are met, a title policy can be issued. The report is for information only; it is not to be confused with a title "binder," which legally obligates the title company for specific insurance. And the title companies normally make no charge for the preliminary report; it is part of their service in anticipation of writing the title insurance policy at closing.

Survey

Whenever a loan is involved, a survey may be considered mandatory. It is a good procedure to require an actual survey on any transfer of real property for the buyer's protection. A survey, which must be made by a registered surveyor, will not only show the exact outline and size of the property but will indicate any encroachments that might interfere with full title. An encroachment could be a building on the property erected too close to a property line in violation of a city code requirement, or it could be a fence belonging to a neighbor erroneously placed on the property being purchased. Such usage by a neighbor establishes rights under the statute of limitations through adverse possession and requires sound legal guidance. Because of this possibility, many attorneys require that a survey be available to them before a deed or a mortgage is drawn up.

The close involvement of the survey with the proper title and the legal instruments makes it easier for the title company to order the survey and include the cost in the closing statement of charges. This can be done after the loan has been approved as one of the steps in the closing process. And this is one of the reasons title companies need a few days to properly prepare for the actual closing.

Insurance

Hazard Insurance. Hazard insurance, which covers any physical damage to the property, is negotiated as a part of the sales agreement with the effective date and delivery of the actual policy contingent on closing. As previously outlined in this text, it is important that the insurance company be acceptable to the mortgage company involved. When the loan has been approved, it is necessary to so advise the insurance agent, a communication which is usually handled as part of the services of the real estate agent. The mortgage company needs to know the exact amount of the premiums for the first year and the insurance agent to whom they must be paid so as to advise the title company on distribution of the loan proceeds.

Mortgage Insurance. Mortgage insurance, when required, is handled entirely by the mortgage company. The method of payment is determined during the loan negotiations, and the premium to be paid at closing is turned over to the mortgage company for remittance to the insurance carrier, be it private mortgage insurance or FHA insurance.

Credit Life Insurance. Mortgage life insurance is a matter between the borrower and his own choice of an insurance carrier. It is not required in residential loans and is not involved in closing procedures. Sometimes such a requirement for life insurance becomes a requirement in larger commercial loans where the successful operation and, thus, the loan repayment depend heavily on one or two individuals.

Title Insurance. The title company handling the closing furnishes the title insurance, which is a routine procedure. Rates for such insurance are set by the state insurance commission and are well known in advance. The amount of insurance cannot exceed the sales price for the property. It is the seller's responsibility to prove his title and pay the insuring costs for the owner's policy. Concurrently, a title insurance policy is issued to the mortgagee, which cost is paid for by the borrower (buyer).

Property Taxes

The determination of taxes due at closing always creates some questions. At most closings, this information is obtained by the title company from the court house records. Under the time pressures that most title companies work with, the actual figures are not available very much prior to the formal closing.

What the mortgage company asks is that one, two, or three months' taxes be held for the escrow account and that the title company guarantee taxes paid to date of closing. Title companies exercise great care on this point, as a tax lien at any time will take precedence over a first mortgage lien.

Real estate brokers are often asked for an exact accounting of closing costs at the time a sale is consummated, but this involves a determination of the current tax assessment and the mortgage company's escrow requirements. A prior year's tax statement gives a good base for estimate but is always subject to change, usually higher. Taxes must be prorated between buyer and seller to closing date. Since taxes are due and payable annually at the end of the year, the seller is asked to pay his proportionate share at closing for the time he has occupied the property.

Prepaid Interest

Another expense at closing that is difficult to determine precisely in advance is the prepaid interest. On mortgage loans interest is normally paid *after* the money has been used; the regular monthly payment on a house loan covers interest for the *preceding* month, plus a reduction in the principal. In order to adjust a payment date to the first of each month (or other agreed monthly date), the borrower is expected to pay the interest on his loan from closing date to the inception date of his normal monthly payment in advance;

this means the interest from the closing date to the end of the month in which the closing took place. From the first of the following month the interest would accrue, making the first full monthly payment due on the first of the *second* month following closing. Thus, the actual amount of the prepaid interest due cannot be accurately determined until the closing date has been set.

Since interest is now being paid on a loan that may not be funded until several days after closing, an adjustment may be in order. Some mortgage companies, in anticipation of a normal five-day delay in funding, will calculate the interest due, not from the closing date, but from five days after closing until the end of the month when the closing was made. Some companies start the interest at the closing date, even though funds are not released, on the premise that the money has been committed and, therefore, cannot be used for any other purpose during the interim. The FHA and VA, recognizing that abuses in delays can occur and will accrue to the benefit of the mortgage company, have a rule requiring recalculation of the prepaid interest if the loan is not actually funded within five days of closing.

Escrow Accounts or Trust Accruals

Because the cash to establish certain deposits is required at the time of closing by all mortgage companies, the funds needed have come to be classed as a part of the closing costs. The deposits are to assure the lender that there will be adequate funds on hand to pay *future* taxes and insurance charges. These deposits are also referred to as "prepays" or "prepaid items."*

The mortgage company collects one-twelfth of the annual property taxes and insurance costs (both hazard insurance and the FHA or private mortgage insurance premium if involved) as a part of each monthly payment. Therefore, in order to make sure that sufficient money is on hand by the

---

* The escrow account may be likened to a bank deposit owned by the borrower, but under the complete control of the mortgage lender. It is held for the purpose of paying taxes and insurance owed by the borrower. It should not be confused with the escrow fee which is a small service fee charged by the title company for some of the work performed at closing.

date taxes or insurance payments are due, a cushion is needed. Due dates may not coincide, or there may be a slow payment on the part of the borrower. So the mortgage companies ask for one to three months of these charges to be placed on deposit, depending on the policies of the lender and the time of the year. The deposit remains the property of the borrower and is recoverable at payoff of the loan.

Discount

The charge known as the *discount* is one of the least understood costs associated with closing and, as a result, creates more irritations and hard feelings than any other factor. It is simply a charge for the use of money precisely the same as interest would be. For clarification it might be compared to a down payment for the purchase of a car, with the balance paid in monthly installments.

The origin of discounting goes back to the efforts of the government to freeze an interest rate in a fluctuating market. And, since the government cannot loan the money itself, the job devolves on private sources of money to fund government underwritten loans. The private sources have to meet the competition of market interest rates and, in order to produce nearly comparable yields to the investor on a fixed interest rate, a system of discounting the loan has been developed. It amounts to a certain percentage reduction of the total loan that is funded; each 1% of the loan amount is called *one point*. As the spread between market interest rates and the government specified rate increases, so the points needed to balance are increased.

So far, this procedure would not seem too complicated, but the incongruity becomes apparent in that the government refuses to recognize the realities of the market. And, further, in attempting to protect the purchaser-borrower, the FHA and VA have established the requirement that no discount can be paid by him. From the government's point of view, a discount is regarded as an unnecessary charge for the privilege of using the government insurance or guarantee of payment. From the lender's viewpoint, it is difficult to justify to the association members, trust fund, or stockholders whose money is being loaned, that they should accept a discount substantially under the market rate for comparable conventional loans.

The most obvious answer to resolve the dilemma would be to let the fixed government rates float with the market, a system that has been proposed by many high officials; or to use a direct subsidy of points, a system that has been accomplished through HUD's tandem plan.

But for our purposes, a portion of the loan cost on FHA- and VA-type loans is expected to be paid by the seller as a part of his selling cost, and it does increase the potential market for the seller. A growing use of discount is coming into conventional lending, but with conventional loans there is no such arbitrary rule placing this cost on the seller.

Miscellaneous Costs

In addition to the larger items of cost involved in closing, there are several smaller charges incurred. The *recording fee* is for the purpose of recording with the county the new deed, the new mortgage or deed of trust, and any releases of prior liens that are being paid off at closing. The recording fee, usually charged for by the page, is another item that cannot be determined precisely until the exact number of pages involved is known. The *escrow fee* is another expense consisting of a set charge made by the title company for its services in handling the loan and for providing security for the instruments.

Copies of any property restrictions are normally requested and are furnished by the title company. These are necessary for both the lender and the new owner to know exactly what the subject property might be limited to in its usage. The title company also draws from the county a certificate of the taxes due on the subject property. The costs for reproducing these public records are simply passed on to the buyer or seller, as the case may be, at the time of closing.

Depending on what cost items may have been paid in advance or at time of a loan application, there could be some additional charges remaining to be paid at closing. These would include an appraisal fee, credit report, and photos of the property, all charges associated with securing the mortgage loan and normally paid by the purchaser-borrower.

Attorney's Fees

Each party to the transaction is free to employ his own attorney and, in case of any legal questions or disputes, should certainly be encouraged to do so. On most residential property sales, both buyer and seller tend to rely on the selection of attorneys by the title company and/or the mortgage company. The interests of both companies parallel the principal's interest in assuring proper transfer of title and security of the mortgage instruments. It is common practice to rely on the title company to have its own associated law firm prepare all instruments, as it is the title company who actually guarantees that proper title has been passed. The fees involved are divided between the buyer and seller, as they may agree; normally, the seller pays for the warranty deed and any title clearing instruments (releases, etc.), and the buyer pays for the note and mortgage instruments needed to secure the loan.

Finance Fees

The charge by the mortgage company for handling the loan processing and funding is called a finance fee, a service charge, or occasionally, loan brokerage. The charge is 1% to 1½% of the loan amount and is normally paid by the buyer.

Sales Commission

The charge by the real estate agent for selling the property is usually listed as the *commission* and is whatever fee the seller has agreed to, ranging from 5% to 8% of the sales price.

Closing Charges

On the following two pages are first, *a Seller's Statement* and second, a *Purchaser-Borrower Statement* that show the speci-

USLIFE TITLE COMPANY of Houston

Seller's Statement

Settlement Data on Property Known as

Lot 6, Block 4, Blackacre Subdivision
Harris County, Texas

File No. 89642
Closer Smith
Date 2/27/74

Seller John Doe et ux Mary   Purchaser Paul Rae et ux Sue

Item	Deductions		Credits	
Selling Price:			$	
Plus—Insurance . . . . Mo's @			46	000 00
Loan Reserves Transferred				
Other				
Other				
Gross Balance Due Seller			$ 46	000 00
Less—Consideration Received Heretofore	$			
Agent's Commission Johnson Real Estate Co. (6%)	2 760	00		
1st Lien Note Safety Savings Assn. (3/2/74)	23 428	76		
2nd Lien Note				
Other Liens				
City Taxes Paid for 19				
State and County Taxes Paid for 19				
Other Taxes Paid for 19				
All Taxes Prorated (1974) 1 mo. 27 days @ 45.62 mo.	88	16		
Interest Prorated from . . . . to Date				
Rents Prorated . . . . @				
Title Policy . . . . Owners X . . . . . . Mortgagee	250	00		
Tax Cert	7	50		
Escrow Fee	7	50		
Attorney Fee for Drawing Papers . . . James Jones	35	00		
Filing Fees . . . . Release $ X . . . . Other $ . . .	3	00		
Other				
Other				
Other				
Other				
Total Deductions			$ 26	579 92
Net Balance Due Seller			$ 19	420 08

The data shown above is based on figures obtained from other sources and USLIFE Title cannot guarantee the accuracy thereof. Tax prorations are based on figures showing on last tax due date or estimates of the current year's taxes, and in the event of any change for the current year all necessary adjustments will be made between the undersigned and the Purchaser.
The foregoing is approved and disbursements as shown are authorized.

Seller _____

Seller _____

Seller
Formerly DALLAS TITLE COMPANY of Houston
5M1073

Mailing Address—After Closing _____

Figure 14–1

Purchaser's Statement

Settlement Data on Property Known as	
Lot 6, Block 4, Blackacre Subdivision Harris County, Texas	File No. 89642 Closer Smith Date 2/27/74

Seller   Purchaser

Item	Credits		Debits	
Purchase Price:	▶		$ 46 000	00
Plus—Proration of Hazard Insurance				
Loan Reserves Transferred to Purchasers Account				
Survey			45	00
Title Policy—Owners . . . . Mortgagee X			15	00
Escrow Fee			7	50
Attorney Fee—Drawing Papers James Jones			35	00
Filing Fees—Deed $ X . . . . DT$ . . . . X . . . . DT$ . . .			14	50
Certified Restrictions			10	00
XXXXXX Amortization Schedule			1	00
Other Private Mortgage Insurance premium			207	00
Loan Company Fee 1½% brokerage			621	00
Loan Origination Fee				
1 Year's Hazard Insurance Premium Protection Agency, Inc.			253	00
2 Mo. Hazard Insurance @ 24.00 per mo.	$ 48	00		
5 Mo. XXXXXXX Maintenance @ 5.67 per mo.	28	35		
5 Mo. Tax Deposit (1974) @ 45.62 mo.	228	10		
____ Mo. Tax Deposit				
____ Mo. Tax Deposit				
Interest To End of Month 2 days @ 10.06	20	12	324	57
Total Debits	▶		$ 47 533	57
LESS—Consideration Paid Heretofore Earnest money	750.00			
1st Lien Note XYZ Mortgage Company	41,400.00			
2nd Lien Note				
Proration of Taxes from Seller (1974) 1 mo. 27 days @ 45.62	88.16			
Proration of Interest from . . . . to Date				
Proration of Rents				
Other				
Total Credits	▶		$ 42 238	16
Balance Due by Purchaser	▶		$ 5 295	41

The data shown above is based on figures obtained from other sources and USLIFE Title cannot guarantee the accuracy thereof. Tax prorations are based on figures showing on last tax due date or estimates of the current year's taxes, and in the event of any change for the current year all necessary adjustments will be made between the undersigned and the Seller. The undersigned hereby acknowledges receipt of the original of this statement.
The foregoing is approved and disbursements as shown are authorized.

_____   Purchaser

Purchaser
Formerly DALLAS TITLE COMPANY of Houston
5M1073   Mailing Address—After Closing

Figure 14–2

fic items that are normally charged to each party involved.

For a good generalization in allocating charges, the seller is expected to pay for all the costs of delivering a good title and the warranty deed; the purchaser-borrower pays for all costs involved in securing his mortgage loan. The big exception to this rule is the loan discount when an FHA or VA commitment is involved; the government agencies specifically forbid the purchaser-borrower to pay these costs, and they must be carried by the seller.

One of the problems in giving more specific rules for guidance in the allocation of closing costs is that there are not too many fixed requirements; this is somewhat a matter of negotiation. And it is not unusual for a builder or an anxious seller to agree to pay *all* closing costs, absorbing these costs in the selling price as an expense like advertising or sales commissions.

FINAL CLOSING INSTRUCTIONS

Mortgagee's Closing Instructions

Once a loan has been approved, the mortgage company prepares a sheet of instructions for delivery to the title company handling closing procedures. The instructions detail such items as the correct legal name of the mortgagee, the name of the trustee for the deed of trust, the terms of the mortgage note, and special requirements to be included in the mortgage or deed of trust (that is, if the mortgage company is not submitting its own forms for a note and mortgage), specific instructions on monthly payments to be given to the borrowers, details of the escrow requirements, and details of disbursement procedures. Along with the instructions the mortgage company will send the buyer-seller affidavits as may be required, which certify to the actual down payment (cash and/or property exchanged) and to the use of the loan proceeds, which must be acknowledged by the notarized signatures of all buyers and sellers. Also, a truth in lending statement is prepared for the purchaser-borrower signature at closing. Some mortgage companies require certifications of occupancy (for homestead information), and the forms vary between companies according to how their legal counselors interpret the state laws.

The instructions of the mortgage company invariably call for a certain amount of work on the part of the title company closing the loan, if only as a means of clarifying the loan requirements. This is in addition to the other details of closing that a title company must handle, such as assembling the title information, preparing or reviewing the note and deed of trust, verifying tax requirements, and determining the insurance payments needed.

It is advisable to allow a title company a reasonable time for its work in preparing for a closing. A forced deadline can induce errors and omissions.

Setting the Closing

When the mortgage company has approved the loan and prepared its closing instructions, it is the responsibility of the real estate agent, or agents, involved to arrange a mutually agreeable closing time. The title company will usually specify a time that a closer (the trained specialist who handles the actual closing) is available, and the agent can then seek an arrangement with both buyer and seller. Closings can be accomplished with separate meetings, the buyer at one time and the seller at another, leaving the title company to escrow the instruments and consideration until the procedure is completed and distribution can be made.

It is easier for the title company and for the agents involved, as well as providing greater clarity for both buyer and seller, to arrange for a single meeting. Although a closing is no place for negotiations, if any misunderstanding should crop up, it can be more readily resolved if all parties are immediately available for decisions.

DISBURSEMENT OF FUNDS

In many parts of the country, a closing is just that; instruments are signed and funds are disbursed before anyone leaves the closing table. In some areas, it is more common to execute and acknowledge the instruments at the closing but delay the disbursement of funds until later.

The purpose for any delay in releasing funds is twofold: first, to give the lender an opportunity to make a second review of all instruments and to verify proper signatures and acknowledgements, and second, to allow the title company time to clear any checks that may have been submitted by the parties involved before releasing its own disbursement checks. One interpretation of state regulations governing title insurance companies calls *any* check paid to a title company an "escrow receivable," rather than a cash item, until the check has actually cleared the bank. However, there is growing pressure to handle a closing in its proper sequence and not call for the parties to meet until all the loose ends have been accomplished and the money is available for distribution.

On the following page is an example of a disbursement sheet that a title company uses to distribute the funds to the proper parties. Often the title company disburses to a number of individuals and companies (1) as a part of the procedure to assure clear title; (2) in order to pay expenses such as property inspections, an insurance policy, or a survey; (3) to distribute the fees involved in selling and loan processing; and, finally, (4) to pay to the seller what is due to him.

GF No. 89642   Esc. A/C No. _____

Escrow for <u>John Doe et ux Mary</u> to <u>Paul Rae et ux Sue</u>

           SELLER OR MORTGAGOR   PURCHASER OR MORTGAGEE

Property: <u>Lot 6, Block 4, Blackacre Subdivision, Harris County, Texas</u>

DATE	RECEIVED FROM	AMOUNT
2/4	Earnest money – Paul Rae	$ 750.00
2/27	Loan proceeds from XYZ Mortgage Company	41,400.00
2/27	Balance due from Paul Rae et ux Sue	5,295.41
	TOTAL ➡	47,445.41

INSTRUMENTS FILED	CHECKS TO TITLE COMPANY			
	Premiums–OP	A	$ 250.00	
	Premiums–MP Various	A	15.00	
	( )	A		$ 265.00
	Filing Fees	B	17.50	
	Tax Certificates	C	7.50	
	Escrow	D	15.00	
	Restrictions	E	10.00	
	Survey		45.00	
	( )			$ 95.00

DATE	CHECK TO	CHECK NO.	AMOUNT
3/2	USLIFE Title Co. [Invoice No. 6021]	1021	$ 30.00
3/2	USLife Title Co.	1022	330.00
3/2	James Jones	1030	70.00
3/2	Protection Agency, Inc.	1031	253.00
3/2	Johnson Real Estate Co.	1034	2,760.00
3/2	Safety Savings Assn.	1035	23,428.76
3/2	John Doe et ux Mary Doe	1039	19,420.08
3/2	XYZ Mortgage Company (for following)	1042	1,153.57
	2 mos. hazard ins. 48.00		
	5 mos. maintenance 28.35		
	5 mos. taxes 228.10		
	Int. 2/27 to 2/28 20.12		
	Amort. sch. 1.00		
	PMI 207.00		
	Service charge 621.00		
	TOTAL 1,153.57		
		TOTAL ➡	47,445.41

Figure 14–3

GLOSSARY

The following terms are those most frequently used in real estate financing, which are considered essential in understanding the material presented in this text.

Acceleration. A clause in a mortgage instrument permitting demand for full payment of principal upon default of the obligations.

Acknowledgement. For real estate purposes, a signature witnessed or notarized in a manner that can be recorded.

Amortization. The systematic and continuous payment of an obligation through installments until such time as that debt has been paid off in full.

Appraisal. An estimate of property value by a qualified person.

Assessment. A charge against a property owner for purposes of taxation; i.e., the property owner pays his share of community improvements and maintenance according to the valuation of his property.

Assessed Value. Property value as determined by a taxing authority.

Assignment of Mortgage. Transfer by the lender (mortgagee) of the mortgage obligation.

Assumption Agreement. A contract, by deed or other form, through which a buyer undertakes the obligations of an existing mortgage.

Balloon Payment. A debt repayment plan wherein the installments are less than required for a full amortization, with the balance due in a lump sum at maturity.

Basis Points. The movement of interest rates or yields expressed in hundredths of a percent; i.e., a change in yield from 7.45% to 7.55% would be termed an increase of 10 basis points.

Basket Provision. Regulations applicable to financial institutions that permit a small percentage of total assets to be held in otherwise unauthorized investments.

Bond. A form of security that guarantees payment of the face value with interest to the purchaser (lender), and usually secured with a pledge of property or a commitment of income such as a tax revenue bond.

Borrower. A person or company using another's money or property, who has both a legal and moral obligation to repay the loan.

Broker. An intermediary between buyer and seller, or between lender and borrower, usually acting as agent for one or more parties, who arranges loans or sells property in return for a fee or commission.

Capitalization. The conversion of an income stream into a property valuation for purposes of appraisal.

Cash Flow. The amount of cash received over a period of time from an income property.

Chattel. An article of property that can be moved; personal property.

Chattel Mortgage. A type of lien (legal claim) that applies to personal property as distinguished from real property.

Closing. The consummation of a real estate transaction wherein certain rights of ownership are transferred in exchange for the monetary and other considerations agreed upon. Also called *loan closing*.

Collateral. Property acceptable as security for a loan.

Compensating Balance. A minimum balance held on deposit in accordance with a loan agreement.

Commitment. A pledge to grant a loan based on an acceptable application.

Commitment Fee. Money paid in return for the pledge of a future loan.

Conditional Sale. An agreement granting title to property after all payments have been made.

Consideration. The cash, services, or token given in exchange for property or services.

Constant Payment. The payment of a fixed sum periodically, which money is applied to interest, and second to principal reduction, in a manner calculated to amortize a debt.

Constant Rate. Also called *constant,* which is the factor or multiplier used for easy computation of the equal monthly or annual payments to amortize a loan.

Construction Loan. A type of mortgage loan to finance construction, which is funded by the lender to the builder at periodic intervals as the work progresses.

Contingent Liability. The responsibility assumed by a third party who accepts liability for an obligation upon the failure of an initial obligor to perform as agreed.

Contract for Deed. An agreement to sell property wherein title to the property is delivered to the buyer only after all installment payments have been made.

Contract for Sale. An agreement between a buyer and a seller of real property to deliver good title in return for a consideration.

Conventional Loan. A loan that is not underwritten by a federal agency.

Debenture Bond. An unsecured pledge to repay.

Debt. An obligation to be repaid by a borrower to a lender.

Debt Service. The periodic payment due on a loan, which includes principal, interest, mortgage insurance, and any other fees required by the loan agreement.

Deed of Trust. A type of mortgage that conveys real property to a third party for holding in trust as security for payment of a loan.

Deed Restriction. A clause in a deed that restricts the use of the land being conveyed.

Default. The failure to perform on an obligation as agreed in a contract.

Delinquency. A loan payment that is overdue but within the grace period allowed before actual default is declared.

Development Loan. Money loaned for the purpose of improving land by the building of streets and utilities so as to make lots suitable for sale or use in construction.

Discount. The deduction subtracted from the face value of a loan in order to increase the effective yield.

Encroachment. Any physical intrusion upon the property rights of another.

Equity. The ownership interest—that portion of a property's value beyond any liability therein.

Escrow. Property, money, or something of value held in custody by a third party in accordance with an agreement.

Execution. The act of signing by the involved parties of an instrument, usually witnessed or notarized for recording purposes.

Fee Simple. A legal term indicating title to property without encumbrances.

FHA Loan. A loan insured by the Insuring Office of the Department of Housing and Urban Development; formerly known as the Federal Housing Administration.

Fixture. Personal property so affixed to the land as to become a part of the realty.

Foreclosure. Legal action to bar a mortgagor's claims to property after default has occurred.

Gross Income. The total money received from an operating property over a given period of time.

Guarantee (verb). The act of pledging by a third party to assure payment.

Guaranty (noun). A pledge by a third party to assume the obligation of another.

Hazard Insurance. The insurance covering physical damage to property.

HUD. The Department of Housing and Urban Development.

Income Property. Real estate capable of producing net revenue.

Instrument. A legal document in writing.

Interest. The payment for the use of money.

Interim Financing. An in-between (intermediate) loan—the money loaned for construction in anticipation of the permanent loan.

Land Loan. Money loaned for the purchase of raw land.

Late Charge. A fee added to an installment as a penalty for failure to make a timely payment.

Leverage. The capacity to borrow an amount greater than the equity in property. The larger the loan in relation to the equity, the greater the leverage.

Lien. A legal claim or attachment, filed on record, against property as security for payment of an obligation.

Limitations. A period of time as fixed by state statutes within which certain acts are to be performed to render them valid.

Liquidity. The extent to which assets held in other forms can be easily and quickly converted into cash.

Loan. A granting of the use of money in return for the payment of interest.

Loan-to-Value-Ratio (LTVR). The relationship between the amount of a loan and the value of the property pledged.

Marginal Property. Capable of making only a very low economic return.

Maturity. The date that payment on a loan is due.

Mechanic's Lien. Also known as Mechanic's and Materialmen's Lien, or M & M Lien; a claim for payment of labor and/or materials filed on record in the County.

Mortgage. A conditional conveyance of property as security for a debt.

Mortgaging Out. Securing of a loan upon completion of a project sufficient to cover all costs: a 100% loan.

Mortgagee. The lender of money and the receiver of the security in the form of a mortgage.

Mortgagor. The borrower of money and the giver of a mortgage as security.

Mortgage Note. A description of the debt and a promise to pay—the instrument that is secured by the mortgage indenture.

Mortgage Release. A disclaimer of further liability on the mortgage note issued by the lender.

Multifamily Mortgage. An FHA term designating an apartment or any housing with more than four family units.

Net Income. That portion of gross income remaining after payment of all expenses.

Origination Fee. The amount charged for services performed by the company handling the initial application and processing of a loan.

Permanent Loan. A mortgage loan granted for a long term based on the economic life of a property.

Partial Release. The removal of a general mortgage lien from a specific portion of the land that has been pledged.

Personal Property. A possession: any item of value that is not real estate.

Points. A unit of measure for charges that amounts to one percent of a loan. One point is one percent of the subject loan.

Possession. Occupancy: the highest form of "notice."

Principal. The amount of the mortgage debt.

Real Estate. Land and that attached thereto, including minerals and resources inherent to the land, and any man-made improvements so affixed as to become a part of the land. Also known as *realty* or *real property*.

Realtor. A registered word designating a member in good standing of the National Association of Real Estate Boards.

Recording. To file a legal instrument in the public records of a county.

Reversionary Clause. A restrictive provision in a deed to land that causes title to return to the grantor if violated.

Servicing (Loan Servicing). The work of an agent, usually a mortgage company, comprising the collection of mortgage payments, securing of escrow funds, payment of property taxes and insurance from the escrowed funds, follow-up on delinquencies, accounting for and remitting principal, and interest payments to the lender.

Single-Family Mortgage. A mortgage loan on property occupied by one family; and for classification purposes, can include up to four family units.

Spot Loan. Money loaned on individual houses in various neighborhoods, as contrasted to new houses in a single development.

Statutory Redemption. A state law that permits a mortgagor a limited time after foreclosure to pay off the debt and reclaim the property.

Subordination. To make a claim to real property inferior to that of another by specific agreement.

Survey. The measurement and description of land by a registered surveyor.

Sweat Equity. An ownership interest in property earned by the performance of manual labor on that property.

Syndication. The organization of a group of investors for the purpose of acquiring a specific property.

Take-out. A type of loan commitment—a promise to make a loan at a future specified time. It is most commonly used to designate a higher cost, shorter term, back-up commitment as a support for construction financing until a suitable permanent loan can be secured.

Term. The time limit within which a loan must be repaid.

Time Deposits.   Money held in savings accounts not subject to demand withdrawal.

Title.   The legal evidence of an individual's rights to ownership of real property.

Tract Loan.   Individual mortgage loan negotiated for houses of similar character located in a new development.

Trade Fixture.   Personal property, peculiar to a trade, which remains personal even though affixed to real property.

Underwriter.   The person or company taking responsibility for approving a mortgage loan.

Usury.   Excessive interest as determined by state law.

Variable Rate Mortgage.   A type of mortgage agreement that allows for periodic adjustment of the interest rate in keeping with a fluctuating market.

VA Loan.   A loan made by private lenders that is partially guaranteed by the Veterans Administration.

Vendor's Lien.   A lien securing the loan of money used to purchase property.

Warehousing.   The practice, mostly by mortgage bankers, of pledging mortgage notes to a commercial bank for cash used to fund the mortgage loans.

Yield.   The total money earned on a loan for the term of the loan computed on an annual percentage basis.

INDEX

Date Due

MAR 4 '77			
MAR 17 78			
APR 21 78			
DEC 15 '78			
DEC 14 '79			
JUN 10 1983			
JUN 13 1986			
AUG 14 1987			
AUG 17 1993			